LORRAINE KAY

LIVING WITHOUT
CRUELTY

SIDGWICK & JACKSON
LONDON

Just a Snowflake

'Tell me the weight of a snowflake,' a coal-mouse asked a wild dove.

'Nothing more than nothing,' was the answer.

'In that case, I must tell you a marvellous story,' the coal-mouse said.

'I sat on the branch of a fir, close to its trunk, when it began to snow – not heavily, not in a raging blizzard – no, just like in a dream, without a sound and without any violence. Since I did not have anything better to do, I counted the snowflakes settling on the twigs and needles of my branch. Their number was exactly 3,741,952. When the 3,741,953rd dropped on to the branch, nothing more than nothing, as you say – the branch broke off.'

Having said that, the coal-mouse flew away.

The dove, since Noah's time an authority on the matter, thought about the story for a while, and finally said to herself, 'Perhaps there is only one person's voice lacking for peace to come to the world.'

From Kurt Kauben's book *New Fables, Thus Spake the Marabou!*

For Zöe and snowflakes everywhere

Paperback ISBN 0 283 060131
Hardback ISBN 0 283 060654

Typeset by Rowland Phototypesetting Limited, Bury St Edmunds, Suffolk
Printed by Butler and Tanner Limited, Frome, Somerset
for Sidgwick & Jackson Limited
1 Tavistock Chambers, Bloomsbury Way
London WC1A 2SG

CONTENTS

Acknowledgements

This book would never have happened had it not been for the generosity of many individuals who gave freely of their time, expertise, advice and knowledge. I am also indebted to Animal Aid for financial support, and to the companies who donated both cash and products for the photographic work. Either I am more adept at persuasion techniques than I thought, or you all believe, as I do, that the animals needed some good PR. If I have failed to mention anyone below I apologize, and extend my thanks to all who got involved.

My special thanks to: Robert Smith at Sidgwick and Jackson for his faith, and his colleague Gill Paul for straightening out literary defects; Barbara Daly for all her help; Theresa Fairminer for advice and enthusiasm; Trevor 'Form-a-Queue-Please' Leighton for his humour and generosity; Lawrence at Crimpers for a decent hair-do; Jill Furmanovsky, Ron and Leah for being nice; Sue Wade; Joyce Broughton; Dr Vernon Coleman; Penny Pearson; Sheila at MPL; Martin Hensla; Mark Glover at LYNX for the loan of furs and animal traps; Sheffield firms who helped with props: Meadowfayre for dried flowers, Sheffield Scene for cutlery, Filibuster and Booth for antiques, Cookshop for china, and Louie and Liz at the Abbeydale Garden Centre for Chrissie Hynde's 'cage'; Annabelle and friends at the Heaven's Gate Animal Sanctuary; Neil Ashton for his support; Annie and Jane at Image; Helen and Gary for photographic information; the Animal Aid office, particularly Mark, for long-suffering servitude and free accommodation; Helen, Elaine Minto, Elaine Maytum and Gary's mum for being good volunteers.

My personal thanks are due to:

All our celebrity supporters who gave their time, their coffee, their anger and sometimes their tears to tell me how they felt: Richard Adams, Lysette Anthony, Julie Christie, Peter Cushing, Barbara Dickson, David Essex, Peter Gabriel, Uri Geller, Sir John Gielgud, Marie Helvin, Chrissie Hynde, Howard Jones, Carla Lane, Annie Lennox, Joanna Lumley, Linda McCartney, Virginia McKenna, Vicki Michelle, Hayley Mills, Bill Oddie, Kate O'Mara, Carol Royle, Martin Shaw, David Shepherd, Rita Tushingham, Twiggy, Sophie Ward, Toyah Wilcox and Susannah York.

Photographers who waived their fees and often their expenses too, and to their long-suffering assistants and secretaries: Matthew Anker, David Bailey, Neil Barstow, Robyn Beeche, Tim Bret-Day, Ed Byrne, Tommy Candler, Jill Furmanovsky, Ian Kalinowski, Trevor Leighton, Patrick Lichfield, Tony McGee, Stuart McLeod, Bob Marchant, Sanders Nicholson, Karena Perronet-Miller, Alan Shawcross and John Swannell.

Make-up artists who worked for nothing: Linda Burns, Lisa Butler, William Casey, Barbara Daly, Lyn Easton, Theresa Fairminer and Susie Sutherland.

Hair artists who didn't get paid either: Arno, Joseph Carney, Tony Collins, Francesca Crowder, Lawrence Falk, Drew Jarrett and Frank Warner.

Jaleh for styling Vicki Michelle's bath shot; Janet Kay for her beautiful hands; Oded Schwartz for his wonderful cooking and food styling; Sarah Brown for her specially created recipes; Sarah Bounds and *Health Express* for wedding recipes; the helpful bookers at the agencies I pestered, particularly at Camilla Arthur, Sessions, Lynne Franks and Pin-up; Chalk Farm Studios for free use of facilities; Alton Towers Management; Circus Hassani; Linda Tolbert, model with Max Presents, who volunteered for an on-the-spot photo session whilst visiting our photographer; and Bob, the London cabbie who when I told him what this book was about waived the fare across London on my way to a photo session, and gave me helpful suggestions about what to do with bloodsports supporters.

All the companies who supported me and provided free products: All Gain Organics,

ACKNOWLEDGEMENTS

Animal Aid, Barry M Cosmetics, Beauty Without Cruelty, Bodyline Cosmetics, Body Shop, Colourings, Cosmetics To Go, Crimpers, The Dietburger Co., Ecover Products, Fleur, Health and Diet Food Co. Ltd, Holland and Barrett, Homecare Technology Ltd, Honesty Cosmetics, L'Arome, Mange Tout Foods, Meridian Foods, Modern Health Products, Montague Jeunesse, Naturally Yours, Neal's Yard Apothecary, The Organic Wine Company, Pacific Isle, Plamil Foods, Realeat (makers of Vegeburger), Sarakan toothpaste, The Secret Garden, Simply Herbal, Whole Earth Foods, and Yvonne Gray Cosmetics.

All the animal groups who gave freely of their valuable time to answer my questions.

Finally, very special thanks to Col, for putting me up and putting up with me on all those trips to London. I would tell you what a lovely person you are, but you'd get embarrassed. And thanks most of all to Robert for support, for cooking your own dinner whilst I was away, for help with double negatives, and for being pretty amazing anyway.

Extract from 'The Ox' by W H Davies from *The Complete Poems of W H Davies*, courtesy The Executors of the W H Davies Estate and publishers Jonathan Cape Ltd.

Recipes from *Linda McCartney's Home Cooking*, courtesy Bloomsbury Publishing Ltd.

Cosmetic recipes taken from *Natural Appeal* by Pat Wellington & Suzy Kendall, courtesy of publishers J. M. Dent.

Quotation from 'Coverings' by Stella Gibbons, reproduced by permission of Curtis Brown, London, on behalf of the author.

'The Bells of Heaven' by Ralph Hodgson taken from the book *Poems* and courtesy of Macmillan Publishers, Basingstoke.

'A Black Rabbit Dies for its Country' from *The Collected Ewart 1933–1980* (Hutchinsons) by kind permission of the author, Gavin Ewart.

Extract from a poem by Stevie Smith from *The Collected Poems of Stevie Smith* (Allen Lane) by kind permission James MacGibbon, executor, the Stevie Smith Estate.

'Beauty' and 'A Bird in a Cage', by J. O. Salmond and Fay Chivers, reproduced courtesy of the authors, who are both Animal Aid members.

Living Without Cruelty

The Living Without Cruelty Campaign is run nationally by Animal Aid, who have kindly allowed me to use their campaign title for this book. I am pleased to be associated with their peaceful, totally non-violent activities, and am delighted that sales of this book will benefit their work. The work done by Animal Aid covers all the topics discussed in these pages. If you would like to join the campaign, simply contact: Animal Aid, 7 Castle Street, Tonbridge, Kent, TN9 1BH; or telephone 0732-364546 for a free information pack. Supporters receive informative magazines containing recipes, advice and up-to-date information and reviews, with regular expert contributions on health. The annual Living Without Cruelty Exhibition, fast becoming the green event of the year, is staged by Animal Aid in June at London's Kensington Town Hall.

Introduction

This book is for all those people who want the world to be a better place but who feel helpless to do anything about it. Do you say, 'Who am I? I'm just one person. How can I change the way things are?' *Living Without Cruelty* aims to show you just how effective you can be. The choices we make could end animal suffering, increase the quality of our lives through a healthier and saner lifestyle, and leave the world we live in fit for our children to inherit. Sounds too good to be true? It isn't, because *you* can make it happen. If you'd like to replace cruelty with compassion and are sick of reading about exploitation, greed, waste and suffering – then welcome to Living Without Cruelty.

There are many negative things happening in our world, but despite this a growing, ethical, 'green' revolution is struggling to combat the poisoning of the planet and the exploitation of its creatures – human and animal alike. Concepts once dubbed 'cranky', such as alternative medicine and the holistic approach to healthcare, are now ridiculed only by those who cannot profit from them. Interest in healthy eating, concern over food additives and the link between a bad diet and certain diseases have led people to question the advice they once accepted in trust, and both the food and pharmaceutical industries are increasingly being held up to the spotlight of investigation.

In 1975 Peter Singer's book *Animal Libera-*

tion was published, and launched a new awareness and a new ethic: Animal Rights. Ridiculed at first, like all new concepts, the original moral stance broadened into more basic practical questions – could the exploitation of animals on factory farms, in vivisection laboratories and elsewhere be linked in some way to human suffering? Were we, in fact, paying our own price for their exploitation?

Through the medium of television we witnessed the tenderness of a mother seal to her baby, learnt to appreciate the intelligence and beauty of the fox, and saw huge, gentle whales swimming with tiny human divers. And so we were moved to help them when we saw the hunters with their clubs, and the blood on the ice; the fox with bursting lungs; the harpoon gun. In outrage we wrote, we lobbied, we marched. We stopped buying Canadian fish and baby sealskin fur and our sphere of compassion widened to take them in. Gandhi wrote: 'The greatness of a nation and its moral progress can be judged by the way its animals are treated.'

At last we are beginning to appreciate that animals other than ourselves have a right to a life free from pain, suffering and oppression, and a growing number of people are now choosing to reject the products of cruelty, opting for the Living Without Cruelty lifestyle which aims to reduce and eliminate such suffering.

As a lifestyle it represents an ideal. It is not perfect, nor does it pretend to be, yet it offers to each of us the real chance of making our own contribution to that better world, by encouraging us to re-evaluate, to make changes; often just the simple act of reaching for a cruelty-free product over its exploitative competitor. Our individual contribution can be priceless. Collectively, as consumers, we can actively change the emphasis, even against powerful multi-national corporations. Wherever we draw our 'line', whether we ultimately opt for the whole 'package' or take just one or two small positive steps such as switching to free-range eggs or humane beauty products, we can help animals and ourselves to a better way of life.

This book will show you how to create your own personal and positive revolution. There's no sackcloth and ashes to put on, and a halo is not required. Holier-than-thou attitudes have no place in the Living Without Cruelty ethic – *you* determine the changes and the pace, and the facts are presented to allow *you* to make an informed choice, without any off-putting images.

Our celebrity supporters join me in sharing their viewpoints and experiences, and reveal how Living Without Cruelty has changed their lives for the better. We made up the faces of the famous to show just how stunning cruelty-free cosmetics could be, and we created some fabulous foods to tempt even the most intransigent steak-lover (not a nut-cutlet in sight!). Our stars share their favourite 'non-violent' recipes, and we show how cruelty-free cuisine is kinder to your body and your purse as well as to the animals and the environment.

So no matter where you might begin – whether it's goodbye to battery eggs, foie-gras or frogs' legs; a switch to cruelty-free cosmetics; no more furs; or you're thinking about going veggie . . . welcome to Living Without Cruelty. We can testify you'll feel better for it.

Lorraine Kay

Anthropomorphism – the habit of attributing human qualities to non-human forms

I make no apology to my readers for habitually attributing many of the attitudes and feelings which as a human being myself I can identify with in animals. I do not care for the scientific attitudes which strip animals of their capacity to feel and suffer and which strive to eliminate the possibility of their having an emotional or indeed even a spiritual life.

Abusers and exploiters of all forms have long relied on very arbitrary differences in intelligence, capacity to feel pain, perception of time and various behavioural traits in order to continue the particular abuse. I believe that we should not apologize for anthropomorphism, as if it were some awful shortcoming to logical thinking, but simply and commonsensically accept that it is the only way we can appreciate how other life forms suffer with us. I know that animals can and do experience pain, fear, anxiety, stress, panic, concern, depression, boredom, joy and happiness. Some can detect what my inept senses could never begin to realize. They can navigate themselves around the world, call to one another over great distances without the need of a telephone, sing songs and pinpoint both friend and foe by sophisticated scent mechanisms. Some have even learnt some of our own language. They have rich and varied worlds of their own which, by and large, we have been too stupid to perceive, except through forceful intervention. Even then, in our arrogance we judge them by our own dismal standards.

So, along with thousands of thinking people everywhere, I do not need a degree in biology or zoology to know that if my cat cries out in pain it is indeed responding to an injury or hurt of some sort, in much the same way as I would. Scientists who casually describe an animal's screams as 'high-pitched vocalization' will never, in my view, understand the secrets of the lives they plunder, for in hardening their hearts they have lost the ability to look into their victims' eyes and recognize a kindred response. Henry Beston encapsulates my sentiments in *The Outermost House*:

> We patronise them for their incompleteness, for their tragic fate of having taken form so far below ourselves. And therein do we err. For the animals shall not be measured by man. In a world older and more complete than ours they move finished and complete, gifted with extensions of the senses we have lost or never attained, living by voices we shall never hear. They are not brethren, they are not underlings; they are other nations, caught with ourselves in the net of life and time, fellow prisoners of the splendour and travail of the earth.

1 Food for Thought

The Ox

Why should I pause, poor beast, to praise
Thy back so red, thy sides so white;
And on thy brow those curls in which
Thy mournful eyes take no delight?

I dare not make fast friends with kine,
Nor sheep, nor fowl that cannot fly;
For they live not for Nature's voice,
Since tis man's will when they must die.

So, if I call thee some pet name,
And give thee of my care today,
Where wilt thou be tomorrow morn
When I turn curious eyes thy way?

Nay, I'll not miss what I'll not find,
And I'll find no fond cares for thee;
So take away those great sad eyes
That stare across yon fence at me.

W. H. Davies

Why think at all about meat-eating?

Most people who think about vegetarianism see it primarily in ethical terms, at least in the first instance. It is the feeling of moral injustice which spurs us to practical action. But this aspect does not necessarily come foremost and there are many reasons for taking a good, hard look at your diet, not least from the health point of view.

Many people, of course, enjoy eating meat. After all, most of us were brought up to savour the taste without actually knowing what we were eating. I certainly did: my mother's roast beef was famous. When we do realize, our minds often discreetly partition off reality to stop us thinking of the origins of our meal. We pick up the sanitized square of red flesh at the supermarket, nice and lean, to carry home for supper; from abattoir to conscience-free cling-film to dinner plate in less time than it takes to kid yourself that it's all humanely done.

Taste is often the only 'excuse' for con-tinuing to eat meat, but habit, ritual, conditioning and family expectations can all make change difficult. Of course, human beings might taste quite succulent, yet 'taste' here wouldn't be sufficient reasoning for their slaughter. Leg of man next to leg of lamb hanging in the butcher's shop window would seem highly unsettling, but somehow the lamb missed out when we handed out the moral codes. Yet we 'ooh' and 'aah' every spring when their new-born innocence gives the farmer a public relations boost before he sends them off to their deaths. We pass the mint sauce and lick our fingers and never hear baa baa black sheep crying for his mother as the slaughterman's hand does the dirty work for us.

As consumers we shape the marketplace and the products within it. The exploitation of animals, humans and the planet itself is closely interwoven. We either support or seek to abolish that exploitation by the choices we make, and animals are the key factor. Food is the most important of our choices, because with animal products we are dealing with life and death itself, and with the responsibility for that. But although ethical considerations underpin the thinking, the weight of evidence against animal consumption is truly overwhelming. Consider what's involved. . . .

Animal suffering

Would you like to spend the rest of your life in the toilet with three or four other people? It wouldn't be much of an existence would it? Yet for 40 million hens, four to a cage 20 inches wide, this is 'life', and 'Farm Fresh' battery eggs are the result. No sunshine, no earth to peck and scratch, no dustbaths, nowhere to run from the bullies in the cage who peck until you're raw even though your beak's been cut off with a red-hot blade. Two million will be unequal to the struggle and die in their cages each year. Old at two, then off to slaughter for soup and sandwich fillings.

Whilst the ladies lay the eggs their biology cannot deny, the 425 million broiler chickens fatten in stinking, windowless sheds, sprayed with drugs to dampen down infection, whilst their hocks burn in the ammonia of their own excreta and artificial weight gain buckles their joints to that of a cripple. Twenty-five million will die every year before slaughter, in the hell of the broiler sheds. Twenty-nine million turkeys suffer under similar conditions, and queue for the stunner to usher in their season of goodwill. Ducks too have fallen victim to factory production methods, and thousands of ducklings die to satisfy our yearning for a weekend taste sensation with some orange sauce.

Geese are increasingly being raised for pâté production. Although force-feeding is illegal in Britain, importing foie-gras from force-fed birds is not. The process of *gavage* forcibly delivers 6 lb of salted fatty maize daily into each bird, which lives in a 10 × 15 inch cage. Some farms secure an elastic band around the throat to prevent the bird retching up the food, as you would do if you'd been fed 28 lb of spaghetti – the human equivalent.

Quail, those tiny bodies now adorning supermarket counters, are the current trendy meal for the nouveau caterer and are yet more victims of the factory farm. Frogs' legs, another item for the up-market menu, are mostly imported from Bangladesh and Indonesia, where the frog's body remains to crawl away to die after the shock of conscious amputation with a crude, sharpened blade. Death comes slowly – up to an hour later. Part of the present demand are the 2.5 million battery rabbits who die annually, never having felt grass under their feet nor sat upright to sniff the air.

Pigs, so intelligent, suffer terribly in their confinement. Unable, like all the animals on the factory farm, to fulfil normal behaviour patterns, they sway to and fro like living metronomes, eaten up with frustration and boredom, unable to play, to root in the dirt or to apply the cool balm of wet mud to their skins. Concrete is their world, the 2 ft-wide farrowing crate their labour ward, their babies the profit motive with 400,000 sows continually impregnated in this country.

I must also mention the 'trash' animals. These are mostly birds born the wrong sex for the wrong purpose . . . males who don't lay eggs and who don't fatten quickly enough.

Roughly 40 million day-old chicks suffocate or are gassed to death. Some have their heads crushed against a wooden bar. They're not profitable so become known, unemotionally, as 'hatchery waste'.

Other miseries include tail-docking, castration, ear-clipping and various mutilations and interferences carried out every day, mostly on infants, mostly without anaesthetics.

But some animals have a decent life don't they? There they are, out in the fields all day eating grass. The 'Anchor' cow gaily sings to us, and she and her sisters swing their legs in time to the music. The meadow is sunny, full of daisies and clover. In another advertisement, old-timers yearn for the 'taste of the country' and a wistful, Thomas Hardy landscape nostalgically suggests peace and harmony as the cows saunter off to a life of bovine contemplation. But it's not quite like that in real life.

The cow has a natural lifespan of twenty-five to thirty years, but only survives an average of five. Her body, genetically interfered with, now produces twice the amount of milk it did thirty years ago, from udders routinely infected

with painful mastitis and so heavy that she can hardly walk to the milk parlour. After three or four pregnancies, with her milk yield falling, she is considered clapped out and sent to be turned into meat pies after a short life of denial and anguish. Her babies would have been sent away, unweaned, often with their umbilical cord still in place. They would have ended up in veal units for a fourteen-week life in the semi-dark; or, if weak and uneconomic – so-called 'bobby calves' – sent to slaughter, where in their desperation they suckle the slaughterman's hand for comfort; or they might have been given the third option – to replace their mother in the dairy herd as the cycle begins again. Beef animals see up to eighteen months of life being fattened before the trip to the abattoir; an increasing number are now raised inside, on concrete slats.

Newspapers marvelled at the story of Blackie, the cow who, in 1983, escaped one night and walked seven miles through country lanes to be reunited with the eight-week-old calf taken from her that day at market. But why the surprise? Do we hold a monopoly on maternal feeling? Would we not cry if our babies were snatched from our arms?

Personal contact with animals establishes a bond. You wouldn't consider eating your cat or dog (it might taste OK) because you've come to care about its welfare, know when it's ill, and recognize its moods, wants and needs. It's difficult to do this with farm animals. They're distant, removed from your immediate circle of concern. With factory farming they're totally removed – out of sight, out of mind. Ditto the abattoir. Ditto Auschwitz, Buchenwald, Belsen.

But their suffering isn't diminished, nor their deaths less traumatic, simply because we protect our sensibilities from the gore. The crucial question we need to ask ourselves is a pragmatic one: 'If I could stop the axe from falling, would I?' A switch to a vegetarian diet lifts the death sentence from between twenty-five and forty animals every year. That's just for one person.

All humanely done

And after this life, what then? Do we really believe that the death of a 'food' animal is akin to having the dog put to sleep? A slaughterhouse does what its name suggests: it is a place of carnage. There is fear and anticipation of the unthinkable, then terror, hopeless struggling, pain, shock, endurance and ultimately, death. There is no place for the word 'humane'.

Investigative writer Andrew Tyler visited one of the UK's 'top-notch', EEC-licensed slaughterhouses and witnessed the typical deaths of three hundred pigs. In his disturbing report he noted that 'speed, forced by a piece-rates system, was the essence and many a rule on welfare and hygiene was trampled on the way. Where the animals would not co-operate in their own slaughter, and even when they did, they were punched, kicked and cursed the way women are cursed: "Cummon you dozy bitch . . . you stupid c——t!"'

Pre-stunning, the process supposed to render animals unconscious, has been described by one Leeds pathologist as 'a farce', with over a third of animals standing helplessly wounded and fully conscious whilst the gun is reloaded. Tyler described the stunning of pigs with electric tongs:

As the first dozen are driven into the stunning pen, one urinates on the trot and makes a screeching noise I hadn't heard before. Blood and mucus flies from his snout, the eyes close, the front legs stiffen and when Hammond [the slaughterman] opens the tongs he falls, like a log, on his side. He lies there, back legs kicking, as Hammond turns to the next candidate. Most huddle against the entrance with their rumps towards him, heads passively bowed, snout to snout. They wait quietly until Hammond clamps another and then a couple break from the huddle and sniff a fallen comrade.

He tells me that the tongs should be held on for a minimum of seven seconds to ensure a proper stun before the throat is cut. But Hammond, urged on by his mates further along the slaughterline, is giving them 1½ seconds or less.

There is just one more waiting for the tongs, a small, quiet creature who, from her position near the gate, looks me directly in the eye, breaking my heart. Hammond chases her a few steps. The tongs first ineptly clamp her neck, her eyes close in a strange blissful agony. The tongs are adjusted and like a rock she falls.

The routine tightens up when the inspectors call, but, as Hammond stated: 'They only have to look at the graph of the weekly kills to see we're taking three times as long to do half the work. It's just that it has to be seen to be done.'

A recent development has been the slaughter of farmed deer at the abattoir. These particularly nervous, highly strung creatures are processed into veniburgers, sausages or steaks and are sold at outlets such as Waitrose. One Hampshire slaughterhouse manager remarked: 'It's hard enough to get the men to handle pigs properly, let alone deer.' The killing systems, ritual or otherwise, whether for cattle, pigs, sheep or hens, omit the capacity for an easy death – if there ever can be such a thing.

At every turn animals are deprived of almost everything which would make their lives worth living. We have interfered to such an extent that nature is rebelling. We may all, soon, have to pay a price. God knows, the animals have paid theirs.

Human suffering

We've already seen how science is mobilized to increase the farmer's productivity at the animal's expense. Genetics has produced leaner carcasses, which means the animals suffer from the cold and are less hardy. Artificial insemination leads to continous pregnancies which nature would avoid, but which the farmer employs to increase profits, denying the animal even the simple joy of courtship and mating. Science has even created chimeras by mixing species genes to produce 'inventions' which conveniently can be patented like so many bits of machinery. Watch out, brave new world, because we'll be next and on our way to the perfect, unimpaired human race.

But there are more immediate effects to worry about. Intensive farming, in particular, produces its own set of problems. Disease is easily spread in an environment of foetid air, excrement-covered floors and confined spaces. The animals, very often with resistance bred out, are more susceptible to illness; especially vulnerable are infant animals denied the natural antibodies in mother's milk which full-term weaning would have provided. So antibiotics and anti-diarrhoea drugs are added to their feed.

At almost every stage from birth onwards, a pharmaceutical product is dosed into the animals. The market is worth a staggering $2.5 billion in the USA, and the UK is the sixth biggest user of animal 'health' drugs. As one disease is brought under 'control' so another comes along, recently 'VD in pigs'. The cause baffles the farmers, but the antibiotics suppress the symptoms. This lackadaisical attitude to drug usage leads to resistance build-up; now compelling scientific evidence is suggesting that this is being transferred across the species barrier, through the meat we consume. Hence drugs like penicillin, invaluable for so many serious human complaints, could be rendered worthless as the abused factory-farmed animals pass their human-engineered problems in to us. The *British Medical Journal* acknowledged: 'Current regulations on the use of antibiotics in animals bred for food have failed to prevent the rapid emergence of multiple drug resistances.'

Recent salmonella scares must also have undermined public confidence in what they are told by industry. Yet it's estimated that only 10 per cent of cases are notified. Egg production is undoubtedly contaminated and consumption, understandably, has fallen. The withdrawal of contaminated products has almost become a matter of routine. As well as eggs, pâté, cooked turkey, other meat products, soft cheeses and yogurt have all caused serious illness, and in some cases death. A 1989 Ministry of Agriculture report cites some 2 million cases of salmonella per year, with 700,000 linked to chicken and egg consumption. In fact, 70 per cent of food poisoning is attributed to meat and fish anyway. The campylobacter bug alone, according to one Ministry vet, claims some eighty thousand lost working days through the acute pain and diarrhoea it causes. Meat, especially chicken, is a prime source. Listeria, found recently in dairy produce, was also discovered in 60 per cent of chicken – both fresh and frozen – in a study done by the Central Public Health Laboratory.

The government response to this appalling state of affairs is to use consumer disquiet as an excuse to introduce food irradiation – a disastrous backward step. Why bother with hygiene when the germs can be obliterated and the rotting process halted in its tracks with the consumer none the wiser? It would conflict with vested interests to admit that the problems of disease caused by the consumption of meat and dairy products are inseparable from one another. The *Farmer's Weekly* has noted that 'Britain is sitting on a salmonella time bomb', whilst a Ministry of Agriculture spokesman suggested that meat and milk were responsible for 'even more gastroenteritis than salmonella'!

Meat's got the lot!

The ban on growth-promoting hormones came into effect in December 1986, but increasing disquiet suggests that farmers may be flouting the law – which the meat industry itself admits is 'full of holes'. A study on hormone use in the USA pointed out that 'Not only are these compounds capable of bringing about . . . imbalance in the endocrine system . . . but by exciting tissue cells . . . hormones are also able to promote carcinogenesis'. Despite the ban, the *Meat Trades Journal* assured producers that 'science has made sure that there are plenty of new substitutes coming'.

And here's a good one. BST (bovine somatotropin) is a 20 per cent milk-boosting hormone, now undergoing trials, which could prove to be the final straw for the cow, already overburdened with an unnaturally inflated udder. BST-laced milk is already mixed into production, despite having no product licence, and its effects on humans cannot be quantified. The market, though, could be worth $1 billion a year. Professor John Webster of Bristol University's Department of Animal Husbandry has stated: 'The modern dairy cow already works as hard as a coal-miner doing a ten-hour shift. With BST we will be asking her to do the equivalent of a twelve-hour shift.' Yet a spokesman for BST's manufacturers, the drug company Monsanto, said that it was a 'safe and valuable benefit to society'! The fact that the EEC already has more milk than it knows what to do with doesn't seem to suggest the gift of intelligence at the Ministry of Agriculture.

Of course, if we got rid of factory farming and stopped this cruel interference with natural processes, we would eliminate these problems which the system itself has invented and exacerbated and which have led to a surge in agricultural research, costing millions. (Yet more animal cruelty is perpetrated in the laboratory, which results in another mass of contradictions and confusion.)

So far, then, we have drug residue, antibiotic resistance and unknown hormonal activity as possible threats to our health from animal product consumption, not to mention salmonella, campylobacter, listeriosis and gastroenteritis. But there are more delights in store.

Sheep suffer from a brain disease called scrapie. Cattle, fed with sheep protein containing infected brains, caught the disease and have developed BSE (bovine spongiform encephalopathy). Cattle brains, the most easily infected part of a diseased animal, are used in meat pies, pasties and beefburgers. Cattle can carry the BSE virus for years without displaying symptoms. Now a ban has been implemented on the use of beef brains in foodstuffs, including baby food. Fears are that the virus, having crossed from sheep to cattle, may leap the species barrier into man.

Abattoir workers, daily handling carcasses infected with bacteria and disease, are at high risk. A third of all cattle herds in the UK are infected with leptospirosis. The flu-like symptoms in man, often dismissed, can lead to meningitis, kidney failure and jaundice. Studies in both the USA and Britain also suggest that workers in slaughterhouses and meat trade professions suffer significantly from cancers of the bone, mouth and throat. A report by EEC inspectors found British slaughterhouses 'a frightening picture of poor hygiene, slapdash organization and blood and gore all over the floor'. The speed of operation led to cross-contamination of carcasses, guts spilled on to the floors and a general lack of cleanliness, with infected faeces commonly splashed over meat destined, for example, for pork mince.

The killing and gutting over, the flies are free to move in on the annual 1.5 million tonnes of unusable offal, blood, bones and fat, the removal of which is described by renderers as 'vital to public health'. The *Meat Trades Journal* tell us that 'the aroma of freshly cut meat acts as a powerful lure to many unwanted food tasters'. These disease-carrying insects loiter with intent around butcher's shops and abattoirs.

Hidden extras

Meat purchasers get more than they bargain for in other ways too – or less as the case may be. Sausages may contain gristle, sinew, rind and

PETER GABRIEL
'I support Living Without Cruelty. This
planet is not the exclusive property of the
emancipated ape. All the best with it.'

head, not to mention sulphur dioxide to make things look better and last longer. Cooked meat products can use feet, rectum and spinal cord and many products include mechanically recovered meat (MRM), the slurry of eyeballs, noses, lips and snouts, converted from grey to pink by the use of chemicals. The legal definition of 'lean meat' allows a percentage of tail, head, diaphragm and pancreas. And there is nothing legally wrong in companies like McDonald's offering '100% pure beef' burgers which can contain heart, diaphragm, fat, skin, rind, gristle sinew and MRM. Carcasses are also bloated out with injections of water to bump up the weight, and polyphosphate salts are often added which help to retain liquid in the body cells.

The meat industry is the second largest customer of the colouring manufacturers. The most widely used is red 2G, a coal-tar derivative linked with cancer and child allergy and banned from the USA and the rest of the EEC. Other enhancers include monosodium glutamate (MSG), a flavouring linked to dizziness, headache and palpitations; nitrates, to stop rotting, and suspected of causing allergy, hypersensitivity and cancer; and sulphur dioxide, already mentioned, which is known to destroy vitamin B1. Joints of meat can also be doctored, as reported by consumer journalist Jan Walsh, who writes: 'You can bet its colour has been enhanced by gas as well as by clever lighting. Nitrogen, carbon dioxide and carbon monoxide are the favourites.' The Soil Association has estimated that each of us consumes between 6 and 15 lb of additives every year, 'many of which come from meat products'.

Eating your heart out

Bad diet is associated with all the major killer diseases such as heart disease, cancer and strokes, as well as diabetes, diverticular disease, obesity and other disorders. Allergy to certain foods is another disturbing trend, particularly amongst children.

The main causes of heart disease are faulty diet, smoking, overweight, too much alcohol, lack of exercise and excessive stress. These are all preventable factors. Saturated fat in the diet leads to high blood cholesterol, the fatty substance which blocks arteries, leading to heart disease. The Coronary Prevention Group,

Health Education Council and doctors have all recommended eating less meat and dairy produce. All animal food produce contains saturated fat. The *Farmer's Weekly* stated, amazingly, that 'it takes almost a vegetarian diet to make any measurable difference in blood cholesterol levels'. Thanks for the recommendation. A study published in the *Lancet* monitored blood pressure levels in patients on different diets. Blood pressure fell among the vegetarians, but went up whenever meat was introduced! In a Swedish study twenty-nine volunteer patients, all on high blood pressure drug therapy, were placed on a vegan diet (no animal products at all) with chocolate, coffee, tea, sugar and salt all omitted. Exercise was encouraged. A year later, twenty-six of the perservering patients had significantly lowered their blood pressure, cholesterol levels and pulse rates; only six were still on medication. An editorial in the *Times* concluded that 'the benefits of the vegan path seem clear'.

Diet is also thought to cause one third of all cancers; yet a vegetarian diet can protect against the disease. Studies of largely vegetarian population groups, such as Seventh Day Adventists, were reported in the journal *Cancer Research*. Mortality rates for those cancers unrelated to smoking and drinking were 50–70 per cent of those of the general population. The report concluded that the diet did protect, particularly against one of the commonest forms of the disease – cancer of the colon. Professor Richard Doll, writing in *Nutrition and Cancer* and describing the connection between colon cancer and meat consumption, ended with the advice to 'increase consumption of wholemeal bread, vegetables and fruit'. An editorial in the *Lancet*, discussing vegetarians, asked the question, 'Apart from diet what are the other differences . . . which might account for their strikingly low rates of cancers and chronic disorders?' Yet more medical evidence appeared in the *British Medical Journal* in 1982, which noted: 'Women who are vegetarians seem to have lower rates of endometrial and breast cancer than their meat-eating sisters.' It was suggested that this might be due to the lower oestrogen production associated with vegetarian women.

The American Cancer Society noted a close connection between obesity and cancers of the endometrium, gall bladder, uterine cervix, colon, rectum, breast and ovary. Others have shown that obesity, meat and fat consumption and a lack of fibre (all facets of the Western diet) are closely linked to these cancers, the diseases of developed nations. Obesity is also involved in the development of maturity-onset diabetes, which again usually responds to a change in diet. The British Medical Association stated that 'vegetarians have lower rates of obesity, coronary heart disease, high blood pressure, large bowel disorders and cancers and gallstones'. A study confirming this, carried out by two British researchers, found that vegetarians suffer less from diet-related illness, spend less time in hospital and accordingly save the country many millions of pounds a year.

It is clear that adopting a good vegetarian diet can result in a healthier life, with a greater sense of well-being, but even cutting down your meat consumption – one study recommended restricting the consumption of flesh foods to twice a week at most – can bring benefits. When cutting down, try to incorporate some of our changeover recipe ideas to familiarize yourself with vegetarian protein 'equivalents'. Although cutting out red meat initially is a popular recommendation, and, it must be said, a good way to reduce initial consumption, as one American doctor stated, 'What may surprise many people is that dairy products, poultry and seafood also contain a great deal of fat and cholesterol. These foods are not very different from beef and pork in terms of fat and cholesterol, when compared with vegetables, which are cholesterol-free.'

Producers have responded to dietary concerns over fat by retailing an array of low, half and virtually fat-free products which must be preferable to their saturated predecessors, yet it would be unwise to continue to think of milk as the 'complete food' tailor-made for us by nature. Nothing could be further from reality. We've already looked at the animal suffering inherent in milk production, but hidden away from view. Indeed, many people even fail to make the link between pregnancy and lactation, somehow believing that the milk flow is some sort of natural secretion, unconnected with babies.

The human species is the only one which drinks the milk of another, both as a suckling food and in adulthood. Yet cow's milk is designed by nature to nurture and benefit a calf, not a human baby. Its rich protein, mineral and fat content boost the growth of bone and muscle in a creature designed to reach maturity within two years. Human breast milk, with built-in antibodies from mother for the baby, is totally different in composition. Designed for humans, it contains lighter and more digestible protein, and a higher vitamin content to help develop our more advanced nervous system.

It has been estimated that 75 per cent of allergy and 40 per cent of digestive disorders in children can be traced to dairy produce. The majority of adults lack the necessary enzyme, lactase, to digest milk sugars, which then form body mucus. This can lead to disorders such as sinusitis and distressing congestive complaints. Dairy consumption is also linked with eczema and asthma, as well as other major diseases already examined.

All the nutritional components in milk can easily be found elsewhere. Indeed, recent research has found that milk drinking can be counter-productive. Writer Jane Brody warns us that 'calcium absorption is impaired by excessive dietary fat, and large amounts of animal protein result in an increased loss of calcium through the urine'. As she puts it, drinking milk to avoid calcium deficiency 'is like pouring water on a fire to get more heat'.

Over-production of milk has also resulted in by-products finding their way into an incongruous selection of foods and household goods, in an effort to get rid of the stuff. Anybody who reads packets in the supermarket will bear this out – try buying a packet of biscuits which doesn't contain whey.

Embracing the Living Without Cruelty lifestyle benefits both the animals and ourselves individually, but globally there is an even greater connection, and one which needs to be examined in this overall context. Let's look how the circle of suffering expands to bring us back to where we began. . . .

Planetary suffering

The word which concerns us here is 'waste', and in a world of shrinking resources we cannot afford to ignore the implications of an agricultural policy wedded to this phenomenon. Animal agriculture is extremely wasteful. The equation is criminal in a world in which 15 million children die from malnutrition every year and over 500 million individuals are severely malnourished: 3 lb of grain fed to poultry yields just 1 lb of edible meat, while 10 lb of grain given to cattle returns just 1 lb of beef.

Over 90 per cent of UK agricultural land is used to grow animal feed. In addition the EEC imports around 40 million tonnes annually to feed to its animals. Amazingly, about 60 per cent comes from the Third World, which uses some sixty thousand square miles of valuable land to produce food – for Europeans to feed to livestock. In 1984, for example, British animals alone consumed 4 million tonnes, mostly soya.

Worldwide, soya contributes some 15 per cent of total protein yields, with maize, corn, millet, rice, lentils, cassava, chick peas, wheat, beans and vegetables being the traditional staples of Third World countries. In combination with a sensible agricultural policy soya alone, developed into milks, tofu and textured vegetable protein, could do much to halt starvation and bring prosperity to many bankrupt, disadvantaged nations. Instead, powerful multi-national companies are allowed to buy up the land in these poorer countries and monopolize its use for animal feed, exploiting in turn the indigenous population, who are then unable to sustain a traditional harvest. At the height of the Ethiopian famine we purchased £1.5 million worth of linseed cake, cottonseed cake and rape-seed meal from Ethiopia and fed it to our animals. Surely the land which grew those crops could have been put to better use?

Yet the Third World looks to the West as ambassadors of good sense. It is to us that they turn for expertise, medical aid and, in times of famine, food. Whilst not denying the good which has been done and the charitable outpourings from enterprising groups such as Live Aid, it must be recognized that the West, as a whole, has sold the Third World woefully short. We should be assisting them to establish traditional and representative agriculture; instead we sell them factory farming.

Africa has seen a 98 per cent increase in poultry production alone since 1975. By the early eighties African states were annually *importing* 10 million tonnes of grain. Nigeria alone, with a battery flock of 40 million birds, has an industry near collapse which cannot find the maize, soya and fish meal needed to sustain the chickens, which the poor cannot afford anyway. All over the Third World, in Bangladesh, Sudan, India, Tanzania, even Ethiopia, factory farming, the West's Jerusalem, is being expanded. Five hundred thousand Ethiopian broiler chickens already fatten under that sky, and at the height of the famine the government announced plans for 2 million birds. Battery egg plants are also envisaged for Assmara and Eritrea. A spokesman stated that 'our ultimate objective is to develop the production of corn and soya [to feed the chickens]'. Ten acres of land is approximately the size of five football pitches. It will support sixty-one people on a diet of soya beans, twenty-four on a diet of wheat, ten on a diet of maize and two eating cattle meat. Hungry for change?

Not only do we hand over a bankrupt agricultural system, we also share out the diseases which go with eating its products. As Professor James of the Rowett Research Institute states:

> We are already storing up a time bomb in Africa. Cases of high blood pressure in West and South Africa are now increasing at a terrifying rate. If they go on like this, by the year 2000 it will be the largest single budgeting drain on their health sector and in the West we are largely to blame, by sending the wrong sort of food aid and exporting totally inappropriate forms of agriculture.

Once again animal exploitation leads to human suffering, but another fundamental threat awaits.

A hundred acres of tropical rainforest disappears forever every minute of every day. The forest canopy, so closely linked with rainfall and life-giving oxygen for the earth, is being chopped down for the short-term gain of cattle ranching. After a few years the land, now infertile, is useless and more forest is axed for further grazing. With the best land owned by the burger chains, whether former rainforest or not, the local tribes themselves are reduced to clearing the very forest which once sustained them, so that they too can obtain a living. Meanwhile, the planetary weather systems are threatened because of greed and wholesale exploitation.

Pollution is another result of the obsession with animal agriculture. What do you do with the combined excrement of hundreds of cows, or thousands of hens? One answer is the slurry lake: even the name sounds disgusting, and they are. Man-made reservoirs of liquid faeces, open to the air (and any unfortunate victim who might fall in accidentally), are an obvious health hazard and pollution threat, regularly contaminating water courses. The smell from these, and from battery or broiler houses, particularly in hot weather, is enough to make most people gag simply driving past. One town planner summed up the problems at the planning enquiry for a proposed broiler site: 'We are concerned about pollution of air, water and ground by smell, dust, bacteria, vermin, noise, traffic and carting, and methods whereby waste products are disposed of.'

The countryside also suffers in other ways because of animal agriculture. Instead of using straw for bedding (there's no comfort on the factory farm) it's burnt off, causing air pollution, danger and death to wildlife. Hedgerows, vital for their habitat and to prevent topsoil erosion, are ripped out to make bigger fields for bigger machinery to grow bigger crops of barley to put in bigger grain mountains to feed to more factory-farmed animals. The chemical cocktails sprayed on all this unhealthy monoculture simply add to the nightmare, whilst the nitrates ploughed into the exhausted land leak out into our drinking water, bringing another set of health problems.

Water itself is a precious commodity, as recent debates show. Yet pollution from individual factories, a frightening state of affairs in itself, is only the tip of the iceberg when seen alongside the environmental damage caused by the livestock business. First, the animals themselves consume 80 per cent of water supplies worldwide. When you consider that some 60 gallons are needed to produce 1 lb of wheat and that 250 gallons yield the same amount of rice this seems a lot, especially if the harvest is then fed into animals. But what about meat? A minimum of 2000 gallons up to a staggering 6000 gallons of water is needed for your pound of flesh. And then there's the mess to clear up. Chicken processing plants alone use up a million gallons every day to wash away the blood and guts – that's enough water for twenty-five thousand humans.

Slaughterhouses are responsible for heavy pollution as a soup of fat, offal and 2.6 million gallons of blood (enough to fill 260 swimming pools) is swilled primarily down our drains every year. Bernard Matthews and the Milk Marketing Board have both been prosecuted in recent years for local water pollution. Mr Matthews' own 'bootiful' business, which sends 9 million turkeys to their death each year, breached legal waste discharge levels no fewer than twenty-seven times during 1988, polluting the Rivers Way and Wensum. The biggest UK 'carnage' industry is Hillsdown Holdings, with forty red-meat slaughterhouses. One set of North Devon premises was convicted three times in 1988 for river pollution, the abattoir waste and sludge on one occasion turning the river red. Buxted, a subsidiary, were convicted of river pollution in 1986.

In Holland, the writing is already on the wall. Estimates give the Dutch between ten and twenty years before nitrates render all water unfit for drinking. In some parts, notably the south and east, it will be centuries before the watertable recovers to allow consumption. The vast amounts of waste from the very intensive factory farming have devastated the soil, stripping it of its growing potential through excess ammonia and seeping into the water systems. The atmosphere itself is killing trees, and the flat landscape serves to exacerbate the disaster. What price East Anglia?

Throughout the world the life arteries of the planet, our river systems, pour their polluted contents into our oceans where their complex chemistries mingle to create new, unknown 'cocktails'. Great Britain alone discharges 300 million gallons of sewage daily into the North Sea. The sewage sludge from barges, which contains a variety of dangerous contaminants, contributes a further 7 million tonnes annually. Add oil slicks, plastics and massive quantities of unknown chemical wastes and stir gently!

As sea life struggles in this toxic soup, the mammals at the end of the food chain sicken and die as their weakened immune systems allow disease an easy stranglehold. We shall never know how many thousands of seals died in 1988 from the strange viral disease which swept through colonies from the Baltic to the Wash, but the answers to such catastrophes run deeper than the short-term solution of a vaccine. Levels of PCBs (polychlorinated bi-phenyls), heavy metals and other toxins are regularly being found in the tissues of marine life, including fish. We, of course, are also at the top of the food chain and consume fish from the same polluted seas as do the seals and other animals. The fishery industries, responsible for so much wholescale suffering, have over-fished the seas with their huge factory ships until all but fry remain. Apart from the fish, who slowly suffocate to death, the gigantic nets kill thousands of dolphin, porpoises, turtles and other animals in the relentless sieving of the oceans. Fish farming, particularly in river estuaries, is another cause of pollution and suffering.

The points raised here are just an outline of the problem, a mere sketch to illustrate the vicious cycle of events inseparable from animal consumption. Everywhere we look we can see the clumsy interference and plundering greed of humankind, yet by now both the nature of the problem and the means for a solution should be emerging. Professor Williams at Reading University concludes that 'a greater proportion of the diet in industrialized countries will have to be derived from plant products. There is now no other way in which world supplies of primary products, including energy, can meet the pressure of mouths to feed.'

Some years ago, when I used to discuss these issues in school lectures or in debate, one person would always ask why I chose to campaign for animals at the expense of people. Even now, critics voice the same argument. Animal rights? What about human rights then, aren't you interested in that? I hope I have gone some way to answering that question.

New beginnings

Mums and little ones

A great deal of progress has been made over the past decade with regard to attitudes towards vegetarian mothers-to-be, although some reactionary, outmoded attitudes still exist within the medical profession towards vegan mums. As with any diet, as long as you're aware of your needs during pregnancy and eat sensibly, you should have no problems at all.

Pregnancy is a natural state, not an illness. Unfortunately the swing towards convenience birthing and the increase in the number of caesarian deliveries, coupled with unnecessary intervention, has led many women to feel more like patients, helplessly taken over by a technological birth machine. It is as well to prepare yourself in advance for both the delivery itself and the baby's nutritional needs. The National Childbirth Trust and the Laleche League will help you with natural childbirth methods and preparations for trouble-free breast feeding.

It is essential that you include foods rich in calcium, iron and vitamins A, B, C and E. A daily multi-vitamin tablet will provide some extra 'insurance' in case you miss out on your food intake on any particular day – through morning sickness, for example. Go for as many natural, unrefined foods as possible, such as brown rice and pastas and stoneground wholemeal bread. With doctors regularly prescribing iron tablets during pregnancy, which tend to exacerbate the tendency towards constipation as the baby grows, it's vital to include as much natural fibre in the diet as possible.

Try to get your food wherever possible from organic sources, and avoid products which contain chemical additives such as colourings and flavourings. Wash all non-organic fruit and vegetables especially well to remove as much pesticide residue as possible. Try to avoid strong stimulants such as tea and coffee; drink herb teas for a refreshing change. Raspberry leaf tea is reputed to contribute to an easier delivery! Also aim to cut down on white flour and sugar products. Avoid alcohol, especially in the early months; and for the sake of your own as well as your baby's health, give up smoking. Studies have shown a link with smoking and cot-death syndrome as well as late miscarriage, and the hazards of alcohol on the unborn have been known since Greek and Roman times.

Mothers-to-be are bombarded with advertising from companies intent on securing their allegiance to a particular baby product, be it a food or 'health' preparation. Powdered baby milk companies often provide hospital freebies which nursing staff use on newborns within the ward nursery. Notify the doctor if you don't want your child to be fed on a cow's milk formula. Human breast milk, designed by nature, is the complete baby food and should therefore be first choice. Early preparation will help overcome difficulties and allow you to take the right, relaxed approach to this natural, shared moment of mother-and-child communion. Stress and worry, as well as medical problems, can interfere with the milk supply, but the breast operates on a 'supply and demand' principle. Milk therefore can be expressed by hand to ensure your baby receives your own milk on a continuous basis and to keep production going until suckling can take place again. Mother's milk contains antibodies which help protect your child from infection and provides the best start to a new life. A breast-feeding mother will need an extra five hundred calories daily to keep her supply going and supply the extra vitamins, protein, fats and carbohydrates needed.

If you cannot breast feed for any reason or the supply is inadequate, you will need an infant formula. Allergies can occur with cow's milk formula, so consider soya. Unfortunately only one soya preparation is available to mothers: Ostersoy from Farley's, which should be obtainable from most high street chemists. This is obviously one area where manufacturers are still failing to respond to consumers' needs. Comparisons made between cow and soya formulas have indicated that infants with acute diarrhoea recover better on the soya, so availability is important. Consumers should beware of soya preparations such as Wysoy which contain beef fats, so are not even vegetarian.

Ordinary soya milks should not really be introduced until weaning has commenced and then, not as a substitute for the baby formula. Start with a sugar-free variety to help prevent the development of a sweet tooth later on.

It is worth noting that a great deal of concern has been expressed as to the activities of many powdered baby milk companies, notably Nestlé's, who with subtle advertising messages have been promoting their products to the detriment of breast feeding. This has led to disastrous consequences in some Third World countries, where poorly educated, impoverished mothers are being seduced into believing that bottle feeding, with its 'modern, Western' connotations, is superior to a mother's nipple. In areas of poor sanitation where sterilization is difficult this has led to an increase in diarrhoeal diseases as well as death through malnutrition, as mothers drastically dilute the formula they cannot really afford to make it last longer. Along with other multinationals, Nestlé's are heavily involved in South Africa and also sponsor vivisection in the USA. When the British company Rowntree Mackintosh were taken over by Nestlé's, the much respected Rowntree Charitable Trust immediately disposed of its Rowntree shares.

Solid foods should not be introduced until at least three months of age, preferably four to six months if your milk supply is plentiful. Although there are excellent prepared vegetarian baby foods available, if possible try to get into the habit of preparing your own in batches. If you have a blender or liquidizer this is a simple matter, and mini-meals can be frozen in advance. In this way, time is saved as well as expense.

A simple food such as well-mashed ripe banana or some sieved cooked carrot makes a good start to weaning. Don't forget to give your baby boiled water to drink, too, but don't sweeten it with sugar. At around five months or so introduce pureed lentils with vegetables, baby cereals, wholemeal rusks and pureed fruits such as apple. Try a little soya yoghurt, too, in tiny quantities. Supervise any finger-foods to avoid choking. At six months three small meals daily along with any soya milk top-up can be introduced. Avoid strong seasonings, especially salt and sugar. Thin slices of wholemeal bread can be started, spread thinly with honey, yeast extract or Veeze 'cheese' spread. Soups and grated cheese can also be introduced.

If you intend to use them, remember that some children are allergic to eggs, so try not to introduce them into the diet until your child is at least eight months old. Free-range are best, but even so, use them very sparingly and make sure they are well cooked. The dangers of salmonella from egg consumption as well as infections such as listeriosis in other dairy produce may prompt mothers to avoid such foods altogether. Soya equivalents exist for all dairy produce; their consumption lessens the risk of allergy too.

Information on the nutritional aspects, together with an excellent selection of recipes for infants, is now available in several mother-and-baby books specially created for vegetarian mothers-to-be. These are listed on p. 65. Both the Vegetarian and the Vegan Societies offer advice and literature on the practical and nutritional aspects of infant feeding.

For those times when convenience matters, such as a train journey or a holiday abroad, there are several products worth looking at. Granose make a range of organic baby foods which are really good. At 80p upwards they are more expensive than non-organic brands, but of course are free from pesticide residues and other 'hidden extras'. Beech-nut is an American product range, available in selected health store outlets, which offers an extensive vegetarian choice. Heinz, Cow and Gate, and Boots all do sweet and savoury dishes which are suitable for vegetarian babies. Cheese and egg selections are numerous, although the cheese will probably not be vegetarian and the eggs will inevitably be battery. However, quite a few varieties are animal-free. These are:

Boots

Stage 1: Savoury mixed vegetables (instant)
Mixed vegetable savoury variety (jar)
Garden vegetable casserole (granulated)
Golden vegetable hotpot (granulated)
Stage 2: Country vegetable bake (instant)
Savoury vegetable casserole (jar)

Cow and Gate

Stage 1: Apple dessert (ready-to-eat)
Apple and banana dessert
Apple and orange dessert
Fruit delight dessert
Vegetable and rice casserole (trial-sized ready meal)
Stage 2: Vegetable casserole with pasta (ready meal)
Pineapple dessert

Heinz

Savoury cans: Carrot and tomato
Golden vegetable
Mixed vegetable
Spring vegetable
Winter vegetable
Dessert jars: Apple
Apple and banana
Apple and blackcurrant
Apple and orange
Fruit salad
Pear and cherry
Apple and apricot
Apple and pear
Mixed fruit

Fresh salad foods can be introduced at around one year of age, along with ground, not whole, nuts. Children should be pretty much integrated into the family eating regime at eighteen months.

Suggested baby menu for an eight-month-old child

BREAKFASTS
Diluted fresh fruit juice
Baby muesli with soya milk or
Porridge or
Soya yoghurt with fruit puree and wheatgerm
Wholemeal toast with sugar-free smooth peanut butter

LUNCHES: MAIN COURSE
Steamed vegetables pureed with egg, cheese, Veeze or lentils or
Pureed bean stew with vegetables cooked with yeast extract such as Natex and Vecon vegetable stock or
Pureed lentils or split peas with vegetables or
Vegetable medley pureed with brown rice and soy sauce to taste or
Cauliflower cheese or Veeze or
Macaroni savoury with cheese or Veeze

PUDDING
Soya yoghurt or
Stewed fruits or
Soya desserts or
Fresh fruit

TEATIME
*Wholemeal bread with Natex/peanut
butter/tahini/vegetarian
pâté/Vecon/Veeze/grated cheese/cottage
cheese/sugar-free fruit spreads
Fresh fruit*

Making the Living Without Cruelty Switch

Most of us cannot afford the luxury of spending a lot of time learning how to devise lots of new dishes. Many people think that a diet without the familiar 'look' of meat-based foods as a centrepiece may be rather dull and that a lot of effort may be required in order to switch over to a vegetarian diet. Happily, both are false premises. Forget about being marooned in the kitchen for hours on end waiting for the beans to cook and of being in uncharted culinary waters whilst you serve up endless variations on the filled jacket potato. Don't throw away your old ideas and cookbooks – just adapt. Later on, at your own pace, you can bring in new and unfamiliar taste combinations and begin to wean yourself away from thinking about meat as the essential component in eating.

This gradual approach is especially important if you have a family. What so often occurs is that one or two members of a family decide, often suddenly, to go vegetarian. Often it's the children who begin to feel uneasy about eating animals. The cook of the family is faced with a dilemma. One – or two – dishes to cook at every meal? It's at this stage that principles often come into conflict with practicalities, and clashes occur.

Animal Aid's Youth Group receive many letters every year from children forced to eat meat, who feel they are in an intolerable situation at home and are upset and angry at their parents' attitude. Some children give in at this stage and write to say they are longing for the day when they can leave home and decide for themselves what they'll eat. Others remain firm, initially living on vegetables alone, until their parents relent. One child wrote: 'My mum thinks that without meat your body won't get the necessary things . . . and my dad used to work in a slaughterhouse and is now a butcher and thinks vegetarians are round the twist.' Another wrote in desperation: 'I'm worrying my mother sick as I just can't bring myself to eat meat *and I don't want to*. We visited the doctor for information, but he didn't agree with me going vegetarian as I'm only fourteen. When I see animals in fields, then think of them being slaughtered, I just know I can't carry on. Please help and please don't say I must eat meat.'

Hopefully, such situations resolve themselves quickly and a child's decision to be a vegetarian – a mature step to take, especially in the face of derision – should be respected, not obstructed. Nutritionally, parents need not worry. Medical writer Dr Vernon Coleman, himself a vegetarian and former GP, says: 'An enormous amount of today's illness can be traced back to the consumption of meat and meat products. The wisest and healthiest diet would include very little meat or no meat at all.'

When you consider the appalling diet currently fed to most British schoolchildren, parents should be delighted to have their children turning their backs on a largely junk-food and fat-laden diet of chips, burgers and high-calorie sweets and pop. This results in a high dose of saturated fat with little essential B and C vitamins or fibre. Fears for the health of the next generation appear to be confirmed, as post-mortems on child road accident victims reveal that most children already have arterial (heart) damage caused by their intake of saturated, mostly animal, fats.

A 1988 Gallup Poll commissioned by the Realeat Co., who make Vegeburgers, found that 1.3 million children under sixteen were already vegetarian or avoiding red meat completely, and the numbers are increasing. A *Which* report covering the North Yorkshire education authorities showed that children wanted 'more vegetarian food, less greasy food and less fattening food'. Yet 66 per cent of young veggies still prefer to take a packed lunch because at many schools they're only offered 'chips and beans'. In response to this situation Animal Aid, the Vegetarian Society and the Athene Educational Trust launched the Choice Campaign – for 'the right to choose a healthy vegetarian meal at school'. Special menu planners, meal promotions and literature are provided for school caterers; this has resulted in a great boost for healthy eating. Some education authorities, notably Nottingham, Sheffield and Avon, are now serving wholefood school lunches with more vegetarian selections. Make sure your school knows about Choice.

Back at home, however, the problem remains – what to cook. The following ideas will help solve this dilemma, at least initially, and should please everyone – vegetarians, meat-eaters and especially the cook. If the lone veggie happens to be the one planning the family eating, these recipes will be especially useful in persuading the reluctant to move over towards a cruelty-free diet.

The Living Without Cruelty lunchbox

If you thought it would be cheese sandwiches all the way, then think again!

SANDWICH FILLINGS

Cheeses with pickles/salad/relish etc.
Veeze
Vegetarian pâtés – huge selection including Tartex, vegetable, nut and tofu spreads
Tivall slicing sausage
Peanut butters
Sugar-free fruit spreads
Bananas
Yeast extract
Vecon
Free-range egg with Waistline mayonnaise

SALAD BOX

Mix selections of salad greens/cucumber/tomato/raw carrot/gherkin/celery/beetroot/brown rice/cooked mixed beans in dressing/nuts/olives/cooked new potatoes/fresh coleslaw/beansprouts/onion etc.

SAVOURIES

Sosmix scotch egg
Sosmix roll
Vegetarian pasty
Slice of cold nut roast
Cold, cooked Vegeburger
Portion of quiche
Sliced nuttolene roll

Cooked falafel
Vegetable samosa
Hummus
Flask of vegetable soup
Whole Earth Pasta Pot
Stuffed pitta bread

BREAD, BISCUITS AND PUDDINGS

Wholemeal/granary bread and rolls
Wholewheat crackers/sunflower margarine
Hedgehog organic crisps
Packet of nuts and raisins
Wholegrain crunchy bar
Dried apricots, figs, dates etc.
Fresh fruit
Home-made cake
Pot of soya dessert
Carton of soya yoghurt

DRINKS

Carton of juice
Juice mixed with naturally carbonated mineral water
Soya milkshake drink

Basic change-over recipes and ideas for busy lives

There are umpteen vegetarian cookery books now available, and the choice can be quite overwhelming. Many are very good – but some are awful. My own list of recommended books is on p. 65. Included here, with recipes as examples, are the culinary ideas you need to make 'going veggie' a simple task. Meat-eating family members will be amazed. Indeed, I've fed members of my own family on these tried and tested versions, often for several weeks at a time, before it finally dawned on them that they *weren't* eating meat! Astute cooks should serve in silence, wait for the empty plates, and not let on – preferably for a month or two – as you slip in the cruelty-free dinners and replace the meat. When the carnivores find out, preferably after weeks of eating non-meat pies, pasties and casseroles, you will be able to smile to yourself when they say, 'I thought it tasted a bit funny, but I didn't like to say anything!' This may seem a bit mean, but is based upon personal experience.

I do recognize that many vegetarians do not like to eat anything which actually resembles meat. This is fair enough, and it's an easy matter to replace TVP (Textured Vegetable Protein) products with beans and pulses. These make tasty alternatives anyway. Yet for newcomers encountering prejudice or a difficult home situation, faced with living alone or simply with being a cook conditioned through years of being in the 'meat-and-two-veg rut', TVP-associated foods offer an easy solution to 'mixed' catering problems and are an excellent advertisement to meat eaters who believe you'll fade away on a vegetarian diet.

A wide range of TVP products are available and come in both unflavoured and 'meat'-flavoured varieties – usually 'beef' and 'pork'. The granules are used for 'mince' recipes such as cottage pie and bolognese sauce. The chunks make superb pies, casseroles, stews and curries. There are even TVP 'steaks'. All TVP products need 'hydrating' and the best results come from soaking in a flavourful marinade rather than just hot water. Pre-flavoured sausage and burger mixes are also widely available.

Included in this section are favourite recipes from celebrities who've adopted the Living Without Cruelty lifestyle. They demonstrate the versatility of compassionate cooking with warming winter casseroles, quick family feasts, one-man, one-pan creations and a few naughty-but-nice dinner party treats. Try them out on your big kids!

INCREDIBLY VERSATILE SAVOURY MINCE BASIC RECIPE

1 large onion
2 medium carrots, scrubbed
4–6 mushrooms
vegetable oil
¼ red pepper, chopped and deseeded
¼ green pepper, chopped and deseeded
salt and pepper to taste
1 packet unflavoured or savoury soya mince (TVP)
1 tablespoon tomato puree
1 teaspoon yeast extract e.g. Natex
1 vegetable stock cube

Chop the onion, carrot, and mushroom and sauté in a little hot vegetable oil until the vegetables just begin to brown. Add the peppers, seasoning and soya mince. Mix thoroughly and continue to cook gently for 5 minutes, stirring to prevent sticking.

Make a stock with the tomato puree, yeast extract, stock cube and enough hot water to make ¾ pint (400ml). Pour it over the mince mixture, stir and cover. Simmer until the vegetables are tender, the mince soft and swollen and the mixture thick. You may need extra water as the TVP will absorb quite a lot of the stock.

If you need to thicken, make a 'gravy' mix with wholemeal flour and Bisto powder (not granules) in equal quantities, mixed to a smooth paste with a little water. Slowly stir it into the mince until the desired consistency is reached.

Use in your favourite recipe or in the ideas below. This recipe serves 2–4, depending on use.

ITALIAN AND HERBY

Serve with your favourite pasta and sprinkle with grated Parmesan.

Substitute olive oil for vegetable oil
To basic mince add:
2 cloves garlic, crushed (add to the sauté)
1 teaspoon oregano
2 teaspoons basil
Extra tomato puree (optional)
1 small can plum tomatoes, chopped

MEXICAN AND SPICY

Serve with a big, crisp salad and a chilled fruit juice cup.

To basic mince add:
½–1 level teaspoon chilli powder, depending on how far you want to travel!
1 small cup sultanas
1 small can red kidney beans, rinsed
Extra tomato puree
1 small can tomatoes

Serve with rice, or use less stock and thicken to a stiff mix with a little wholemeal flour. Use to stuff tortilla shells and heat through in a hot oven.

SHEPHERD'S PIE

Serve with green vegetables.

To basic mince add, if desired:
1 small turnip, diced
1 small parsnip, diced
1 teaspoon dried parsley
You'll also need:
Boiled potato
Vegetable margarine
Soya milk

Pre-heat the oven to 220°C (425°F/gas mark 7). Place the cooked mince in an ovenproof pie dish and top with the potatoes, creamed with vegetable margarine and a little soya milk if wished. Bake until crisp and golden on top.

REALLY AMAZING CORNISH PASTIES

50 per cent wholemeal shortcrust pastry
2–3 large potatoes, well scrubbed
Cold, cooked savoury mince
1 small cup thawed frozen peas (optional)

Pre-heat the oven to 200°C (400°F/gas mark 6). Roll out the pastry and cut it into teaplate-sized circles. Finely chop or grate the potatoes into the mince and add the peas. Mix thoroughly. Place sufficient filling into each circle to fill the pasty without it bursting in the oven. Brush the edges with water, stick them together and crimp in the usual way. Place on a greased baking sheet and glaze with milk or beaten egg if wished. Cook until golden brown and serve hot or cold.

CHEATING MINESTRONE

Serve with grated cheese and crusty bread for lunch.

Leftover Italian mince mix
½ cup wholemeal macaroni
1 vegetable stock cube or *1 teaspoon Vecon vegetable stock*
2 bay leaves
2 tablespoons brown rice

Place all the ingredients in a large pot with sufficient hot water to make a light, brothy soup. Bring to the boil and simmer for about 20 minutes, until the rice and macaroni are tender.

DELECTABLE CHUNKS WITH RED WINE CASSEROLE (FOR MEAT EATERS WHO THINK YOU LIVE ON LETTUCE AND NUT CUTLETS)

This dish will impress anyone. It's great for a special dinner where you have to cater for both veggies and meat eaters. Serve, sprinkled with plenty of chopped fresh parsley, with sauté new potatoes, petits-pois, asparagus spears and soft, wholemeal rolls. It's very rich, so any dessert should be light and fruity. Serves 4–6.

2 teaspoons dried thyme
1 teaspoon dried basil
1 teaspoon dried parsley
3 dessertspoons tomato puree
freshly ground black pepper
Vegetable stock e.g. Vecon
1 bottle red wine
8–10 small onions, preferably pickling size
Olive oil
2 tablespoons Sizzles bacon-flavoured soya mix
1 packet unflavoured or *savoury soya chunks (TVP)*
2 large carrots, sliced
10 button mushrooms, wiped
1 small red pepper, deseeded and finely chopped
1 small green pepper, deseeded and finely chopped
1 heaped teaspoon yeast extract e.g. Natex
1 large can plum tomatoes
1 large aubergine
2 courgettes, sliced
Sea salt

First, make a marinade by combining the thyme, basil, parsley, tomato puree, black pepper, ½ pint (275 ml) of the vegetable stock and ½ pint (275 ml) of the red wine. Set aside.

In a medium saucepan, sauté the whole onions in a little olive oil with the Sizzles mix until browned. Set aside. In a large ovenproof casserole, heat a little more of the oil and tip the soya chunks into it when hot. Flash fry, stirring continually. The chunks will crisp slightly and soak up the oil. Add the chunks to the prepared marinade and leave to soak.

In the same casserole, heat a little more oil and sauté the rest of the vegetables except the aubergine and courgettes. Cover with a 50–50 stock of red wine and vegetable stock and add the yeast extract. Bring to the boil and simmer for 5 minutes. Add the can of tomatoes. Remove from the heat.

Heat the oven to 200°C (400°F/gas mark 6). Halve the aubergine lengthways and place it on an oiled baking sheet at the top of the oven. Cook until soft and browned, but be careful not to burn the skin. Chop it into large chunks when it is cool enough to handle.

Combine in the casserole the onions and Sizzles mix, the soya chunks in their marinade, the courgettes and the aubergine chunks. Turn down the oven to 180°C (350°F/gas mark 4) and place the covered casserole in the centre. Cook for approx 45 minutes to 1 hour, until the chunks and onions are tender. Use extra wine and stock if necessary to prevent drying out, but the casserole should be thick in itself without the need to add flour-based thickeners. Adjust seasoning as necessary.

OTHER IDEAS FOR HUNKY CHUNKS

Use TVP beef-flavoured or plain chunks in all recipes previously made with stewing steak, such as hot-pots, stews, meat pies and curries. Marinade plain chunks in tomato puree, herbs and a yeast extract gravy to add flavour, or alternatively a chilli-based or curry sauce in spicier dishes.

Pork-flavoured chunks can also be used for casseroles with a difference, adding apples, cider, pineapple and stuffings to create a variety of tasty and interesting dishes. Here are two of my own.

OLD-FASHIONED 'MEAT' AND POTATO PIE WITH THYME

Wholemeal pastry can now be purchased frozen or chilled, puff or shortcrust. Both Sainsbury's and Jusrol make puff pastry without animal fat. Serve this dish with lightly cooked green vegetables. Serves 4.

1 dessertspoon tomato puree
1 dessertspoon yeast extract e.g. Natex
Freshly ground black pepper
1–2 teaspoons dried thyme
1 sachet Protoveg beef-flavoured chunks
A little sunflower oil
2 cloves garlic, finely chopped
1 large onion, chopped
1 large carrot, sliced
4 medium mushrooms, quartered
2 medium potatoes, scrubbed and diced
Sufficient wholemeal pastry for a 10 inch (25 cm) square ovenproof dish or large pie plate (sides and top only)

Pre-heat the oven to 200°C (400°F/gas mark 6). Place the puree, yeast extract, pepper and thyme into a bowl and add the chunks. Just cover with boiling water and leave to soak, stirring to ensure the chunks are well covered. In a little oil sauté the garlic and onion. After 2–3 minutes add the carrot, mushrooms and potatoes. Continue cooking for 5 minutes, stirring to prevent sticking. Add the chunks along with the gravy and mix well, adding extra water if necessary. Cover and bring to the boil. Reduce to a low simmer and cook till the chunks and potato are tender. The gravy should be thick without the need for flour-based thickeners. Set aside.

Roll out the pastry and line the sides of your greased dish or pie plate. Cut out the top. Fill the dish with the prepared filling and moisten the pastry around the edge to fit on the top. Crimp the sides and decorate with leftover pastry as desired. Bake for 40 minutes or until the crust is golden.

'PORK' AND CIDER SAUCE WITH STUFFED APPLES

This is delicious accompanied by green beans or peas. Serves 4.

1 sachet pork-flavoured Protoveg chunks
Approx. 2 pints/1.1 litres dry Blackthorn cider
2 cloves garlic, finely chopped
1 large onion, chopped
2 sticks celery, finely sliced
8 baby carrots, trimmed and scrubbed
8 oz/225 g button mushrooms, wiped
2 bay leaves
1 teaspoon chopped parsley
sprig of fresh rosemary
A little oil for frying
4 Bramley cooking apples, washed and cored
1 packet country stuffing mix or home-made sage and onion stuffing
1 tablespoon raisins, washed
Freshly ground black pepper
Brown sugar to taste

Pre-heat the oven to 190°C (375°F/gas mark 5). Marinade the chunks in 1 pint (600 ml) of the cider. Sauté the garlic, onion, celery, carrots, mushrooms and herbs in a little oil for 5 minutes. Add the chunks in their marinade to the vegetables and remove from the heat. Set aside for the flavours to mingle.

Meanwhile, score the apples around their middles with a sharp knife to allow the skins to separate during cooking. Make up the stuffing, adding the raisins, and pack this into the apples. Arrange the apples in an open ovenproof dish. Spoon around them the chunks and vegetables, adding extra cider if necessary to prevent sticking during cooking. Grind fresh pepper over the dish and sprinkle the tops of the apples with a little brown sugar. Bake in the centre of the oven for 45 minutes to 1 hour, until the chunks and vegetables are tender and the apple tops puffed yet still whole. Cover with foil if the apples brown too easily.

LINDA McCARTNEY'S WINTER HOT-POT

Working mum Linda McCartney loves cooking for her vegetarian family. This is a favourite winter dish and a great way to cook soya chunks. Accompany with creamed potatoes or rice, plus green vegetables or a salad. Serves 4.

2 oz/50 g margarine
1 large onion, chopped
4 medium carrots, chopped
4 medium potatoes, cubed
2 cloves garlic, crushed
2 sticks celery, chopped
½ red pepper, chopped and deseeded
1 small packet TVP chunks or 8 small vegetable burgers, cubed
1 × 14 oz/400 g can chopped tomatoes
vegetable stock or water to cover
2 tablespoons soy sauce
salt and freshly ground black pepper to taste

Melt the margarine in a large pan and lightly brown the onion. Add the other vegetables and sauté for a few minutes. Add the chunks and brown for 3 minutes over a gentle heat. Add the tomatoes and stock. Season with soy sauce, salt and pepper. Cover and simmer for 30–40 minutes, until well cooked and thickened. Add extra stock a little at a time during cooking if the mixture seems too dry, as the TVP will absorb a proportion of the liquid.

Sausages with style

You don't have to forsake this traditional and much-loved treat if you change to a vegetarian diet, because there are so many tasty – and healthier – options available. All of them can be used in your favourite recipes.

Look for Sosmix, Sosfry and Vegebanger. These dry mixes are simply added to water and become 'sausage meat'. They are great for shaping into thin flatties as sausage burgers; 'sos-shapes' on sticks for parties; bangers for breakfasts, hot dogs and hot sandwiches with whole-grain mustard; wrapped around a free-range egg for 'Scotch eggs' (great for picnics cold or with salads); in pastry for sausage rolls; and in all your favourite savoury recipes. They are especially good for stuffing vegetables like giant tomatoes and flat field mushrooms. Herbs, garlic, onion, mushrooms and fresh tomatoes can be added and the mixture roasted in a loaf tin to make a savoury 'loaf' to slice, good hot or cold.

Because the mix is dry it can be kept in the cupboard – unlike meat, which needs refrigeration – and there's no risk of the product 'going off' after a few days. The cooked product also freezes well. The fat content is very low and what there is mostly comes out during cooking, so you rarely need to add any at all.

For a spicier, smoked taste like frankfurters look for the frozen party and hot-dog sausages from Tivall (see the barbecue recipes on page 56). Actress Vicki Michelle uses the party-sized 'franks' to make a cruelty-free version of the French sausage cassoulet. A frozen slicing sausage is also available for sandwiches. This makes great canapés too and can also be made into battered fritters. Vegebangers also come ready-frozen.

VICKI MICHELLE'S VEGGIE CASSOULET

Vicki, who plays Yvette in BBC1's hit comedy *'Allo 'Allo*, serves this garlicky French hot-pot to non-vegetarian dinner guests who, she says, always ask for more! Serve with hot garlic bread and a glass of robust red wine. The cassoulet can be made the day before and kept in the fridge (this actually improves the flavour). For an eco-nomical everyday version use baked beans with the sausages and add any leftover cooked vegetables to the dish before placing in the oven. Serves up to 8.

2 large onions sliced
4 cloves garlic, finely chopped
Sunflower oil
2 carrots, scrubbed and sliced
8 oz/225 g mushrooms
3 medium potatoes, scrubbed and roughly diced
1 teaspoon thyme
1 teaspoon chervil
1 teaspoon basil
Freshly ground black pepper
4 cups assorted cooked beans (black-eye, haricot, red kidney, aduki)
1 medium can tomatoes
2 pints/1.1 litres Vecon vegetable stock
Freezer-sized pack Tivall vegetarian cocktail sausages
1 dessertspoon tomato puree
1 glass red wine (optional)

Pre-heat the oven to 180°C (350°F/gas mark 4). In an oven-proof casserole, sauté the onion and garlic in a little oil till browned. Add the carrot, mushrooms and potatoes and cook for a further 5 minutes, stirring to prevent the potato sticking. Add the herbs and season with pepper. Add the beans and tomatoes. Cover with the stock and slowly bring to the boil. Add the sausages cut in half, the tomato puree and the wine, if used. Remove from the top of the cooker and cook in the oven for about 1½ hours, until the ingredients are tender and the stock thickened. The sausages will swell.

Burgers without cruelty

The advertising for most of the biggest burger chains like McDonald's is aimed primarily at children. Perhaps they are aware of the danger of a falling market in future years as more and more young people realize what a 'burger' really is and opt for a cruelty-free diet. Burger chains such as Wimpy now offer beanburgers in an effort to attract 'mixed' families, but beware – animal fats may still be used to cook both burgers and french fries. Fast foods in general are not particularly healthy and contain large amounts of fat and additives as well as being animal-exploitive (see what you might be getting in your take-away on page 18). But there is no reason why you can't enjoy a burger meal Living Without Cruelty-style.

Look for Vegeburgers, available as a dry mix or ready-frozen from health stores and supermarkets. These are really delicious and come in herb and chilli flavours. Kids love them.

Burgermix and Dietburger are also very tasty dry mixes and much 'meatier' in texture and appearance. Serve in the usual way in a wholemeal sesame bun with salady bits and relish. The best-tasting ready-made 'pickles', which really enhance the taste, come from the Whole Earth Co. Their tomato relish and sweet-corn pickle are unbeatable; all the ingredients are natural and largely organic.

Holland and Barratt shops with freezer sections usually have a good selection of 'sausages', 'burgers', ready-made meals and other convenience foods which can be useful on busy days. They are also really helpful in adjusting your cooking habits and the family's meal expectations. As already stated, there is little point in discarding all your favourite recipe ideas when they could easily be adapted, and the convenience products mentioned can make life easier when catering for both vegetarians and meat eaters in the family.

Lots of love
Howard Jones

HOWARD JONES
'My reasons for Living Without Cruelty are simple and have nothing to do with intellectual arguments – I just don't want to be party to killing and suffering. I think the violence we do to animals affects us all, so for me, vegetarian food is simply "Non-Violent Cuisine".'

HOWARD JONES'S 'BIG HOJO'S'

Here's a simple and delicious recipe for making your own veggie burgers – the kinder alternative to Big Mac's. Make a big batch and freeze the mixture in flat burger shapes ready for frying. They're good for the barbecue, too. The quantities given here make 12 burgers. Rock musician Howard owns a vegetarian restaurant called Nowhere in New York's Greenwich Village. Serve the burgers in a sesame seed bap with, to quote Howard, 'copious chips, browned onion rings, peas, tomato ketchup, mustard and a pint of Guinness!'

2 tablespoons vegetable oil and extra oil for frying
1 large onion, chopped
½ teaspoon coriander
8 oz/225 g mixed unsalted nuts
½ teaspoon dried parsley
3 oz/75 g fresh wholemeal breadcrumbs
1 oz/25 g rolled oats
1 teaspoon yeast extract e.g. Natex
¼ pint/150 ml vegetable stock
1 free-range egg
A little flour for coating

Heat the 2 tablespoons of oil and gently fry the chopped onion until soft but not brown. Stir in the coriander and cook for a further minute. Remove from the heat. Finely chop the nuts and stir them into the onion mix along with the parsley, breadcrumbs, oats, yeast extract and stock. Beat the egg and stir it in. Divide the mixture into 12, making each portion into a flat burger shape. Roll them in flour, then chill for 1 hour in the fridge before gently frying in a shallow frying pan for 10 minutes on each side.

Other proteins

TVP-based 'meat' replacements undoubtedly make it easier and more convenient to make changes in your diet. They are certainly cheaper than their meat equivalents, but there are a host of other plant proteins which will make your cooking even more diverse and save you pounds over the cost of flesh foods. These highly nutritious staples have a long shelf life and do not require refrigeration.

Nuts are the butt of all the boring wisecracks made about the vegetarian diet. Many people would be surprised to discover that most veggies have never had a nut cutlet or would wish to eat one. Yet nuts are so delicious and useful: not only can they be eaten raw with dried or fresh fruit as a snack, or used in salads, rice dishes and desserts, but ground and mixed with herbs, cereals and fresh vegetable purees they become fantastic mixes which can be 'roasted', meatloaf-style. Each nut variety imparts its own unique flavour and delicate oils to the dish. Nut mixtures can be shaped into burgers or rissoles, used as pasty or pie fillings, as well as baked in a loaf tin or ring mould for both hot and cold slicing. Totally versatile and quick to make and cook, these 'roasts' can be used for every occasion from Christmas dinner to a summer picnic.

Pulses

These are beans, of which there are umpteen varieties each with a different flavour and texture; green, brown and red lentils; split peas and chick peas.

Dried beans need a 10–15 minute boil to eliminate toxins, followed by slow cooking in fresh water. This need not be a drawback if you think ahead. Pre-soaking overnight cuts down cooking time, and batch-cooking bean-based meals for the freezer makes these very economical proteins too good to miss out on. For emergencies, tinned varieties are now available in most supermarkets – the familiar baked (haricot) beans, red kidney, barlotti, black-eyed, aduki and butter beans, and chick peas. Most, unfortunately, have salt and sugar added, so if you do use them remember to cut out your own seasoning.

Lentils cook very much faster than beans – red ones take only about 15 minutes. Lentils make wonderful thick soups and spicy curried dhals. With a chunk of good wholemeal bread the soups are a meal in themselves, and a big panful makes a cheap and highly nutritious family lunch.

Lentils and beans, combined with herbs and vegetables, can be used to create alternative lasagnes, hot-pots, cottage pies, flans and pasties. Use chick peas to make your own falafel or garlicky hummus. Fantastic!

Whole grains

We all know about brown rice. That's the glutinous mass over which vegetarians pour a suspicious brown slop called vegetable curry. This rather quaint, stereotyped image has clung to vegetarianism over the years and goes with the nut-cutlet, rabbit's-ears, come-to-Jesus-sandals and lentil-burger figure. This ancient relic has now more or less been laid to rest as cruelty-free living spreads its message. Whilst the meat industry seems intent on portraying its consumers as a cretinous bunch of thicks (Wot No Meat?), vegetarianism took off as consumers began to realize that the 'brown rice brigade' might have something worth looking into. Brown rice, hand in hand with wholemeal bread, has really been the 'pivot' which has educated us into thinking 'whole' about our food.

Now we can buy wholemeal pastas and macaroni as well as barley, oats, rye, buckwheat, millet, bulghur wheat and quinoa grains. Some of these may seem unusual and unfamiliar, but all have a contribution to make to a satisfying and diverse menu. As you become familiar with creating new savoury dishes, you will discover that these grains have a role far beyond that traditionally assigned to them in bread making. Wheat can be used to make delicious roast mixes, while bulghur is a great alternative to rice or potatoes and is especially good for salad dishes and savoury puddings.

Something quick

Apart from bangers and burgers and other similar foods, supermarkets are beginning to introduce convenience ready-meals approved by the Vegetarian Society. Look for the VSUK's 'V' symbol on packaging. As with any dish, not all are to everyone's taste. Some are fairly bland and lack character, but try them for yourselves. They are certainly a welcome development for students and bed-sit dwellers with limited cooking facilities, and equally good for holiday self-catering and other days when you need to get away from the kitchen. Prices seem to be around £1.20 a portion upwards for one. Tasty ones that I'd recommend are:

Sainsbury's Savoury Pie (beef-type) made from Quorn mycoprotein
Sainsbury's Lentil and Vegetable Roll in wholewheat pastry

Sainsbury's vegetable samosas (deli counters)
Sainsbury's Cornish Vegetable pasties
Sainsbury's vegetable pizzas (freezer)
Marks and Spencer's Ratatouille

Other convenience foods which have a place in my store cupboard/freezer are:

Falafel mix by Fantastic Foods
Granose nut roast in foil bake-dish
Granose tinned nuttolene
Sosmix
Vegeburgers
Protoveg TVP chunks and mince
Granose soya desserts
Sainsbury's Vive non-dairy ice cream (freezer)
Sainsbury's puff pastry cases made with non-animal fats

Price comparisons

Wastage will include shrinking, fat release, and inedible gristle and sinew	No waste
Stewing steak £2.66 lb	TVP 'beef' chunks 52 p lb
Beef mince £1.28–£1.98 lb	TVP mince 52 p lb
Sausage meat From 82p lb	Sosmix 65p lb
Beefburgers (4) From 90p	Vegeburgers (4) 59p

We live in an age of fast foods and convenience eating and our health undoubtedly suffers as a result. But quick doesn't have to be unhealthy. Although some of the convenience foods mentioned are invaluable, they shouldn't be relied upon totally. Indeed, their expense limits them to occasional use when the need arises. By the time it takes to reheat a frozen ready-meal (or even a chilled one) you can heat up a little sesame oil in a wok and stir-fry some mushrooms, cauliflower and broccoli florets,

---

Weekend eating: Based on two days' meals for a family of four

Chicken: 3 lb £1.70–£2.50	**Nut roast:** £1–£2.50
Beef: topside joint £2.68 lb (£6.00–£8.00 for joint)	**Vegetarian Christmas roast:** £3.37 max
Beef: brisket joint £1.80 lb (£4.00–£6.00 for joint)	**Beans:** 28p–69p lb depending to variety
Pork: leg joint £1.20 lb (£4.50–£6.50 for joint)	**Lentils:** 35p–49p lb
Pork: lean belly £1.15 lb (£3.50 for joint)	**Chick peas:** 38p lb
Lamb: leg £1.68 lb (£6.00–£8.00 for leg)	**Bulghur wheat:** 43p lb
Lamb: large shoulder 68p lb (£3.00–£4.00 for shoulder)	**TVP chunks** (unflavoured): 77p lb dry weight – makes over 3 lb when cooked
Turkey: 64p lb (£2.50–£9.00 for bird)	**Nuts:** From 55p lb (peanuts) to £4.75 lb (cashews)*

* Brazils, walnuts and pecans average 90p lb, hazelnuts £1.35 lb. Cashews are more expensive but you would only need ½ lb for a family-sized nut roast which would cater for two days' meals.

---

onion, carrot, chopped peppers, mange-tout, flaked almonds and a little shredded fresh ginger. Shake over some soy sauce and squirt with a freshly cut lime and you've got a meal to set your taste buds singing – about 20 minutes from start to finish. So my recommendation is – get a wok. You'll find out what vegetables really taste like.

HAYLEY MILLS'S FAMILY SUNDAY LUNCH: LENTIL LOAF ROAST

This delicious roast is simple to cook and very economical, and a firm favourite with Hayley Mills's family. It makes a great centrepiece surrounded by your favourite Sunday-lunch vegetables, and will also slice cold for a second meal if required. Up to 8 portions.

8 oz/225 g lentils
2 onions, chopped
1 clove garlic, crushed
Vegetable oil
2 cups wholemeal breadcrumbs
4 oz/100 g cheese, grated
1 teaspoon chopped sage
1 teaspoon chopped thyme
1 tablespoon chopped parsley
Salt and freshly ground black pepper
2 free-range eggs, beaten

Pre-heat the oven to 180°C (350°F/gas mark 4). Cook the lentils in three times their volume of water, which should take about 15 minutes. Meanwhile fry the onion and garlic in the oil, and when soft add to the breadcrumbs in a mixing bowl. Add the cheese, herbs, salt and pepper and mix. Finally add the eggs and the cooked lentils and mix thoroughly. Place in a well-greased loaf tin and cook for 40 minutes, until firm.

ANNIE LENNOX'S SPICY LENTIL SOUP

Serve with hot naan or granary bread for a filling lunch or supper.

2–3 tablespoons sunflower oil
½ teaspoon turmeric
½ teaspoon coriander
½ teaspoon cumin
¼ teaspoon cayenne (chilli) pepper
2 cloves garlic, finely chopped
2 large onions, finely chopped
2 carrots, grated
1 stick celery, finely chopped
8 oz/225 g dry weight green or brown lentils, washed and pre-cooked
2 pints/1.1 litres vegetable stock e.g. Vecon
Salt and pepper

Heat the oil in a large pan and fry the spices, garlic and onion gently for 1 minute. Add the other prepared vegetables and sauté until softened and beginning to colour. Add the cooked lentils and mix well. Cover with the stock. Bring to the boil, then cover and simmer gently for 1 hour until the ingredients have softened and the soup is thickening. Season to taste. The soup can be eaten as it is, or liquidized for a creamier texture.

RITA TUSHINGHAM'S BEANY BAKE

Actress Rita Tushingham likes using a variety of coloured beans to give this dish its taste and visual appeal, but any combination of beans will do. Serve with a crunchy salad and garlic bread. Serves 4.

1 large onion, finely chopped
8 oz/225 g mushrooms, wiped and thinly sliced
3 cloves garlic, finely chopped
Olive oil
1 large aubergine, sliced, covered in salt (to remove bitterness) and rinsed
1 lb/450 g cooked beans – a combination of red kidney, green flageolet, white butter bean and black-eyed or aduki beans is very good (the beans should be tender, not mushy)
1 teaspoon oregano
1 teaspoon basil
Freshly ground black pepper
Sea salt
6 ripe tomatoes, thickly sliced
1 cup single cream
3–4 oz/75–100 g wholemeal breadcrumbs
3 oz/75 g cheese, grated
2 oz/50 g walnuts, roughly chopped

Pre-heat the oven to 200°C (400°F/gas mark 6). Sauté the onion and garlic in a little olive oil until soft but not browned. Add the aubergine slices and brown. Mix the cooked beans with the herbs and season well. Toss the beans with 1–2 tablespoons olive oil.

Oil a large ovenproof dish and cover the base with a layer of tomatoes. Cover this with a third of the mixed cooked beans, then sliced mushrooms, aubergine and sautéed onion and garlic. Repeat the layers, finishing with the remaining third of the beans. Pour the cream over the dish and sprinkle with breadcrumbs. Cover with the grated cheese and chopped walnuts. Bake for 45 minutes–1 hour until deep golden and bubbly.

MARIE HELVIN'S NASI GORENG

This delicious, quick Indonesian meal is a tried and tested favourite which Marie confesses to eating, not just for lunch or supper, but at breakfast-time too! Stir-frying keeps the vegetables nice and crunchy. To vary the flavour you can add other vegetables, especially roots, as well as nuts and seeds. Serve on hot plates, with a fried egg in the centre, and garnish liberally with fresh coriander.

Japanese soy sauce
Tomato ketchup
Red chilli pepper (cayenne)
1 large onion, chopped
Garlic, finely chopped
Sunflower oil
Fresh spinach leaves, roughly chopped
String beans, topped and tailed and halved
Carrots, sliced
Cauliflower, broken into small florets
White cabbage, shredded
1 cup cold, pre-cooked Japanese or 'pudding' rice per person
1 free-range egg per person
Fresh coriander

Prepare sufficient vegetables for the number of people you are feeding. The average-sized wok will stir-fry ingredients for roughly two people only – more becomes unwieldy.

Make the sauce by mixing equal quantities of soy sauce and ketchup – about 3 dessertspoons of each will cover sufficient vegetables for two. Add chilli pepper to taste, as hot as you like! The sauce should be sweet, but strong-flavoured.

Sauté the onion and garlic in a little sunflower oil till softened. Turn up the heat and add the other vegetables. Stir-fry, continually turning the vegetables and add a little more oil if required – there should be no residual oil at the bottom of the wok. After 3–4 minutes, the vegetables will begin to 'sweat' their juices and gloss over. They should retain their crispness. At this point, add the cooked rice and mix well. Continue turning the mixture for 1 minute until the rice is heated through. Spoon the sauce over the top, stirring, until the vegetables and rice are coated and a rich red/brown colour. Do not make the mixture wet by adding too much sauce.

Keep hot while you fry the eggs to your taste.

DAVID ESSEX'S HIGH-SPEED VEGETABLE CRUNCH

A busy musician and actor, David often caters for himself. This is a typical man's recipe based on the principle of the ubiquitous fry-up. But it's an altogether healthier and delicious version. Quick and easy, this recipe adapts to whatever vegetables you have available, and is perfect after a busy day. Make as much as you can eat!

Garlic, finely chopped
Olive oil or vegetable fat
Cauliflower florets
Broccoli florets
Cold cooked waxy potatoes, chopped
Courgettes, chopped
Fresh tomatoes, chopped
Button mushrooms, chopped
Onion, chopped
Carrot, chopped
Red and green peppers, chopped
Nuts, chopped
Chilli sauce
1 cup vegetable stock
Mature vegetarian Cheddar cheese, grated
1–2 slices wholemeal bread, crumbled

Sauté the garlic in the oil and add the cauliflower and broccoli. Cook for 5 minutes, stirring continually. Add the other vegetables and continue to cook and stir until they begin to brown and 'sweat' their juices. Add the nuts. Use just enough oil to prevent everything burning. Add chilli sauce to taste. Turn into an ovenproof casserole, and pour stock over the top. It should just moisten the dish, not swamp it. Cover with grated cheese and crumbled wholemeal bread. Grill on a high heat until browned and bubbly. Serve immediately.

DAVID ESSEX
'For me, the key to everything is "naturalness". Humans and animals need to live their lives without interference, and with dignity. Factory farming robs animals of any chance of that, but there's a level of consciousness in the streets which is helping to overthrow these systems.'

CHRISSIE HYNDE'S BAKED MACARONI CHEESE

Rock singer Chrissie is well known for speaking out against both human and animal abuse and is a director of the environmental group Ark. These favourite supper recipes are taken from *Linda McCartney's Home Cooking*, written with Peter Cox and published by Bloomsbury. Serves 4.

12 oz/340 g macaroni
1 free-range egg
1 pint/570 ml milk or *soya milk*
1 oz/25 g butter or *vegetable margarine*
10 oz/285 g vegetarian Cheddar cheese, grated
Salt and *freshly ground black pepper*

Pre-heat the oven to 180°C (350°F/gas mark 4). Lightly boil the macaroni for about 5 minutes until half cooked. Whisk the egg and milk together in a large jug. Melt the butter or margarine and add it, with the grated cheese, to the egg and milk. Stir well. Place the strained, lightly cooked macaroni in a greased baking dish. Pour the egg and cheese mixture on top. Sprinkle with salt and pepper and stir well. Press the mixture down evenly and bake, uncovered, for 30–40 minutes, until the top is brown.

NIÇOISE GREEN BEANS

This goes well with the macaroni dish above.

2 tablespoons olive oil
1 medium onion, chopped
2 sticks celery
1 lb/455 g French green beans
1 × 14 oz/397 g can chopped tomatoes
4 tablespoons vegetable stock or *tomato juice*
1 bay leaf
½ oz/15 g fresh parsley, chopped
Salt and *freshly ground black pepper to taste*

Heat the oil in a large frying pan and gently sauté the onion and celery until lightly browned. Boil or steam the French beans until tender (about 10 minutes). Drain and set aside. Add the tomatoes, stock, bay leaf and parsley to the sauté. Stir well and simmer this sauce for 20 minutes, uncovered. Season to taste. Add the cooked beans to the sauce and stir well. Bring back to a simmer and cook for a further 2 minutes. Serve immediately.

BARBARA DICKSON'S QUICK SUPPER PASTA

After a tiring day in the recording studio, singer Barbara Dickson doesn't want to spend too long in the kitchen. This 'meal-in-a-moment' is so simple, yet the flavours are fresh and zingy. Serve with a tomato salad sprinkled with fresh basil.

Mushrooms, sliced
Garlic, crushed
Olive oil
Pesto (basil sauce)
Fresh Parmesan, grated
Fresh noodles (tagliatelle)

Sauté the mushrooms with the garlic in a little olive oil until browned. Cook the fresh pasta in lots of boiling water for 4 minutes. Drain and add the garlic mushrooms and pesto to taste. Then sprinkle with the grated Parmesan.

CARLA LANE'S HOT 'N COLD POTATO CAKES

Writer Carla Lane makes up her cooking as she goes along, according to what's in the kitchen. This cheap and easy dish can be adapted to whatever you have available and is ideal for using up left-over vegetables.

4–6 potatoes, peeled and washed
Salt and *pepper*
Knob of vegetable margarine
Mature Cheddar cheese, finely grated, to taste
1 large onion, chopped
2 teaspoons mixed herbs
2 oz/50 g peanuts, roughly chopped
½ cup thawed frozen peas

Boil the potatoes until tender, but not mushy. Strain them, and mash really well with the margarine until creamy, adding seasoning to taste. Combine the remaining ingredients until evenly blended. Make into flat cakes and serve in one of the following ways.
(1) Cold with chopped parsley on top, with a big mixed salad.
(2) Topped with extra cheese and a tomato slice and browned under the grill. Accompany with vegetables and a spicy tomato sauce.

(3) Thicken the mixture with a handful of oats, shape and fry in hot oil until golden and crisp on the outside. Nice with baked beans for a nourishing tea which the kids will love.

PETER CUSHING'S BEETROOT AND ONION SUPPER SPECIAL

Actor Peter's two favourite flavours are combined here to make a filling and easy-to-prepare evening meal. Serve hot in individual bowls, sprinkled with chopped fresh mint if desired, and with a chunk of fresh granary bread. Busy mums could adapt this recipe by incorporating any left-over vegetables, turning it all into an ovenproof dish, sprinkling thickly with grated cheese and putting under a hot grill until bubbly. Serve with salad and hot garlic bread.

4–6 medium beetroots, cooked
2 sticks celery, scrubbed
2 large onions, roughly chopped or 8–10 pickling onions whole
2 large potatoes, pre-boiled for 10 minutes
Sunflower oil
Freshly ground black pepper

Dice the beetroot and finely slice the celery. In a large pan sauté the onion until just turning brown. Add the beetroot and celery. Turn down the heat and cook for 2 minutes. Chop the potatoes into chunks and add to the pan. Season with pepper. Cover and cook on a very low heat until the potato is tender, stirring every few minutes to prevent sticking.

TWIGGY'S PASTA QUILLS WITH FOUR CHEESES

This pasta dish is ideal for an informal meal. Accompany with salad and garlic bread. Serves 4.

2 oz/50 g butter or vegetable margarine
½ oz/15 g flour
8 fl. oz/225 ml milk or soya milk
2 oz/50 g Mozzarella cheese, thinly sliced
2 oz/50 g Gruyère cheese, thinly sliced
2 oz/50 g Cheddar cheese, thinly sliced
2 oz/50 g Edam cheese, thinly sliced
Salt and freshly ground black pepper
14 oz/400 g pasta quills
Parmesan cheese
Fresh parsley, chopped

Melt the fat in a saucepan and stir in the flour. Cook for 1 minute, then gradually blend in the milk to make a sauce. Bring to the boil and cook for 2 minutes. Stir in the cheeses and cook over a gentle heat until melted. Season with salt and pepper.

Meanwhile, cook the pasta in plenty of boiling, lightly salted water as directed on the packet. Drain, then toss the pasta in the hot cheese sauce. Either serve immediately, sprinkled with Parmesan and fresh parsley, or bake in an ovenproof dish, covered with a liberal sprinkling of Parmesan, at 220°C (425°F/gas mark 7) until golden on top. Garnish with the parsley to serve.

CAROL ROYLE'S AUBERGINE PIE

Actress Carol Royle, star of *Life without George* and Dennis Potter's *Blackeyes*, says this is a family favourite. It's one of those easy meals which look good whatever the occasion, and is excellent for informal entertaining. Accompany with a crunchy courgette and tomato salad in vinaigrette, and warm pitta bread. Serves 4.

2 lb/1 kg aubergines
8 fl. oz/225 ml olive oil
1 onion, chopped
1 clove garlic, crushed
1 lb/450 g tomatoes, skinned and chopped
4 oz/100 g cottage cheese
5 oz/150 g low-fat yoghurt
Salt and pepper
1 oz/25 g Parmesan, grated

Slice the aubergines, sprinkle them with salt and leave in a colander for 1 hour. Drain and pat dry with kitchen paper. Pre-heat the oven to 180°C (350°F/gas mark 4). Heat 2 tablespoons of the oil in a pan. Add the onion and fry until softened. Add the garlic and tomatoes and simmer, uncovered, for 5–7 minutes. In a bowl, mix together the cottage cheese and yogurt, seasoning to taste. Heat the remaining oil in a frying pan and cook the aubergine slices until golden on both sides. Drain on kitchen paper.

In an ovenproof dish arrange one third of the aubergines and cover with half the tomato mixture. Top this with half the yogurt mixture. Repeat the layers, finishing with the remaining third of aubergines. Sprinkle with the grated Parmesan and cook in the oven for 35–40 minutes.

MARTIN SHAW'S TAHINI VEGETABLE STEAMER

Actor Martin recommends this meal as excellent for cleansing the system and it's great for slimming. If liked, a little cold-pressed olive oil can be added to 'sauce' the vegetables, as can cubes of plain tofu to make a more substantial meal. Use whatever vegetables you have available.

Potatoes/kohl rabi/carrots/sweet potatoes/parsnips/Jerusalem artichokes/turnips/swedes, all diced
Celery chunks/whole button mushrooms/green and red pepper chunks/green beans/fresh peas
Lettuce or spinach leaf 'parcels'
Freshly ground black pepper
Tahini (sesame seed spread)
Tamari or shoyu (fermented soy) sauce
Fresh herbs to serve

Fill the steamer with all the prepared vegetables except the lettuce/spinach, putting root vegetables in the bottom as they take longer to steam. Season lightly with freshly ground black pepper if liked. Steam for about 10 minutes until the vegetables are just tender, not squashy. After 5 minutes' steaming, add the lettuce/spinach. Drain. Return the vegetables to the empty steamer, spoon over tahini to taste and shake shoyu or tamari over them to add colour and flavour. Serve sprinkled with your favourite fresh, chopped herbs.

VIRGINIA McKENNA'S 'SALAD-IN-A-BOAT'

Born Free actress Virginia uses this idea for vegetarian family get-togethers. This dish serves up to six and would make a lovely centrepiece for a summer dinner party, served with parsleyed new potatoes. Alternatively, the 'boat' could be filled with a variety of fillings and served hot or cold, cut into thick wedges.

¼ pint/150 ml water
5 tablespoons sunflower margarine
¼ teaspoon salt
2 oz/50 g flour
3 free-range eggs
3 oz/75 g Swiss cheese, grated
Egg-vegetable salad (see below)
1½ cups small spinach leaves
8 cherry tomatoes

Pre-heat the oven to 200°C (400°F/gas mark 6). In a large pan heat the water, margarine and salt, stirring until margarine melts completely. Remove the pan from the heat and add the flour, beating until well blended. Return to the heat and cook for about 1 minute, stirring until a ball is formed and a film forms on the bottom of the pan. Remove from the heat again, and beat in the eggs one at a time until the mixture is smooth and glossy. Add the cheese and mix well. Spoon into a greased 9-inch/23 cm round tin which has either a removable bottom or spring-release sides. Spread the mixture evenly over the base and up the sides of the tin. Bake for 40 minutes until puffed and brown, then turn the oven off. With a wooden skewer, prick the crust in 10–12 places and leave in the closed oven for a further 10 minutes to dry out. Remove from the oven and cool completely before taking the 'boat' out of the tin.

Prepare the egg-vegetable salad described below. Line the bottom and sides of the 'boat' with spinach leaves. Cut each tomato in half. Pile the egg salad into the boat and garnish with the tomatoes.

EGG-VEGETABLE SALAD
¼ pint/150 ml mayonnaise
1 teaspoon Dijon mustard
¼ teaspoon ground cumin
1 cup thinly sliced raw cauliflower
4 oz/100 g raw mushrooms, thinly sliced
1 cup thawed frozen peas
1 cup thinly sliced celery
2 spring onions plus their tops, thinly sliced
4–6 hard-boiled free-range eggs, coarsely chopped

Stir together the first three ingredients in a bowl until well blended, then add everything else.

PETER GABRIEL'S FAVOURITE TARTE AU MOUTARDE
Vegetarian rock musician Peter Gabriel can't resist this flavour-filled savoury pastry. Try serving it with a green salad tossed in a honey and fresh herb dressing, and buttered new pota-toes. You won't need a big piece as it's quite rich, but you'll wish you had room for 'seconds'!

9-inch/23 cm pastry shell, baked blind
3 tablespoons Dijon mustard
4 oz/100 g Gruyère cheese, grated
1 × 8 oz/225 g can tomatoes drained and chopped
3 free-range egg yolks
⅓ pint/200 ml double cream
Salt and pepper

Pre-heat the oven to 170°C (325°F/gas mark 3). Spread the bottom of the pastry shell with the mustard. Cover with grated cheese and top with the tomatoes. Beat the egg yolks and mix them with the cream. Season and pour into the pie shell. Bake for 1 hour. Leave to rest for 10 minutes before serving.

SOPHIE WARD'S LASAGNE
Actress Sophie enjoys creating dishes for her vegetarian family. This pasta dish is quick and easy to make, so it's great for either family meals or carefree entertaining. Delicious accompanied by a selection of green vegetables or a fresh, crisp salad. For a special occasion, serve with a glass of sparkling Italian red Lambrusco, well-chilled. Serves 4.

Fresh lasagne sheets
Tomatoes
1 lb/450 g spinach
8 oz/225 g Ricotta cheese
1½ oz/40 g margarine
½ pint/275 ml milk or soya milk
1 small onion
1 oz/25 g plain flour
Salt and pepper

Cook the lasagne in plenty of boiling, slightly salted water until 'al dente'. Line the base of a large ovenproof dish with sliced tomatoes, then layer pasta sheets, spinach and Ricotta, ending up with a layer of pasta on top. Set aside and make a béchamel (white) sauce by boiling the milk with the onion in it. Strain, and set the milk aside. Heat the margarine until it foams, then sprinkle in the flour, mixing well together. Add the milk gradually until the sauce is thick and creamy, then add the seasoning. Pour the sauce over the pasta layers and bake for 30 minutes until bubbly and golden on top.

URI GELLER'S FAVOURITE: HUMMUS WITH TAHINI

Freshly made, this simple yet wholly satisfying meal is always on the menu in the Geller household. Served with warm pitta bread it's out of this world!

*1–2 cups Garbanzo beans or chick peas soaked
overnight in water
Juice of 2–3 lemons
Salt
¾ cup tahini
3 cloves garlic, crushed
1 tablespoon olive oil
1 teaspoon paprika
1 tablespoon finely chopped parsley*

Boil the soaked beans in fresh water for about 1 hour until tender. Drain and reserve the liquid, keeping a few beans aside to garnish. Puree the rest of the beans in a blender, gradually incorporating the lemon juice and any reserved liquid needed to produce a creamy consistency. Add the salt, tahini and garlic and mix thoroughly, adjusting the seasoning to taste. Mix the olive oil with the paprika. Place the hummus in individual bowls or in a serving dish. Drizzle the oil and paprika over the hummus and garnish with the parsley and reserved whole beans.

JULIE CHRISTIE'S VEGETABLE PIE

A complete meal in itself under a pastry lid. Serves 4.

*½ cauliflower
1 onion
2 carrots, cooked for 5 minutes
4 oz/100 g margarine
3 courgettes, sliced into chunks
Celery, sliced into small chunks
8 oz/225 g button mushrooms
2 oz/50 g flour
1 pint/0.5 litres milk or soya milk
6 oz/175 g or more Cheddar cheese, grated
8 oz/225 g tinned sweetcorn
Broad beans
1 cup cooked rice
2 free-range eggs, hard-boiled
1 blade mace
Salt and pepper
12 oz/350 g shortcrust pastry made with vegetable fat
Egg/milk wash to glaze*

Pre-heat the oven to 200°C (400°F/gas mark 6). Chop the cauliflower, onion and carrots and fry them in the margarine until golden brown. Add the courgettes, celery and mushrooms and continue frying. Stir in the flour to make a roux and cook for 2–3 minutes. Then gently pour in the milk, stirring continuously. Bring to the boil and simmer for 4–5 minutes. Chop the hard-boiled eggs. Next tip in the cheese, sweetcorn, beans, rice, eggs, mace and seasoning. Cook for a further 5 minutes and place the mixture in a large pie dish. Roll out the pastry and cover the pie. Glaze with the prepared egg wash and bake for 25 minutes.

SUSANNAH YORK'S PASTA (PASTA CASA NOSTRA)

This quick and easy meal, served with plenty of freshly grated cheese, will fast become a family favourite. Serves 5–6. Excellent with a crisp, green salad, lightly tossed in a lemon juice and walnut oil dressing.

*Olive oil
2–3 cloves garlic, chopped
1 onion, chopped
1 green pepper, deseeded and finely diced
½ red pepper, deseeded and finely diced
8 oz/225 g mushrooms, sliced
1 lb/450 g fresh tomatoes or 2 × 14 oz/397 g
cans Italian plum tomatoes (or a mixture of
both), chopped
2–3 bay leaves
Oregano to taste
Salt and freshly ground black pepper
Tomato puree to taste
Vegetable stock or 1 glass of wine
Black olives to taste
Fresh pasta for 5–6 servings (my favourite is green
tagliatelli)*

Bring slowly to the boil a large pan of salted water, to which 1 teaspoon of olive oil has been added. Sauté the garlic and onion with a little olive oil in another pan. When the onion is translucent add the vegetables and sauté for another few minutes. Stir in the tomatoes and herbs. Season with a little salt and plenty of pepper. Add sufficient tomato puree for taste and colour and stir in enough stock or wine to make a thick sauce. Add the olives. Cover and simmer on a very low heat for 5 minutes, adding a little further liquid stock if necessary to prevent sticking.

Whilst this is finishing add the fresh pasta to the boiling water and cook until 'al dente'. This takes about 5 minutes, so both pasta and sauce should be ready together.

BILL ODDIE'S ORANGE PIPPIN SALAD

Funny man Bill is serious when it comes to the natural world and prefers natural foods too. What does he like best? 'Quite simple,' he said, 'an apple. But not any old apple. I don't like those big red ones that taste like candy floss or the yellow ones that are more like cotton wool. I like 'em green' – how appropriate – 'crisp and with a slightly tangy taste, and that means one of the early autumn crop of Cox's Orange Pippins.' Add granary baguettes, a selection of tangy cheeses and a crisp, sparkling glass of cider, and this dish makes a marvellous picnic lunch.

1 head crisp lettuce such as Webb's Wonder
1 bunch watercress
Walnut oil
Freshly ground black pepper
No-egg salad cream such as Waistline
Fresh parsley, chopped
Handful sultanas
2 oz/50 g roughly chopped walnuts
4 Cox's orange pippins, cored and sliced and dripped with lemon juice to prevent browning
Green pepper strips to garnish

Wash and chill the salad greens before chopping them roughly and mixing them together in a large glass bowl. Drip walnut oil over them and add pepper to taste. Toss thoroughly.

In another bowl make a dressing of the salad cream and parsley, adding a little oil and pepper to taste. Fold in the sultanas and walnuts, then add the apples, making sure they are well coated with the dressing. Pile the apples into the centre of the green salad bed. Garnish with green pepper strips.

KATE O'MARA'S AVOCADO DELIGHT

Kate O'Mara, star of *Dynasty* and *Howard's Way*, says she loves the taste of avocado pears. This quick and easy recipe is versatile too. Use as a sandwich filling; as a starter, garnished with a crisp lettuce leaf or mousse–like in an elegant glass with a slice of lemon; as a dip; as a stuffing for cold hors d'oeuvres or a topping/filling for a cold sandwich loaf.

For each avocado you will need:
1 teaspoon lemon juice
2 teaspoons egg-free mayonnaise
2 teaspoons sunflower seeds, lightly toasted
1 tablespoon finely chopped fresh chives
1 small tomato, skinned and chopped
Chopped bean sprouts (optional)

Blend together the avocado flesh, lemon juice and mayonnaise until pureed. Turn into a bowl and fold in the seeds, chives, tomato and bean sprouts, if used. Use immediately to prevent discoloration.

RICHARD ADAMS'S GOOD OLD WELSH RAREBIT

Writer and anti-fur trade campaigner Richard Adams likes simple fare, and this is his favourite. It's good with a fresh tomato salad and spring onions for a nourishing lunchtime treat.

3 oz/75 g Cheddar cheese
Salt and freshly ground black pepper
Dry mustard
Soy sauce
A little milk
2 slices wholemeal toast

Grate the cheese into a bowl and season with salt, pepper and dry mustard to taste. Add a shake of soy sauce and enough milk to make a stiff paste. Spread the mixture on to two freshly made pieces of toast and brown under the grill. Serve at once.

LYSETTE ANTHONY'S FAVOURITE SALAD

Actress Lysette prefers the foods from nature's garden. Simple flavours combine here to create a tasty salad. Use aromatic nut oils to give your salads that extra-special taste – Lysette calls hazelnut oil 'a gift from the gods!' This dish is wonderful with really fresh, hot, crusty wholemeal bread and a glass of your favourite wine.

Ripe avocados
Really good salad tomatoes
Spring onions
Hazelnut oil
1–2 cloves garlic, crushed
Fresh lemon juice
Freshly ground black pepper

Chop the avocado flesh into large chunks, and do the same with the tomatoes and onions. Mix the garlic with some hazelnut oil, lemon juice and pepper. Combine all the ingredients to make a salad.

JOHN GIELGUD'S CUCUMBER SALAD

This salad is totally addictive – once you begin eating, you have to devour it all! It goes well with mushroom and herb burgers, good, crusty wholemeal bread and a crisp, dry white wine.

1 cucumber, peeled
1 clove garlic, crushed
1 tablespoon sugar
1–2 tablespoons white tarragon vinegar
Pinch of salt
1 bunch green dill, chopped
Freshly ground black pepper
½ large carton Greek yogurt
Watercress and tomato wedges to garnish

Slice the cucumber thinly. In a bowl mix the garlic, sugar, vinegar and salt. Mix in the dill and season well with the pepper. Pour the mixture over the cucumber, coating the slices, then add to the yogurt, mixing well. Turn into a serving dish and garnish with the watercress and tomato wedges. Cover with clingfilm and chill thoroughly before serving.

TOYAH WILCOX'S RICH OAT CAKE

Singer and actress Toyah tried this recipe on her family – it lasted about 6 minutes. Serve this high-fibre cake as a special dessert or teatime treat.

5 dessertspoons runny honey
4 tablespoons corn oil
1 teaspoon vanilla essence
4 oz/100 g wheatgerm
4 oz/100 g bran
8 oz/225 g rolled oats
1 heaped teaspoon baking powder
8 tablespoons orange juice
1 free-range egg, beaten
Icing:
2 large blocks half-fat cream cheese
4 tablespoons runny honey
1 teaspoon vanilla essence

Pre-heat the oven to 180°C (350°F/gas mark 4). Grease a large square baking tin. Mix the honey, corn oil and vanilla essence together. Mix separately all the dry ingredients and stir well. Add the orange juice to the dry ingredients, stir in and follow with the egg, and the honey and oil mixture. Stir well. Pour the mixture into the baking tin and bake for 1 hour 20 minutes. When the cake is cooked, the blade of a knife will come out clean when inserted into it.

For the topping, break up the cream cheese with a wooden spoon, adding the honey to make a creamy mixture. Add the vanilla essence and mix well. Place the topping in the fridge.

When the cake is completely cool, turn it out and cover with topping. Store refrigerated.

DAVID SHEPHERD'S APPLE MERINGUE

Wildlife artist David enjoys simple dishes. This versatile dessert also works well with other fruits such as apricots.

2 lb/900 g cooking apples
3 oz/75 g granulated sugar
3 free-range eggs
Pinch of salt
6 oz/175 g caster sugar

Pre-heat the oven to 180°C (350°F/gas mark 4). Peel and slice the apples and stew them in a little water. Remove them from the heat when cooked and stir in the granulated sugar, then puree the mixture. Separate the eggs and stir the yolks into the apple puree, mixing quickly. Place the mixture in a shallow ovenproof dish and set aside.

Whisk the egg whites with the pinch of salt until stiff peaks are formed. Then add half of the caster sugar and whisk until peaked again. Carefully fold in the remaining caster sugar. Pile the meringue on top of the puree to cover and bake until the topping is a light golden colour.

JOANNA LUMLEY'S 'FAT-BOY PUDDING'

Admittedly naughty, this favourite dessert is strictly for special treats and dinner party indulgences. An equally naughty vegan version can be made by substituting thick, home-made soya yogurt and Sainsbury's non-dairy cream which has been whipped thickly. Joanna says, 'Seconds are always requested!' Serve accompanied by really good dessert biscuits such as ratafias, or with tart fruits such as berries or apricots.

Equal proportions of:
Whipped double cream
Thick Greek yogurt
plus
Very dark brown raw cane sugar, de-lumped, for the topping

Carefully fold together the cream and yogurt. Do not beat. When combined, spoon carefully into either a shallow glass serving bowl or individual glass dishes. Smooth the top flat and dredge the sugar thickly over the cream mixture. Place in the refrigerator for 24 hours. The sugar 'melts' to a caramel-like topping which permeates the cream and yogurt mixture.

No heartaches with dairy-free

Cutting down on meat can initially lead to over-reliance on dairy foods. Understandably, these offer ready alternatives which we already know and love – omelettes, quiches, cauliflower cheese, macaroni pudding and so on – but from a health point of view the best move is to incorporate more of the alternative sources of proteins such as TVP, beans and other pulses, perhaps having an egg/cheese dish just once a week.

On the dairy front, go for fat-free milk, but do consider soya milk. I've yet to meet anyone who can tell the difference in tea, although it tends to separate in strong coffee due to the high tannin content of coffee, and this can look a bit off-putting. But for cereals, custards, mash, puddings and such-like it's marvellous. Some milks, such as Plamil, do have a 'taste' which the palate soon adjusts to (a bit like the first time you eat yogurt – you soon get used to it). Plamil is especially good for children and has added vitamins. Other brands vary in taste and there are regular as well as sugar-free and salt-free varieties. Brands such as Granose, Holland and Barrett and Unisoy Gold are excellent and taste very good, especially chilled. Boots, Safeway, Tesco and Waitrose all sell own brands. Most soya milk is equivalent in protein to cow's, yet contains a third less calories and no cholesterol, so is good for slimming and your heart.

Cheese in general is high in saturated fat and should be eaten sparingly. From the humane point of view, vegetarian cheeses are made without animal rennet – the scrapings from a calf's stomach – and are therefore the Living Without Cruelty choice. Prewett's offer an English cheese selection available through most health stores, and most supermarkets have their own vegetarian Cheddar, cottage cheeses and soft cheeses. In some outlets vegetarian Mozzarella, Feta, Edam and Danish Blue are available. Look out for the 'V' symbol and the words 'Made with non-animal rennet'. It's about time that the bigger chains started to offer more varieties of vegetarian cheese as the demand is surely there, especially for reasonably priced English varieties.

Non-dairy cheese spreads are also available: Veeze is the best; another is Fromsoya. They don't taste like dairy cheese, but have a flavour all of their own and can be used in a host of recipes that call for cheese as well as in sandwiches.

Tofu, soya bean curd, is also the fat-free answer for those who love cheesecake. Use it instead of cream cheese in recipes; it's bland, so adapts well in both sweet and savoury situations, and is really versatile. Cauldron Foods make a good one in plain and smoked varieties. Morinaga make a silken tofu which is excellent.

Changing your spreads and cooking fats is one way to cut down saturated fat intake. Butter is high in saturates, so look for a good-quality margarine which is marked 'high in polyunsaturates'. Cheap margarines often contain animal fats and fish oils and can be highly saturated. Health stores sell several brands which are totally dairy-free and low in saturates. Look out for Vitaquell, Vitasieg, Vitelma, Granose sunflower, Suma sunflower and unhydrogenated varieties, and Meridian. The process of hydrogenation turns liquid oils to more solid ones, but in so doing makes the oil become more saturated. Thus margarines which contain unhydrogenated oils will be less saturated (they will also be a lot runnier!). Spreads which carry unhydrogenated and high-in-polyunsaturates labels will be healthier, but a bit more expensive.

Oils can be confusing too. Just 'vegetable oil' can mean palm oil, which is saturated. Go for sunflower, safflower, corn or soya oils. If you can afford it, olive oil is high in mono-unsaturates and is believed to have a beneficial effect on cholesterol levels. The best (and most expensive) is labelled 'unrefined and cold-pressed', which means less factory processing. It is also called 'virgin' oil.

Home-made yogurt can be made easily – with soya milk too. Starter, available from health shops, is the culture you need to start production. Granose, Sojal and White Wave are delicious ready-made dairy-free yogurts.

Soya-flavoured milk drinks and shakes are also available. Sunrise make delicious chocolate and banana chilled shakes and Granose do a range.

Look out also for the Granose and Provamel soya desserts, which are really delicious and like mousse, only better. The vanilla variety is excellent instead of cream for topping fruit. Most health stores also sell soya ice creams in a variety of flavours. Choc-ices are also made, as well as 'cornettos'. Sainsbury's sell a non-dairy ice-cream called Vive which is delicious and very good value. They also sell their own 'non-dairy cream'. This is thick and makes a great dessert topping: try it on the dairy-free trifle recipe. It's very good indeed.

Look no eggs!

Free-range eggs, the humane option to battery eggs, are of course preferable – although, as eggs contain fat and cholesterol, it's as well to keep to two or fewer per week. However, it's so easy to consume more in hidden form such as in cakes and biscuits, so why not try these recipes, or adapt your own, and eliminate the eggs? As a guide, 1 tablespoon of soya flour mixed to a cream with a little soya milk will replace an egg in many baking recipes. Rubbing-in type cake recipes seem to adapt best. Try the egg-free recipes in this section, and you'll begin to see how easy it is to do without these 'indispensable' products.

CHOCOLATE SPONGE
4 oz/100 g light brown sugar
2 dessertspoons cocoa or drinking chocolate
½ teaspoon sea salt
6 oz/175 g plain flour (use unbleached with a 50% wholemeal mix)
1 teaspoon bicarbonate of soda
3 fl oz/75 ml sunflower oil
1 teaspoon vanilla essence
1 dessertspoon cider vinegar
⅓ pint/200 ml cold water

Pre-heat the oven to 180°C (350°F/gas mark 4). Mix the dry ingredients in a mixing bowl. In a jug combine the oil, vanilla essence and vinegar. Add to the dry ingredients and pour the cold water over them. Mix well with a fork, without beating. Pour the mixture into two greased and lined sandwich tins and bake for about 30 minutes, until the sponge is springy to the touch and has shrunk from the sides. Cool completely before turning out.

Fill with a chocolate fudge icing and decorate with chocolate glacé topping and candied orange slices.

Alternatively, use as a basis for a *Black Forest Gateau*. Fill the centre with a cherry fruit spread such as Robertsons sugar-free and whipped non-dairy cream. Decorate with piped non-dairy cream, canned cherries and grated plain chocolate.

Chill thoroughly before serving.

CHOCOLATE DAIRY-FREE TRIFLE

1 chocolate sponge cake
2 tablespoons dark rum
1 large tin mandarin oranges
1 Snowcrest orange flavour jelly
1 pint/0.5 litres chocolate blancmange made with soya milk or 1 carton Granose chocolate soya dessert
1 carton non-dairy cream
6 segments Terry's plain chocolate orange

In a deep glass bowl break up the sponge, spoon the rum over it and leave to soak. Drain the oranges and arrange the fruit evenly on top of the sponge. Use the juice to saturate any dry bits of sponge. Make the jelly according to the instructions on the carton, adding the rest of the juice. Pour it on immediately, as it sets very quickly. Chill. Make the chocolate custard and cool it, or use the Granose dessert. Spoon this over the jelly. Whip the cream until thick and spread it over the chocolate layer. Grate the chocolate orange segments over the top to decorate. Refrigerate for at least 2 hours before serving.

NO-EGG FRUIT CAKE

8 oz/225 g wholemeal flour
8 oz/225 g unbleached plain flour
1 heaped teaspoon mixed spice
1 teaspoon bicarbonate of soda
6 oz/175 g vegetable margarine
6 oz/175 g brown sugar
10 oz/275 g dried fruit, cleaned
10 fl oz/275 ml soya milk
1 heaped tablespoon soya flour

Grease and line an 8-inch/20 cm cake tin. Pre-heat the oven to 170°C (325°F/gas mark 3). Mix the wholemeal and plain flours, spice and bicarbonate of soda thoroughly, then rub in the margarine until the mixture is like fine breadcrumbs. Stir in the sugar and fruit. In a small jug combine the soya flour and 2 tablespoons soya milk until creamy. Make a well in the centre of the dry mix and add the milk and creamed soya flour. Stir well, adding extra milk or water if needed to give a dropping consistency. Place the mixture in the tin, level the top and bake in the centre of the oven for about 2 hours, until firm to the touch and a sharp knife comes out cleanly.

DAIRY-FREE CHEESECAKE WITH BLACKCURRANT TOPPING

6 oz/175 g digestive biscuits
2 oz/50 g vegetable margarine
1 lb/450 g tofu
3 tablespoons soya flour
2 teaspoons vanilla essence
juice and finely grated rind of 2 lemons
2 teaspoons agar-agar
6 oz/175 g brown sugar plus 2 oz/50 g (if using fresh fruit)
1 teaspoon baking powder
1 carton blackcurrant-flavoured soya yogurt
6 oz/175 g fresh blackcurrants or small can blackcurrants
2 tablespoons arrowroot

Pre-heat the oven to 140°C (275°F/gas mark 1). Crush the biscuits finely, melt the margarine and mix them together well. Press the crumb mixture into the bottom of a flan tin or pie dish. In a blender place the tofu, soya flour, vanilla essence, lemon juice and rind, agar-agar, the 6 oz of brown sugar and the baking powder. Whizz for about 20 seconds. Pour in the carton of yogurt and blend for a further 5 seconds. Pour the filling on to the crust and smooth it flat. Bake for about 1 hour, until the filling is set. Cool completely, then refrigerate.

Meanwhile make the blackcurrant topping. Wash the fresh fruit and simmer with the 2 oz of sugar until tender. Thicken carefully with the arrowroot first, mixed to a cream with a little cold water. If using tinned fruit, warm through and thicken in the same way. When the topping is cold, spread it over the chilled cheesecake and return it to the fridge for a further hour before serving.

DAIRY-FREE BANANA ICE CREAM

3 teaspoons agar-agar
¼ pint/150 ml hot water
8 oz/225 g tofu
¼ pint/150 ml soya milk
3 tablespoons apple juice
2 teaspoons honey
2 teaspoons vanilla essence
2 ripe bananas, peeled

Put the agar-agar and hot water into a blender and whizz until dissolved. Add the remaining ingredients and blend until smooth, creamy and thick. Turn the ice cream mixture into a plastic freezer container and place in the freezer. After 2 hours remove it from the freezer and whisk to break up the ice crystals. Return it to the freezer. It will be ready to eat after another hour.

Quiche fillings without eggs

Try these tasty combinations and leave the eggs on the shelf. Each recipe requires a wholemeal pastry case.

SPINACH AND TOMATO PICNIC QUICHE

1 lb/450 g spinach
1 onion, chopped
2–3 cloves garlic, crushed
8 oz/225 g tomatoes plus 2 extra for garnish
A little sunflower oil
1 dessertspoon tomato puree
4 oz/100 g finely ground peanuts
1 dessertspoon soy sauce
Nutmeg to taste
Salt and freshly ground black pepper
4 oz/100 g whole roasted peanuts
1 teaspoon wholegrain mustard
Chopped basil (optional)

Pre-heat the oven to 190°C (375°F/gas mark 5). Cook the spinach and drain it. When cold, chop it finely. Sauté the onion, garlic and tomatoes in a little oil until soft. Add the tomato puree and ground peanuts, together with a little water to make a thick sauce. Add the soy sauce and nutmeg, season to taste, then stir in the spinach. Add the whole peanuts and the mustard. Mix well, adding extra water if needed, but the mixture shouldn't be sloppy. Turn into the pastry case, cover with sliced tomato and sprinkle with basil if liked. Bake for 1–1½ hours.

MAIN MEAL BEAN AND MUSHROOM QUICHE

8 oz/225 g black-eyed beans
8 oz/225 g mushrooms
Sunflower oil for frying
2 teaspoons oregano
½ teaspoon caraway seeds
4 oz/100 g nuts, ground

Pre-heat the oven to 180°C (350°F/gas mark 4). Boil the beans until soft (about 45 minutes). Slice the mushrooms and sauté them in a little oil with the oregano and caraway seeds. Add the ground nuts and a little water until a thick 'sauce' is obtained. Combine with the cooked beans. Bake in the pastry case for 1–1½ hours.

SPICY PEPPER AND TOMATO QUICHE

8 oz/225 g red lentils or yellow split peas
1 × 14 oz/400 g can Italian plum tomatoes
8 oz/225 g onions
2 cloves garlic, crushed
8 oz/225 g mixed green and red peppers
2 teaspoons basil
1 teaspoon curry powder
A little sunflower oil
8 oz/225 g fresh tomatoes

Pre-heat the oven to 190°C (375°F/gas mark 5). Pre-soak the lentils with the tinned tomatoes for 30 minutes, then simmer this mixture with a little extra water until the lentils are soft. Sauté the onions, garlic, peppers, basil and spice in the oil until soft. Add the coarsely chopped fresh tomatoes and lentil mixture. Mix well and bake in the pastry case for about 1 hour.

RED AND GREEN QUICHE WITH APPLE AND RICE

6 oz/175 g brown rice
1 large cooking apple, peeled, cored and chopped
8 oz/225 g tomatoes, chopped
8 oz/225 g curly kale
A little sunflower oil

Pre-heat the oven to 190°C (375°F/gas mark 5). Cook the rice in the usual way. Sauté the apple with the tomatoes in a little oil until soft, add the rice and season to taste. Wash and chop up the kale and simmer in a little salted water until the leaves change colour and reduce their bulk. Drain. Layer the kale and rice mixture in the pastry case and bake until the pastry is cooked and the filling set.

So replacing animal products isn't the daunting task you might have imagined. With a little re-arrangement of shopping habits, the whole exercise becomes simple and far from selling your family or yourself short, you'll be helping yourself to health.

Living Without Cruelty doesn't mean Living Without . . . unless you count 8 lbs of cholesterol-ladened animal fat each year, increased risk of heart disease, strokes, diabetes, gall-stones, various cancers, appendicitis, haemorrhoids, varicose veins, diverticular disease and obesity.

Living Without Cruelty doesn't mean living without

Examined in this section are the traditionally 'sacrosanct' meals usually connected with meat products. Given the cruelty-free treatment, they're healthier and kinder alternatives for you and your family.

English Sunday breakfast

The English breakfast, mainstay of hotels around the UK and the pride of farmhouse B&B, is a tradition many people enjoy, particularly when on holiday. For most of us, the morning routine is often a hurried bowl of cereal or a slice of toast washed down with the obligatory cuppa. Yet breakfast is an important meal, providing the energy to take you through worktime without having to resort to unhealthy fillers in between meals.

As we've seen, the plate of cooked battery egg and factory-farmed bacon, chemically enhanced sausage and fried bread soaked in animal fat is good neither for you nor the animals. But sometimes, especially on Sundays for example, you might like to treat yourself to a 'proper cooked breakfast'. The Living Without Cruelty Alternative English Breakfast is the answer. It's delicious and low in fat, so you can enjoy this weekend treat without feeling guilty.

What's on the menu?

Chilled apple juice
Fruit compote

Sosmix mini-sausages coated in sesame seeds
Grilled mushrooms
Grilled tomatoes
Crispy 'fried' bread
Free-range egg

Sugar-free preserves
Honey
Wholemeal toast and dairy-free vegetable margarine
Pot of decaffeinated tea/coffee
Soya milk

FRUIT COMPOTE

This dish can be made in quantity as it improves with time and has a fridge life of up to 2 weeks (it'll be eaten up long before then!). Great on its own, with yoghurt, on cereals and sprinkled with wheatgerm or muesli.

1 lb/450 g mixed dried fruit e.g. apricots, prunes, apple rings, pears, raisins, sultanas and figs
1 cinnamon stick
A few cloves
A few cardomom pods
Apple juice
2–4 teaspoons honey
Juice and thinly pared peel of 1 lemon

Wash the dried fruit, place in a bowl and add the spices. Mix the apple juice with the honey, lemon juice and rind. Pour this over the fruit and leave to soak overnight. © Oded Schwartz.

Cooked breakfast

Make up the Sosmix in the usual way and roll it into small, evenly shaped croquettes. Coat in a mixture of black and white sesame seeds. Grill carefully on a baking sheet until golden and cooked through. These can be made well in advance. Uncooked, they can be refrigerated overnight for the morning meal; alternatively, make a big batch and cook in the oven in quantity until about three-quarters done. Freeze when cold, then use as required.

The 'fried' bread is a slice of wholemeal, thinly spread with vegetable margarine, then toasted until really crisp. The mushrooms should not be fried – they soak up fats like a sponge – so grill them instead. Likewise the tomatoes: simply season with freshly ground black pepper and celery salt and grill. Alternatively, eat them raw.

If you want an egg, please choose free-range, and remember to eat as few as possible. Brush the pan with a little sunflower oil when frying. Poaching would be an even better alternative.

The vegan cooked breakfast simply substitutes other items for the egg. Try baked beans: Whole Earth make a really delicious sugar-free kind. These are especially good with tofu scrambled 'egg'.

TOFU SCRAMBLED 'EGG'

1 lb/450 g tofu
½ teaspoon onion salt
1 tablespoon soya sauce
½ teaspoon turmeric
2 tablespoons vegetable oil

Mash the tofu and mix in all the other ingredients except the oil. Heat the oil and add the tofu mixture. Stir well until thoroughly heated and 'scrambled'. Serve on toast or with other cooked breakfast dishes.

A wedding feast for compassionate lovers

This menu, designed by cookery expert Sarah Bounds, will appeal to all your guests. The food is visually stunning, healthy and delicious and makes a wonderful buffet spread or sit-down banquet. Do-it-yourself caterers will find this menu especially easy to manage. If your reception is in an hotel, the resident chef will probably be delighted to be presented with the recipes, ready for him to prepare for your special day. Add a colourful selection of cheeses, breads and crackers and some delicious organic wines to complete a memorable and impressive meal.

Appetizers

FRESH HERB DIP WITH CRUDITÉS

12 oz/350 g low-fat soft cheese e.g. quark
3 tablespoons thick-set or strained natural yogurt
3 tablespoons freshly chopped chives
3 tablespoons freshly chopped mixed herbs – choose a mixture of parsley, thyme, rosemary and tarragon
Freshly ground black pepper

Place the soft cheese in a bowl and beat in the yogurt to a smooth but firm consistency. Add the herbs and season with a little pepper. Mix well. Smooth into several small glass or white china serving bowls and chill till required. This dish can be made 24 hours in advance. Vegans could substitute Veeze and soya yogurt for the dairy ingredients.

The crudités should be very fresh and colourful. They can be prepared overnight and kept wrapped and chilled. A good selection would be:

Celery, scrubbed and cut into 2-inch/5 cm lengths
Courgettes, wiped, cut into 2-inch/5 cm lengths, then subdivided into 4 or 6 strips according to width
Cauliflower, washed and separated into small florets
Tiny button mushrooms, wiped clean
Red, green and yellow peppers, de-seeded and cut into 2-inch/5 cm 'matchstick chips'
Carrots, scrubbed and cut into fine 2-inch/5 cm matchsticks
Cucumber, cut like the courgettes into 6–8 sticks

RATATOUILLE WITH MELBA TOAST

This dish can be made up to 48 hours in advance and kept well chilled. The flavour actually improves with keeping. Serve garnished with sprigs of fresh basil.

1 lb/450 g aubergine
Sea salt
4 tablespoons cold pressed or virgin olive oil
2–4 cloves garlic, crushed
8 oz/225 g onion, finely chopped
2 large green peppers, de-seeded and cut into
1-inch/2.5 cm chunks
2 large red peppers, de-seeded and cut into
1-inch/2.5 cm chunks
1 lb/450 g courgettes, cut into ½-inch/1.5 cm slices
2 lb/900 g fresh tomatoes, skinned and chopped
4 teaspoons fresh basil or 1½ teaspoons dried
Bay leaf
Freshly ground black pepper

Wipe the aubergines and cut them into ½-inch/ 2.5 cm cubes. Sprinkle with sea salt and set aside for 30 minutes to draw out the bitterness. Then pat dry with paper towels.

Heat the oil in a large pan and sauté the garlic and onion gently for 2 minutes. Add the aubergine. Continue cooking for another 5 minutes, stirring occasionally to prevent sticking. Add all the remaining ingredients except the fresh basil, if used, which should be added 15 minutes before the end of cooking. Bring gently to the boil, cover and reduce to a simmer until the vegetables are softened. Check during cooking for dryness, and add a little water if necessary. Season with pepper.

Pre-heat the oven to 190°C (375°F/gas mark 5). Make the melba toast by cutting thick slices from a wholemeal loaf. Toast on both sides until golden. Cut off the crusts, then carefully slice through the middle of each piece of toast to create 2 thin slices. Place in the oven until they curl up at the sides. Cut into triangles and serve hot or cold in a basket. Add fresh wholemeal and granary rolls for bigger appetites.

Main courses and accompaniments

SPINACH AND AVOCADO TERRINE

Makes about 8 slices.

Layer 1
1 lb/450 g frozen spinach or 2 lb/900 g fresh
Black pepper
Nutmeg
Layer 2
2 large ripe avocados
2 free-range egg yolks
4 oz/100 g quark or low-fat soft cheese
Layer 3
10 oz/275 g quark or low-fat soft cheese
½ pack Veeze or Fromsoya spread
Black pepper
2 free-range egg whites

Pre-heat the oven to 190°C (375°F/gas mark 5). Line a 1 lb/500 g loaf tin with greaseproof paper. Cook the spinach until soft and press firmly to remove excess moisture. Fresh spinach should be well chopped. Season with pepper and nutmeg, and press evenly into the base of the loaf tin.

Halve the avocados, remove the stone and scoop out the flesh. Mash with the egg yolks and soft cheese. Season and spread over the spinach layer.

Beat the remaining soft cheese with the soya cheese spread and season. Whisk the egg whites until stiff and fold them gently into the cheesy mixture using a metal spoon. Pour on to the avocado layer, smooth and cover. Bake in the centre of the oven for 45 minutes, until firm. Cool in the tin before carefully removing.

CREAMY MUSHROOM VOL-AU-VENTS

The cases can be pre-baked 2 days in advance and kept in airtight tins. The filling can also be prepared the day before. Use ready-made wholemeal or ordinary puff or flaky pastry and make sure there are no animal fats in them. Sainsbury's own brand and Jusrol are well known; others are available through health stores. Each 1 lb/500 g pack will make 4 large cases. Re-freeze the trimmings and use for other purposes – they will not make evenly risen cases.

1 lb/450 g button mushrooms, wiped and finely chopped or, if very tiny, halved
½ pint/275 ml skimmed or soya milk
¼ teaspoon dried thyme or sprig fresh
1½ oz/40 g soft vegetable margarine
4 oz/100 g onion, very finely chopped
1½ oz/40 g unbleached white flour or 81% wholemeal
3 fl oz/75 ml dry white wine
Freshly ground black pepper
3 tablespoons single cream
1½ oz/40 g lightly toasted flaked almonds to garnish
Fresh parsley to garnish

Place the mushrooms in a pan with the milk and the thyme. Bring to the boil. Remove from the heat and cool for 5 minutes. Strain, discarding fresh thyme if used.

Heat the margarine in a pan over a low heat. Add the onion and gently sauté for 2 minutes. Stir in the flour until all incorporated, then slowly add the prepared milk, beating carefully to achieve a silky-smooth sauce. Bring slowly back to the boil. Turn down the heat and gradually add the wine. Add the prepared mushrooms, season and stir in the cream if used.

To serve, reheat the empty pastry cases in a hot oven for 10 minutes. Carefully spoon in the hot filling up to the top of each case. Garnish with the toasted almonds and parsley. Position the pastry lids at an angle and serve at once.

NEW POTATOES

The best choice is Jersey Royal potatoes. This quantity serves 8 people.

3 lb/1.4 kg new potatoes
Fresh mint
Soft vegetable margarine to garnish
Fresh mint sprigs or parsley or chives to garnish

Scrub the potatoes. Place them in a large pan and just cover them with cold water. Add a few pieces of fresh mint, bring to the boil, then reduce the heat to a simmer for about 15 minutes or until tender. Drain the potatoes and discard the mint. Serve in an attractive bowl garnished with the margarine and herbs.

CASHEW NUT RICE

This dish can be moulded, either in oiled individual ramekins or in a ring mould. These can be turned out when ready to serve and attractively garnished with fresh herbs. Alternatively serve it in an attractive glass bowl. It can be made 24 hours in advance, but keep the mixture chilled and well covered to prevent it drying out. Serves 8.

4 oz/100 g onion, very finely chopped
1 stick celery, halved lengthwise, then sliced finely
1 tablespoon sunflower oil
8 oz/225 g long grain brown rice
¾ pint/450 ml water
¼ pint/150 ml dry white wine
Bay leaf
4 oz/100 g cashew nuts
Freshly ground black pepper
Fresh coriander leaves or chervil leaves to garnish

Gently heat the onion and celery in the oil in a pan for 2 minutes. Add the rice and cook for another minute to turn the grains transparent. Stir in the water, wine and bay leaf. Cover and bring to the boil. Reduce to a simmer for 20–25 minutes, according to the type of rice used. The grains should be tender, and if any water remains uncover the pan and turn up the heat for a minute or two. Stir in the cashews and season to taste. Discard the bay leaf. Garnish with the fresh herbs.

MIXED SALAD

Use a good variety of really fresh salad greens, served in a large bowl, lightly dressed.

1 green lettuce, Webb's Wonder or Cos
1 oak-leaved lettuce
1 head radicchio
1 bunch trimmed watercress
½ cucumber
1 red pepper, de-seeded and sliced into rings
1 yellow pepper, de-seeded and cut into rings
1 bunch radishes, trimmed and halved
Dressing
3 tablespoons sunflower oil or safflower oil
1 tablespoon white wine vinegar or cider vinegar
Pinch of mustard
Freshly ground black pepper

Wash the greens thoroughly, tearing any large leaves in half, and arrange them in a bowl with the watercress, scattering the smaller radicchio in the centre. Add the remaining ingredients to make a colourful mixture on the green bed. Place all the dressing ingredients in a jamjar and shake vigorously. Drizzle the dressing over the salad just before serving, turning the centre ingredients carefully in order to coat them.

Desserts

FRESH FRUIT TART

Use a large, shallow flan dish. The case is baked blind and the filling really needs to be freshly prepared on the day.

5 oz/150 g wholemeal flour
1 oz/25 g ground almonds
3 oz/75 g soft vegetable margarine
1 free-range egg yolk
A little free-range egg white for glazing
Filling
8 oz/225 g tub strained Greek yogurt
Few drops vanilla essence
1 free-range egg white
3 tablespoons sugar-free apricot jam
1 tablespoon boiling water
1 teaspoon lemon juice
Fresh fruit: grapes, de-seeded and halved/sliced kiwi fruit/raspberries/sliced banana/sliced strawberries/canned mandarins in their own juice

Pre-heat the oven to 200°C (400°F/gas mark 6). You will need a shallow 8–10-inch/20–25 cm flan dish. Combine the flour and almonds in a large mixing bowl and rub in the margarine to achieve a crumb mixture. Chill for 15 minutes, then add the egg yolk and enough cold water to mix to a smooth dough. Roll out the pastry, grease the dish and line it with the pastry. Glaze with a little egg white and bake blind for 10–15 minutes. Either remove from the flan ring or keep in the dish for serving.

Prepare the filling by whipping the yogurt with vanilla essence. Stiffly whisk the egg white and fold it into the yogurt. Make the glaze by mixing the jam, boiling water and lemon juice. Pass through a sieve.

When ready to serve, spread the yogurt cream over the pastry base, arrange the fruit attractively and spoon the glaze over the top to cover.

Vegans could omit the egg from the pastry, substituting 1 tablespoon soya flour in the dry ingredients. Omit the creamy base and increase the fruit content. Use a vegan yogurt, flavoured with a little runny honey, as a pouring cream over the tart.

STRAWBERRY CHOUX

A light, healthier version of profiteroles. Serves 8–10.

½ pint/275 ml cold water
4 oz/100 g soft vegetable margarine
5 oz/150 g wheatmeal 81% farmhouse flour, sieved
4 free-range eggs, beaten
1½ lb/675 g fresh strawberries
¼ pint/150 ml whipping cream
12 fl. oz/350 ml strained Greek yogurt

Pre-heat the oven to 220°C (425°F/gas mark 7). You will need 3 baking trays. Place the water and margarine in a large saucepan and bring to the boil. Remove from the heat and beat in the flour immediately, all at once. Beat until a smooth and glossy paste is achieved and allow to cool slightly, before adding in the eggs one at a time, beating thoroughly between each addition.

Place heaped teaspoonful of the mixture on the greased baking trays and bake for 15 minutes at the top of the heated oven until firm and golden, then reduce the heat to 190°C (375°F/gas mark 5) and continue to cook for about 10 minutes until the puffs are firm, without 'give'. Slit with a sharp knife to release the steam and return to the oven for 5 minutes to dry out. Cool on a wire tray. These puffs can be baked in advance and frozen.

To fill, chop half the strawberries and combine them with the whipped cream and yogurt. Fill puffs with this mixture and serve, piled up with the remaining whole fruits.

Cheeseboard

For information on dairy and non-dairy vegetarian cheeses, see page 47.

Organic wines to complement the feast

A wonderful organic wine to drink throughout the meal is Bacchus, an inexpensive substitute for champagne at around £5 a bottle; available in Brut and Demi Brut. A fragrant, semi-sweet sparkling wine which would go well with the sweetness of the wedding cake is Clairette De Die at £5.49 a bottle.

The Barbecue

A cruelty-free selection of mouth-watering and seductive-looking dishes for summer eating. Great for outdoor entertaining and *really* finger-lickin' good!

FOR THE GRILL

Vegeburgers – chilli-style
Sosmix burgers – basic mix with finely chopped mushroom and fresh herbs added
Tivall vegetarian 'frankfurter' sausages
Tivall golden crumbed 'Schnitzel'

VEGETABLE KEBABS

A colourful mixture of raw onion quarters, raw beetroot chunks, sliced courgettes, whole tomatoes, mushrooms, pepper chunks, pineapple cubes, Cauldron smoked tofu chunks, Sosmix balls flavoured with minced onion and garlic, and Vegeburger balls – herb and vegetable style pre-cooked for 10 minutes in a hot oven before skewering.

MARINADE

Use this special marinade for the tofu and as a baste whilst grilling the kebabs:

4 tablespoons thick, natural soy sauce
4 tablespoons runny honey
2 tablespoons sesame oil
2 tablespoons rice vinegar
2 cloves garlic, finely chopped

Mix together before use.

RAW VEGETABLE PLATTER WITH TOMATO SAUCE DIP

On a large flat platter arrange a bed of washed curly salad greens, leaving the centre free. Arrange on the salad greens clusters of prepared pepper strips, baby corn, button mushrooms, red and green olives, whole cherry tomatoes and vegetarian Feta cheese slices.

TOMATO SAUCE

1 cup Whole Earth tomato sauce
1 tablespoon tamarind paste
1 tablespoon chopped herbs – parsley, basil, dill
Tabasco to taste

Mix the tomato sauce with the tamarind, then add the chopped herbs and tabasco. If necessary, add a little sea salt. Decorate with more chopped herbs. Serve in a bowl in the centre of the platter of vegetables.

VEGETARIAN CHEESE DIP

8 oz/225 g vegetarian curd cheese
3–4 tablespoons yogurt or cream
2 tablespoons chopped fresh herbs – thyme, lemon balm
Juice and grated rind of ½ lemon
Black pepper

Mix the cream cheese with the yogurt. Use more or less to achieve a thick, creamy consistency. Add the other ingredients and mix well. Adjust the seasoning, adding a little sea salt if necessary. © Oded Schwartz.

MOZZARELLA HOT BREAD

Granary baguettes
Vegetarian Mozzarella cheese

Line a roasting tin with foil and pre-heat the oven to 200°C (400°F/gas mark 6). Slash the baguettes crossways without completely cutting through. Insert slices of cheese. Pack baguettes into tin and cover with foil. Bake until the cheese is melted into the slits and bubbling out. Serve hot.

Organic Wines: Mas de Gourgonnier – Coteaux d'Aix en Provence les Baux AC, rosé, 1987, £3.50. A rich, deep vibrant pink, this fruity organic wine is highly recommended. It is dry without too much red wine depth to offend white wine drinkers, yet gutsy enough for red wine fans. Serve well chilled in big goblets as a delicious accompaniment to this tastebud-tingling outdoor meal.

Exotic and spicy informal dinner party

This meal is the answer when you want to serve something special and non-vegetarian friends are coming for dinner. It should impress anyone whose idea of Eastern eating is a burnt nugget of tandoori chicken! Serves 4. Recipes © Oded Schwartz.

SWEET AND SOUR VEGETABLES

2 tablespoons ghee or vegetable margarine
1 teaspoon cumin seeds
2 tablespoons finely grated ginger
2 green chillies, sliced
½ teaspoon ground black pepper
¼ teaspoon asafetida
½ pint/275 ml plain yogurt
3 tablespoons tamarind paste
4 oz/100 g brown sugar
1 pineapple, trimmed and cubed
3 carrots, sliced
2 teaspoons mango powder
2 teaspoons paprika
2 teaspoons ground coriander
10 oz/275 g tofu or pressed paneer (Indian soft cheese)
3 courgettes, thickly sliced
4 tomatoes, quartered
3 stalks celery, diced
2 teaspoons sea salt
3 green plantains, sliced or 4 potatoes, scrubbed, cubed and deep-fried
6–8 baby sweetcorn

Heat the ghee in a large pan and fry the cumin seeds. Add grated ginger and green chillies. Stir for 1 minute, then add the ground pepper and asafetida and fry for a further 30 seconds. Pour in the yogurt and simmer for a few seconds. Add the tamarind paste, brown sugar, pineapple, carrots, mango powder, paprika and coriander. Bring to the boil to allow the mixture to thicken, stirring to prevent sticking.

In another pan, deep-fry the tofu until golden. Drain on kitchen paper and set aside.

Add the courgettes to the first pan and cook until half done, then add the fried tofu, tomatoes, celery and salt. Stir and add green plantains, if using. Otherwise wait to add the potatoes until the tofu has absorbed some of the sauce. Cover the pan and continue to cook until all the ingredients are tender.

SPICY SPINACH WITH TOFU AND RAITA

1 lb/450 g fresh spinach, washed and de-stalked
1 tablespoon vegetable oil
2 teaspoons ground coriander
½ teaspoon turmeric
¼ teaspoon cayenne pepper
Pinch of asafetida
3 tablespoons water
8 oz/225 g cubed, deep-fried tofu or uncooked paneer
1 teaspoon sea salt
½ teaspoon sugar

Chop the spinach into small pieces. Heat the oil over a medium heat and fry the spices. Add the spinach and the water. Cover and cook until the spinach is tender – about 8–10 minutes. Add the tofu, salt and sugar. Stir, and cook for another 5 minutes. Serve with raita drizzled over.

FRESH CUCUMBER RAITA

½ cucumber, grated
½ pint/275 ml plain yogurt
Freshly ground black pepper
Sea salt to taste
¼ teaspoon garam masala

Combine all the ingredients, and chill well before serving.

GOLDEN SPICED VEGETABLE FRITTERS

5 medium carrots, scrubbed
4 oz/100 g chick-pea flour
2 tablespoons coarsely chopped walnuts or hazelnuts
1 tablespoon grated fresh coconut
1 tablespoon chopped fresh parsley or coriander leaves
2 fresh chillies, de-seeded and chopped
1 teaspoon garam masala
½ teaspoon turmeric
½ teaspoon sea salt
¼ teaspoon baking powder
Vegetable oil for deep-frying

Grate the carrots finely to make about 9 oz/275 g. Place with all the other ingredients in a large bowl and mix with just sufficient water to make a thick paste which holds together well.

Heat the oil for frying. Fry teaspoon-sized lumps of mixture, 8–10 at a time, until golden on both sides. Each batch should take 4–5 minutes. Remove with a slotted spoon, drain on kitchen paper and serve hot.

RICE WITH COCONUT

10 oz/275 g basmati brown rice
Just under 1 pint/525 ml water
6 oz/175 g brown sugar
½ teaspoon cardamom seeds, finely ground
5 oz/150 g grated coconut, lightly toasted plus a little extra for garnish
2 oz/50 g pistachio or cashew nuts, toasted
2 oz/50 g raisins
1 teaspoon vegetable margarine
A few green pistachio nuts to garnish

Soak the rice for 1 hour, then drain. Place the water, sugar and cardamom powder in a medium pan and bring to the boil. Add the rice and bring to the boil again. Simmer for 2–3 minutes, then reduce to a very low heat, cover tightly and cook for 10 minutes. Lift the cover and quickly add the remaining ingredients without stirring. Cover again and continue cooking for about another 10 minutes until done, uncovering for the last 2–3 minutes to allow the steam to evaporate. Stir to blend all the ingredients and serve on a platter, decorated with a little extra toasted coconut and some greener pistachios for colour.

What to drink
A delicious organic lager is available from Vinceremos of Leeds. Pinkus lager from Münster, West Germany is around 85p a bottle and is sold by the case (24 bottles for £20.50). It is made solely from organic and natural ingredients. The company also stock a selection of other beers, not organic but made without any additives. These include Skopsko Export, Flag Pils, Pilsner Urquell and Clausthaler Low Alcohol. Prices range from 42p to 73p for a 33 cl bottle and all are sold in 48-bottle cases. Discounts are available.

Sarah Brown's elegant evening feast
This is a dinner party menu that is suitable all the year round, especially when you are looking for a light but rich meal. There is a flavourful mari-

naded salad to start, followed by a crisp filo pastry pie filled with a Stilton and spinach mixture. Serve this with new potatoes, or small jacket potatoes, a fresh tomato sauce and carrots tossed in butter with a little parsley. To finish there is a subtle-flavoured mousse made from lime and pawpaw.

MARINADED MUSHROOMS WITH HERBS

For the marinade
2 fl oz/50 ml olive oil
1 tablespoon white wine vinegar
2 tablespoons chopped fresh basil
2 tablespoons chopped parsley
2 teaspoons sun-dried tomato paste
Plus
8 oz/225 g button mushrooms
1 tablespoon olive oil
1 bunch spring onions, trimmed and chopped
6 oz/175 g cherry tomatoes
2 oz/50 g black olives, stoned

Mix all the ingredients for the marinade thoroughly in a screw-top jar and put to one side. Heat the olive oil and cook the mushrooms briefly until they just begin to soften. Put them into a bowl and pour the marinade over them. Add the remaining salad ingredients and leave for at least 2 hours. Serve the mixture in individual dishes and garnish with watercress or parsley.

FILO PIE WITH SPINACH AND STILTON

2–3 oz/50–75 g pine kernels
1 lb/450 g spinach
2 fl oz/50 ml olive oil
1 onion, chopped
2 cloves garlic, crushed
2 free-range eggs
2 oz/50 g Stilton cheese
3 oz/75 g soft curd cheese
3 tablespoons chopped fresh parsley
½ teaspoon grated nutmeg
salt and black pepper
2 fl oz/50 ml butter
½ packet filo pastry

Pre-heat the oven to 200°C (400°F/gas mark 6). Roast the pine kernels for 5–8 minutes at 180°C (350°F/gas mark 4). Then set them aside. Wash the spinach, squeeze it dry and shred roughly. Heat 1 tablespoon of the olive oil and fry the onion until it begins to soften, then add the garlic and cook for one minute. Then add the spinach, cover the pan and cook for 6–8 minutes or until the spinach is tender. Remove from the heat. Drain well, then puree the leaves. In a separate bowl, beat the eggs, crumble in the Stilton and add the curd cheese, parsley and nutmeg. Mix in the spinach puree and season the mixture well.

Melt the butter and remaining oil in a small pan. Brush a deep gratin dish tin with this mixture, lay a sheet of filo on top, brush again, then continue with half the sheets, brushing in between with plenty of the butter and oil mixture and sprinkling some pine kernels in the layers. Spread the filling over the top and then continue to layer up the remaining sheets. Cut a few slashes in the finished pie, as this will help the top layers to crisp. Bake for 40–50 minutes or until well browned. Serve warm.

LIME AND PAPAYA MOUSSE

2 limes
2 free-range eggs, separated
2 oz/50 g sugar
4 fl oz/100 ml whipping cream
1 small ripe pawpaw

Grate the limes carefully, avoiding the white pith, and squeeze them well to remove the juice. Beat the egg yolks, then add the lime peel, juice and sugar. Cook over a medium heat, stirring constantly. Leave to cool. Beat the cream until stiff, then stir it into the cooled lime mixture. Cut the pawpaw in half, remove all the seeds, scoop out the flesh and puree it until smooth. Add the puree to the cream mixture. Beat the egg whites until quite stiff. Stir 1 tablespoon into the pawpaw cream, then fold in the rest. Spoon into glasses and serve chilled.

Organic wines to complement
Alsace Gewurztraminer – a powerfully flavoured, spicy white wine, good for first and main course. Serve chilled. £5.65
or
A chilled Provence Rosé: Mas de Gourgonnier to drink throughout the meal. £3.79.

A Cruelty-Free Christmas

This mouthwatering Christmas spread ushers in a season of true goodwill towards both men and animals. Serves 4–6.

SIMPLY STUFFED RAW VEGETABLES

These delicious mouthfuls won't fill you up!

12 oz/350 g vegetarian curd cheese
1 tablespoon capers, very finely diced
½ red pepper, very finely diced
2 tablespoons very finely chopped gherkin
4 oz/100 g whipped double cream or whipped yogurt
or melted margarine
2 tablespoons finely chopped mixed fresh herbs
2 ins/5 cm fresh lemon grass, finely chopped
Black pepper and tabasco to taste

Mash the cheese, adding a little milk if too thick. Add all the chopped ingredients. Fold in the cream, yogurt or margarine. Season to taste. Use to stuff small raw vegetables – cherry tomatoes, button mushrooms, celery chunks etc. – or small fruits such as apricots. © Oded Schwartz.

THE CRANBERRY CROWN

½ oz/15 g sunflower margarine
1 small onion, peeled and finely chopped
4 oz/100 g mushrooms, wiped and diced
1 teaspoon rosemary
1 teaspoon thyme
½ teaspoon ground nutmeg
2 teaspoons wholewheat flour
¼ pint/150 ml red wine plus ¼ pint/150 ml dark
vegetable stock (or use all stock)
1 teaspoon yeast extract
1 tablespoon tomato puree
4 oz/100 g ground walnuts
2 oz/50 g unsalted peanuts, ground
5 oz/150 g breadcrumbs
1–2 tablespoons tahini
1–2 tablespoons shoyu
Black pepper
4 oz/100 g fresh cranberries
4 oz/100 g dried apricots, soaked overnight in a
mixture of brandy and orange juice (brandy can be
omitted if preferred)
1 tin artichoke hearts

Garnish and glaze
Sosmix
Dried herbs
Extra cranberries
Watercress
Honey

Pre-heat the oven to 190°C (375°F/gas mark 5). Melt the margarine and gently fry the onion till soft. Add the mushrooms, herbs and spice and cook for 5 minutes in a covered pan. Sprinkle the flour over the top and cook for 2 minutes. Add the wine, stock, yeast extract and tomato puree. Bring to the boil, stirring constantly, and cook for 5 minutes.

In a separate bowl mix the nuts and breadcrumbs. Add the mushroom mixture, tahini, shoyu, cranberries and drained apricots cut in half. Mix well and season to taste. Prepare a well-greased ring mould approx 10 ins/25 cm in diameter. Pour half the mixture into the tin and press down. Arrange the artichoke hearts evenly around the ring so they will be in the centre of the mixture. Cover with the remaining nut mix and press down carefully to exclude any gaps around the hearts. Bake for approx 45 minutes until firm to the touch. Cool slightly before turning out on to a heated flat dish.

To garnish the crown, make Sosmix and herb balls, rolled in sesame seeds and baked until crisp; you can also use fresh cranberries and washed watercress sprigs. Glaze the crown with melted honey before serving.

Serve with traditional vegetables – roast potatoes and parsnips, and a lightly cooked medley of sprouts, carrots, celery and courgette chunks. Accompany with a jug of piping hot vegetarian gravy.

RICH GRAVY SAUCE

½ small onion
2 mushrooms
Vegetable oil for frying
1½ pints/900 ml rich vegetable stock from cooked fresh vegetables
1 teaspoon yeast extract e.g. Natex
1 dessertspoon tomato puree
1 dessertspoon wholemeal flour mixed to a cream with a little cold water
1 teaspoon soy sauce
Freshly ground black pepper

Mince the vegetables and sauté until brown in a little oil. Add the stock and bring to the boil, adding the yeast extract, tomato puree and pepper. Simmer for 2–3 minutes, then reduce the heat and carefully stir in the flour to thicken. Cook, stirring continually, for another 2 minutes. Add the soy sauce and serve.

ODED'S CHRISTMAS PUDDING

This is rich and absolutely delicious, and one pudding goes a long way. Makes three 3 lb/1.5 kg puddings.

12 oz/350 g mixed peel
12 oz/350 g raisins
12 oz/350 g sultanas
12 oz/350 g currants
12 oz/350 g grated apple
12 oz/350 g grated carrot
1 lb/450 g washed bulghur
8 oz/225 g brown sugar or honey or molasses
4 oz/100 g glacé cherries
4 oz/100 g crystallized ginger
Juice and grated peel of 1 lemon
Juice and grated peel of 1 orange
1 oz/25 g mixed spices – cinnamon, cloves, allspice etc.
½ pint/275 ml ale
8 free-range eggs
12 oz/350 g vegetable suet or margarine or solid grated cream coconut
Brandy

In a huge, clean bowl combine all the ingredients except the brandy. It makes a very soft mixture. Pour into well-greased pudding basins, cover closely and steam for 4–5 hours. Let the pudding cool down. Open it and pour some brandy over it. Cover again. This pudding keeps well, but periodically it must be looked at and anointed with a bit more brandy!

Before serving, steam for as long as possible – 6–7 hours – so put on the pudding before you do anything else. By the time dinner is served, the pudding will be ready. Serve with really cold custard sauce. © Oded Schwartz.

Petit fours for after dinner
As a sweet treat stuff dates and figs with marzipan and decorate with almonds. Place each in a paper sweet case.

Organic wines for a festive occasion
Windesheimer Rosenburg-OmP-Gewürztraminer Kabinett 1986, Konrad Knodel (Nahe). At under £5 a bottle, this is an excellent wine for the starter course; it has a light, medium flavour and a pale green-gold colour.

Hautes-Côtes de Nuits AC 1985, A Verdet. This powerful burgundy perfectly complements our main course and costs around £7 a bottle.

Clairette de Die AC 'Cuvée Spéciale', Achard-Vincent. A light, sweet fizz that's great with the pudding and has good acidity. Serve in a flute. £5.99.

More information
The National Childbirth Trust
Alexandra House
Oldham Terrace
London W3
01-992 8637
Natural childbirth information.

LaLeche League
Spitalfield
Commercial St
London E1
01-247 0165
Breast feeding information, advice and support.

The Baby Milk Action Coalition
6 Regent Terrace
Cambridge
CB2 1AA
0223 464420

The 'Choice' Campaign
Parkdale
Dunham Rd
Altrincham
Cheshire
WA14 4QG
Four-week vegetarian menu planners for school caterers, plus free campaign pack for children.

The Vegetarian Society
53 Marloes Rd
Kensington
London W8 6LA
01-937 7739
and
Parkdale
Dunham Rd
Altrincham
Cheshire
WA14 4QG
061-928 0793

Members receive magazine, *The Vegetarian*. Separate publication, *Greenscene*, caters for younger members, with the SCREAM campaign (School Campaign for Reaction Against Meat), specially for young veggies at school. VSUK offer extensive publications list, especially recipe books, nutritional and practical advice, catering courses for professional and home cooks, local contacts. 'V' symbol on approved products.

The Vegan Society
33–35 George St
Oxford
OX1 2AY
0865 722166
Members receive magazine, *The Vegan*. Publishes own titles including *The Cruelty-Free Shopper* and eating out/where to stay guides. Practical and nutritional advice on the vegan diet.

London Vegans
7 Deansbrook Rd
Edgware
HA8 9BE

The London Food Commission
88 Old St
London EC1V 9AR
01-253 9513
Publishes *The Food Magazine* quarterly. The LFC is independent and offers unbiased information on food, and critiques of the industry and all eating/health-related matters. Invaluable if you want to know what 'they' don't want you to know.

Vegfam
The Sanctuary
Lydford
Devon
EX20 4AL
082 282 203
Works within the Third World to establish non-exploitive, representative, plant-based agricultural projects.

Find Your Feet
13–15 Frognal
London NW3
01-354 4430
Helps local people in the Third World produce a rich, versatile leaf nutrient by means of a simple, easy-to-make machine. Projects worldwide.

Enough
London House
Queens Rd
Freshwater
Isle of Wight
PO40 9EP
0983 754419
Funds vegetarian projects in the Third World and promotes a non-meat diet on ethical, economic and ecological grounds. Gandhi said, 'There is enough for every man's need, but not for every man's greed.'

Compassion in World Farming
20 Lavant St
Petersfield
Hants
GU32 3EW
0730 64208
Campaigns against all factory farming in favour of humane, sustainable and planetary beneficial

agriculture. CIWF Youth Group is called Farm Animal Rangers.

The Athene Trust
3a Charles St
Petersfield
Hants
GU32 3EH
0730 68070
Educational trust to promote harmony between humans and the rest of creation. School info-packs, videos and other resource materials for educators and students.

Chickens' Lib
PO Box 2
Holmfirth
Huddersfield
HD7 1QT
0484 683158
Specifically concerned with birds reared on factory farms.

The Free Range Egg Association
37 Tanza Rd
London NW3 2UA
01-435 2596
Find out your nearest suppliers by contacting FREGG.

Foodwatch
Butts Pond Industrial Estate
Sturminster
Newton
Devon
DT10 1AZ
0258 73356
Specialist mail order product and information service for those suffering food allergy and environmentally related health problems. Many totally animal and additive-free lines not usually available in shops.

GR Lane Products Ltd
Sisson Rd
Gloucester
GL1 3QB
0452 24012
Vitamin supplements available made without animal products.

Quest Vitamins (UK) Ltd
Premier Trading Estate
Dartmouth Middleway
Birmingham
B7 4AT
021-359 0056
Vitamin supplements available made without animal products.

Cauldron Foods
4 Conduit Place
Bristol
BS2 9R1
0272 632835
Tofu savoury products.

The Dietburger Co Ltd
21 Holmbush Rd
London
SW15 3LE
01-788 3629
Manufacturer of Dietburger.

Granose Foods Ltd
Howard Way
Newport Pagnell
Bucks
MK16 9PY
0908 211311
Extensive range of vegetarian products including tinned and packaged ready-meals and convenience items. Nuttolene; roast mixes; cakes and puddings, soya products including milk, drinks, yogurts and desserts; margarines, pâtés and spreads.

Haldane Foods Ltd
Unit 25
Hayhill Industrial Estate
Sileby Rd
Barrow-upon-Soar
Leicestershire
LE12 8LD
050 981 6611
Hera soups and savoury products; Sojal non-dairy yogurt; Direct Foods range of Protoveg TVP products including Sosmix, Burgermix, TVP mince and chunks, Sizzles and other savoury products.

Health and Diet Food Co. Ltd
Seymour House
South St
Godalming
Surrey
GU7 1BZ
0483 426666
Holly Mill bakery products, Hugli soups and stock cubes, Pompadour herbal teas and Luaka range of decaffeinated tea.

Hedgehog Crisps
Unit 4
Severn Farm Industrial Estate
Welshpool
Powys
SY21 7DF
0938 555053
Organic potato crisps in a range of flavours. The company donate a percentage of their profits to the Wildlife Hospital Trust.

Holland and Barrett
Canada House
Byfleet
Surrey
KT14 7JL
0932 336022
Biggest chain of health stores presently retailing in the UK. Sell most of the foodstuffs mentioned in this book as well as their own range of products which include dried fruits and nuts, ready-snacks and meals, baked goods, soya milk and TVP products.

Leisure Drinks Ltd
24 Willow Rd
Trent Lane
Castle Donington
Derby
DE7 2NP
0332 850616
Alcohol-free range of wine, vermouth and beers. Juices, nectars and tomato cocktails.

MacSweens of Edinburgh
130 Bruntsfield Place
Edinburgh
EH10 4ES
031-229 1216
Vegetarian haggis!

Mange Tout Foods
18 Clanwilliam Rd
Deal
Kent
0304 363862
Vegetarian ready-meals with taste, wholesome ingredients and decent portions. Competitively priced and should be more widely available.

Modern Health Products Ltd
Phoenix House
Davis Rd
Chessington
Surrey
KT9 1TH
01-397 4361
Natex yeast extract and Vecon vegetable stock. Also make Gelozone, a non-animal setting agent.

Plamil Foods Ltd
Plamil House
Bowleswell Gardens
Folkestone
Kent
CT19 6PQ
0303 850588
Range of soya non-dairy produce including milks, cream, Veeze cheese spreads, chocolate, rice pudding and pease pudding.

Provamel
Vandemoortele (UK) Ltd
Ashley House
High St
Hounslow
TW3 1NH
01-577 2727
Provamel soya milks, drinks and desserts.

The Realeat Company (see Haldane Foods)
Vegeburgers and Vegebangers, both available as dry mixes or ready frozen. The dry burger mix is especially good and very versatile.

Tivall Kibbutz Lochamei Hagetaot
MP
Ashrat
Israel
Vegetarian convenience foods with taste. Frankfurter-type sausages, slicing roll sausage, breaded 'Schnitzel', savoury pastry slice.

JOANNA LUMLEY
'That we can process animals as if they were
so many nuts and bolts in a factory just
chokes me up. So as I discovered these
things, I changed the way I shopped.'

Joanna Lumley

The Living Without Cruelty English Sunday Breakfast
Chilled juice and delicious fruit compote
Low-fat cooked dish with Sosmix mini sausages, grilled tomato
and mushrooms, unfried 'fried' bread and optional free-range e
See pages 51–2 for recipes.

SOPHIE WARD
'Becoming vegetarian has definitely been beneficial for me. I feel stronger mentally and physically. The migraines I used to have stopped when I changed my diet. My baby will be vegetarian, of course, and grow up Living Without Cruelty.'

The Barbecue
Hot and spicy cruelty-free savouries: Schnitzel, bangers and burgers with
vegetable kebabs. Hot mozzarella bread and a colourful dip-and-dunk
vegetable platter.
See pages 56–7 for recipes.

BARBARA DICKSON
'I say to my son, "We don't eat animals
Colm, because we love them." There's
nothing in meat you can't get elsewhere in
your diet.'

Exotic and Oriental
Sweet and Sour
vegetables/Spicy
spinach with tofu and
Raita/Golden spiced
vegetable fritters/Rice
with coconut
See pages 57–8 for
recipes.

The Wedding Feast
Appetizers: Fresh herb dip and crudites/
Ratatouille with melba toast. Main course:
Spinach and avocado terrine/Creamy
mushroom vol-au-vents with new potato,
mixed salad and cashew nut rice. Dessert:
Fresh fruit tart/Cheeseboard.
See pages 52–6 for recipes.

Cruelty-free
Christmas
Peace on earth and
good will to man and
beast!
Simply stuffed raw
vegetables/Cranberry
Crown Roast and all
the trimmings/Oded's
Christmas pudding
See pages 60–1 for recipes

MARIE HELVIN
'I want to know my cosmetics have been tested humanely and reliably. Testing them on animals is not only a farce, but a sad reflection on those who continue with these cruel and out-of-date experiments.'

CAROL ROYLE
'I think it's just a fluke that I was born a human animal. I could just as easily have been born a white rabbit having chemicals dripped in my eyes. Putting yourself in the animals' place means you identify with their suffering.'

VICKI MICHELLE
'Animals will continue to suffer until big business realizes that we consumers will have none of it. It's up to us, because the animals can't help themselves. Cruelty-free companies have proved their products are safe and every bit as good. The others could all stop testing on animals tomorrow if they cared enough. At the moment, they obviously don't care enough.'

FOOD FOR THOUGHT

Whole Earth Foods Ltd
269 Portobello Rd
London W11 1LR
01-229 7545
Range of quality products including pickles, relishes and sauces, preserves, Pasta Pots, baked beans and dressings. Many products organic. Lots of taste without additives of any kind.

Write to the above listed companies for a selection of free product information and recipe leaflets.

Reading

Books to inform you
Animal Liberation, Peter Singer, Palladin/Avon/Thorsons.
Food for a Future, Jon Wynne-Tyson, Thorsons.
Assault and Battery, Mark Gold, Pluto Press.
Living Without Cruelty, Mark Gold, Greenprint.
The Politics of Food, Geoffrey Cannon, Century Hutchinson.
Why You Don't Need Meat, Peter Cox, Thorsons.
Chicken and Egg: Who Pays the Price?, Clare Druce, Greenprint.
The Meat Machine, Jan Walsh, Columbus Books.
The New 'E' for Additives, Maurice Hanssen, Thorsons.
Food Irradiation – The Facts, Tony Webb and Dr Tim Lang, Thorsons.

Books to help you
NEW LITTLE VEGGIES
The Vegetarian Baby, Sharon Yutema, Thorsons.
Rose Elliot's Vegetarian Mother and Baby Book, Fontana.
Weaning Your Baby with Wholefoods.★
Good Children's Food, Christine Smith (veggie cook book for children), Century Hutchinson.
Some People Don't Eat Meat, Jane Inglis (a book for children about being vegetarian), Oakroyd Press.
Full of Beans, Evelyn Findlater, Thorsons (recipes for children to cook themselves).
Wholefood Children's Packed Lunches★
Children's Wholefood Party Recipes★
First Foods, VSUK.

NEW BIGGER VEGGIES
Vegetarian in the Family, Janet Hunt, VSUK.
The New Vegetarian, Michael Cox and Desda Crockett, VSUK.
Vegetarian Student, Jenney Baker, Faber and Faber.
The Caring Cook – Cruelty-Free Cooking for Beginners, Janet Hunt, The Vegan Society.
The Single Vegetarian, Marlis Weber, Thorsons.
SPECIALITY/PROFESSIONAL
The Vegetarian Barbecue, David Eno, Thorsons.
The Vegetarian Lunch Box, Janet Hunt, Thorsons.
Sarah Brown's Vegetarian Microwave Cookbook, Dorling Kindersley.
The Compassionate Gourmet, Janet Hunt, Thorsons.
Cordon Vert, Colin Spencer, Thorsons.
Jean Conil's Cuisine-Végétarienne Française, Thorsons.
Vegetarian Catering, Richard Davies.
Catering Without Meat, Barbara Davidson, Food and Futures.
★Booklets available at 45p each from:
The Wholefood Cookery School
16/18 Bushloe End
Wigston
Leicester
0533 883701

Guides
The Cruelty Free Shopper, The Vegan Society.
The Vegan Holiday and Restaurant Guide, The Vegan Society.
Where to Eat if You Don't Eat Meat, Annabel Whittet, Whittet Books.
Staying Vegetarian, Lynne Alexander and Oliver Fulton, Fontana.
Sarah Brown's Vegetarian London, Thorsons.

The Vegetarian Society (VSUK), run a variety of cookery courses. These range from an introductory one-day basic course, speciality day and weekend practicals (including one for children's meals), and a complete four-part diploma course, leading to the award of the 'Cordon Vert'. Courses for catering staff throughout the UK. Details from VSUK.

Arguments against meat consumption

- Inseparable from death and suffering.
- Full of saturated fat, which is harmful to health.
- Adulterated with drugs, hormones and other chemical residues.
- Often contaminated with faecal material and teeming with bacteria.
- Risk of food poisoning.
- Consumption can contribute to diseases such as coronary heart disease, high blood pressure, certain cancers and other degenerative disorders.
- Wasteful to produce.
- Environmentally unsound.
- Very expensive.
- Product shrinks to lower weight when cooked.
- Careful cooking needed, especially for cheaper cuts.
- Needs refrigeration immediately, or freezing to prevent rotting.
- Only keeps for a few days before going off, even when chilled.

Arguments for meat eating

- You might like the taste (this is not actually an argument).

Arguments for living without cruelty

- No killing involved.
- Better for you and your family's health.
- Promotes a real feeling of well-being and an affinity with the natural world.
- Contributes to a better environment.
- Reduces the chances of contracting illnesses such as food poisoning, and helps protect against degenerative diseases.
- Very cost-effective.
- Less wasteful in every way.
- Nutritionally superior diet.
- Actually saves the country money through reducing illness (healthy people make fewer demands on health services).

Arguments against living without cruelty

- Slight effort required.

Linda McCartney

The Living Without Cruelty switch came twenty years ago for Linda when she became vegetarian; yet, like most of us, her conventional, middle-class upbringing in a New York suburb included meat eating. 'I was crazy about animals,' says Linda. 'I would rescue injured creatures and carry them home. I knew they suffered, yet was unaware I was eating animals. One day, I suddenly realized I was eating something's leg. It was later on that I discovered shooting, hunting and the other atrocities. Animals are so similar to us. They have legs, hearts and eyes, and so do we. And like us, they too suffer. We have animals at home – sheep, horses, ducks, chickens, dogs and cats. I couldn't turn around one day and say to my chicken, "I just ate your auntie."'

The McCartney children, Heather, the oldest, and her brother James are both vegetarian, but they have to take a packed lunch to school because the catering is so awful – chips and beans! 'They love the luncheon soya roll for sandwiches. The other kids say, "Hey, can I have *your* lunch?" Lots of the kids at school want to change, but are stopped by their parents. They should respect and help their children if they want to go vegetarian, and nowadays it's no trauma at all. It's not cranky food, and there's so much choice available. I love cooking – pastas, rice dishes, macaroni, soyburgers and big stews. Cook them with *fun* instead of saying "I can't be bothered." *Be bothered* – you're saving an animal's life! I just adapted all my favourite recipes at first, and now I don't need a cookbook. Just use your imagination and get out of the meat-rut. Being vegetarian is never boring.'

Linda's own schooldays were happy, but she admits to being a 'terrible student'. She was living in the north-west of America when a friend persuaded her to attend photography classes. She had to borrow the camera and a roll of film, but found she was a natural and people liked the pictures. It all started from there and as with music (she started from scratch with Wings, encouraged by Paul) she learnt by experience. On stage, Linda uses mainly Beauty Without Cruelty cosmetics and the family buy their toiletries at Body Shop.

'Wherever we go, especially TV studios, we get them to stock cruelty-free. I find make-up artists are totally supportive. The products are

LINDA McCARTNEY
'We're concerned about many issues from nuclear power to waste pollution, but I concentrate on animals. They need a good lawyer!'

Linda McCartney

great, and nice to wear because they really make you feel a better person. We try to use non-exploitive products wherever possible – Ecover for household cleaning, and so on. Even the dogs are vegetarian and very healthy on Happidog! We also support alternative medicine. Homoeopathy saved me from persistent throat infection when repeated antibiotic doses had failed.

'We're concerned, of course, about many issues from nuclear power to waste pollution, but I concentrate on animals. They need a good lawyer! When I look at how we're soiling our own nest, and how politicians are making a mess of things, I get so angry. When I see a fur coat, say at a party or a reception, I just can't bring myself to speak to the wearer. How dare we murder something to wear its skin. God, it's so offensive! At school my daughter was confronted with animal dissection, a totally unnecessary waste of an innocent life. She refused to dissect and eventually they had to find her an alternative. She passed her 'O' level biology without dissection. You just have to hold out for what you believe is right.

'I think we need to show people the love and the wonder of animals, not just the horror, because there are so many dreadful negatives. We must appeal to humankind not to treat them with contempt, or, worst of all, indifference. Stay open-minded and soften up your emotions. Of course you need to be aware of the suffering, but hopefully people will listen and not get their backs up. Perhaps then they'll say, "This Living Without Cruelty makes sense!" I don't want to preach it to the point where people turn off – that's my biggest worry, people saying, "Did you hear her going on about vegetarianism? What a bore . . . pass me another steak." '

Joanna Lumley

Joanna, born in Kashmir when her father was stationed there whilst serving in the Indian Army, has always retained a love of the East.

'I've always approved of the "live and let live" attitude of many Eastern traditions. Although we came to live in England when I was eight and I went to boarding school, I've been back since and it's as beautiful as I remembered it – an area of lakes and quiet and swooping

kingfishers. I went to an Anglican school and it too reinforced my awareness of beauty – the gardens and the countryside made nature an important part of my growing up. I think education is where "responsibility building" must begin, so that we realize we can change things and are responsible for our actions. We can't just live our lives by passing the buck and letting somebody else do it, whatever "it" may be.

'I was a model for a number of years and met Celia Hammond, who even then was rescuing cats and dogs. It was the sixties and the steak and salad diet was fashionable. I was halfway through a steak, the fork on its way to my mouth, and a wave of revulsion hit me. It was as if I suddenly realized it was flesh, as opposed to meat. I became vegetarian and I found my health improved. I eat masses of raw, or virtually raw, vegetables and I found that potatoes, pastas, rice and real bread – all the things we were told make you fat – didn't result in weight gain on the veggie diet. I found my taste buds getting sharper and the most amazing thing was the money.

'Giving up meat saved me pounds every week. This meant I could try out exotic fruits and vegetables, buy really good oils and the slightly more expensive free-range eggs. I was eating a much better and more varied diet, but still spending less. I love cooking and I gave my imagination free rein, trying out lots of new things like sorrel and nasturtium leaves and flowers in salads.

'Sometimes I made "traditional" meals with convenience items such as Sosmix and Vegeburgers. I've made the most terrific shepherd's pies using Burgermix and served them up to meat eaters, and they're the biggest hit – with seconds all round for everyone.

'To begin with, like most people I never thought about where things came from. I had a fur coat, ate meat and used make-up. It never entered my mind how these things were produced. You see a jolly picture of a pig walking along with a pitchfork over his shoulder and a pork sausage on the end, or turkeys laughing and smiling and urging you to stuff them with Paxo. The advertising is designed to stop people putting two and two together. People doing their shopping see labels like "Farm fresh" or "From Nature's Garden" and they think "That's a good thing to have." They don't realize they're buying battery eggs or food processed in a factory which has never seen a garden, let alone a natural one, free from pesticides. We should have labels which clearly state "Factory-farmed produce". What about "Eggs from chickens who have never seen the light of day"? At least then people would know what they were buying.

'The first big horror which I read of was the LD50 test where animals are poisoned to death with products. It struck me as the most appalling piece of madness I'd ever read – apart from the cruelty, what point was there to it all? And then I discovered factory farming. The scale of it, at every level, I find almost unbearable. That we can process animals as if they were so many nuts and bolts in a factory just chokes me up.

'So as I discovered these things, I changed the way I shopped. I found I could buy three really nice cloth bags to go with different outfits for a fraction of the cost of a leather one. I wish manufacturers would make more really nice linen shoes – that's an area which needs attention. There are plenty of really nice materials available, many of which look like leather, but they don't seem to make them into shoes . . . yet! I have an absolutely stunning fabric fur and you can get plastics which look as beautiful as real tortoiseshell or bone for buttons, combs and jewellery. What's the point in having something of ivory if you have to go round telling everyone what it is because it looks just like the plastic sort?

'I don't believe it's right to kill animals to look pretty. We can look beautiful in our own way – we don't have to take from animals to do it. We can all eat, live and clothe ourselves perfectly well without any cruelty. Living Without Cruelty isn't second-best.'

Barbara Dickson

Barbara spent her first seventeen years in Dunfermline, before moving to Edinburgh where she established herself on the folk circuit. The theatre gave her the big break she needed when she appeared in Willy Russell's *John, George, Paul, Ringo and Bert*. The play moved to London, and it's been her home ever since. 'I left school having failed the 11-plus, which made me lose confidence and under-achieve. With only the prospect of office work, I was determined to prove myself artistically and defy the stigma of failure.' With

over eleven albums, umpteen stage appearances, capacity houses on tour and several TV specials, she has proved her point.

Married with two young children, Colm, now three (pictured) and Gabriel, one, Barbara is bringing them up vegetarian. 'To me, the most important thing is truth, and it's vital that children have the truth about things like factory farming and what meat really is. The word "bacon", for instance, has no origins. It is a remote term for a piece of dead pig, and that's not truthful. I say to my son, "We don't eat animals, Colm, because we love them. Would we eat the cat because we love the cat? No, so we don't eat sheep or cows or pigs either."

'When people ask me why I concern myself with animal issues when there are "more important" things to do I always say, "Look, people who don't care about animals, don't care about each other. If you're aware about what happens to animals, then you become more caring about everything, not just about the animals themselves." A whole society is pushing round a supermarket trolley loaded down with products which aren't legitimate in a civilized world – animal-tested cosmetics and household products, fur coats, battery eggs and all the other dreadful products of factory farming.

'Living Without Cruelty is helping people to realize what's involved in the products they're eating. It's important to give people the facts which they would otherwise be denied, especially as animal consumption is so closely connected with illnesses such as heart disease and food poisoning. I read every packet I buy to avoid additives and stick to as much fresh wholefood as possible. I make a lot of really crunchy stir-fries with the vegetables barely cooked, and love to create dishes with fresh pasta and fresh tomato and herb sauces. I never get bored in the kitchen.

'Colm loves the veggie pâtés on toast. These are great for kids. A lot of children are natural vegetarians and hate meat. To make them eat it is ridiculous. There's nothing in meat you can't get elsewhere in your diet. Colm and Gabriel are so healthy on their veggie diet and they love it.

'I took Colm on tour with me when he was a baby and we found that hotels are getting much better at offering decent vegetarian selections. Holiday Inns are very good, for example, and more have abandoned the cheese salad/

mushroom omelette offerings of the past and are serving real vegetarian dishes as the demand grows.

'When on stage I need really vibrant colours and lots of make-up. I use Body Shop avidly and I find it's a good professional make-up. I don't wear fur. People who do so think it gives them status where they have none. Instead of shouting status and importance, wearing fur simply shouts their stupidity and arrogance.

'So don't be overwhelmed by the awful cruelties and injustices. When I watched *The Animals Film* on TV, it upset me to watch the horror of animal exploitation and I felt impotent. The scale of it is so vast, but Living Without Cruelty, with its bright educational campaign for children and its totally positive approach, points the way in an uplifting and practical manner. We really can make the world a better place!'

Uri Geller

Uri became a phenomenon when he appeared on British TV in 1973 and demonstrated his ability to bend cutlery using 'psychic energy'. Since then, thriving on the predictable controversy and ridicule, he has become a rich man – using his powers to locate precious minerals for mining corporations. But behind the showman's image there is a serious and intense commitment to the animal and environmental movements. Fifteen years ago he made a commercial for a Japanese running machine.

'Afterwards we all went to a Japanese restaurant and I discovered tofu. It all started

from there. Until then I ate junk food and weighed 180 lb! I began reading about vegetarianism, health and nutrition. Within a year I'd cut out all meat, as did my family. I began to feel so much better.'

Uri began by eliminating red meats, then poultry and fish, and is now virtually vegan, using minimal dairy produce. 'Everything is better since becoming vegetarian – stamina, vitality, endurance and flexibility. My body feels clean, and spiritually I feel stronger. Exercise plays its part too – I run every day and work out. But at the end of the day, it's not really the health aspects – that's a bonus. It's the killing. I think animals experience the same pains and anxieties as human beings. When the family became vegetarian it was a major step in our adherence to "spirituality" – that we don't kill animals. I'm Jewish, but I believe in one God for all of us, and that includes animals. We may not understand how animals think – the closest we can appreciate their intelligence is with dolphins, and even then we compare our brains with theirs. We are so arrogant. How do we know that dogs, sheep or pigs don't think or calculate or fear?

'When I was young I knew nothing about animal slaughter – ritual or otherwise – but I discovered it through discussion, books and films and realized I was contributing to their suffering by eating meat. So humane education is vital, especially for children. I can't predict what my kids, Daniel and Natalie, will be doing when they're twenty, but I'm making sure they're aware of animal suffering and why we're vegetarian.'

URI GELLER
'Everything is better since becoming
vegetarian . . . my body feels clean.'

Only Skin Deep

Tortured
Twitching
Lonely and
afraid

Caged
Unloved
Killed
for a Beauty Aid

J. O. Salmond

The animal testing issue: how you can help

As more and more people begin to realize the truth about the unreliability of animal research, their use in testing cosmetics and toiletries for safety begins to border on the farcical. Yet still the tests go on, despite widespread condemnation from the public, animal advocates and scientists themselves. The only ones left defending the egg on their faces are those who carry out the tests and the governments who are still archaic enough to accept them.

In 1988, 16,989 animals died testing such products in British laboratories. Procedures include acute and chronic toxicity experiments, where chemicals are forcibly administered to the animals. The heavily criticized and scientifically obsolete LD50 is one such poisoning test which requires half the test animals to die in order to achieve a neat little figure for the bureaucrats (the 'Lethal Dose'). The procedure causes obvious suffering because the animals are literally being 'poisoned', although in many instances animals die from having their body systems overloaded with massive amounts of a substance.

In one reported LD50, animals were force-fed the human equivalent of 4 lb of lipstick formulation. One animal died from intestinal obstruction, not the toxicity of the product. In another experiment the equivalent of 7 pints of melted eye shadow was administered to rats. One UK laboratory reported wrapping mice in kitchen foil and 'grilling' them under ultra-violet lights to simulate sunburn when testing a sun cream. The animals were observed over a 96-hour period and the report concluded that the longer exposure times led to more burning! A wax product used in make-up, fragrance and hair colourants, was dosed into animals by stomach tube – the human equivalent of 1½ lb of chemical. The animals began salivating, bled from the nose and mouth and had diarrhoea. As the test progressed they became emaciated and unkempt. They had congested lungs and kidneys and solid wax in the stomach. LD50s in animals are usually entirely irrelevant for assessing human lethal doses.

Irritancy tests such as the infamous Draize eye and skin tests are the other main type of experiments included in these shameful statistics. Chemicals are instilled into the eyes of conscious rabbits held in stocks. The test can proceed for up to seven days, and as their eyes are physiologically different from ours they cannot produce enough tears to wash the substance away. Rabbits are cheap, easy to handle and, unfortunately for them, they have big eyes.

This is one area where consumers have a powerful role to play, and companies who don't toe the cruelty-free line are as vulnerable to pressure as any other business whose only interests are profits. The answer is simple – switch brands to cruelty-free, then write and tell the company that until they too pledge publicly that they will never use animals again, you will be boycotting their products.

So who is and who isn't cruelty-free? How do you know? Is there a laid-down criterion?

With no legislative guidelines as yet, and the growing insistence on 'green' products, the resultant boom in demand for ecologically sound and exploitive-free shopping has led to a race with companies trying desperately to prove to the consumer that they are the 'greenest' and nicest manufacturers. In such a situation there are bound to be companies whose PR has turned colour overnight ahead of their products. Manufacturers claiming to be 'cruelty-free' could be equally suspect.

For instance, supermarkets who sell own brand cosmetics and toiletries which claim to be cruelty-free are indeed responding to the push which demands the end of animal testing on such goods, yet it is almost impossible for their products to be vetted and approved because most are made by other companies on their behalf. Consumers may read disclaimers on packaging, then wonder why the company name fails to appear on a list of approved products. Because of reasons like internal confidentiality retailers such as Sainsbury's, for instance, refuse even to name the company who make their J-range, so animal groups who compile a list of acceptable companies find it next to impossible to investigate such products. A more open attitude here would surely give the customer greater confidence and, in turn, would benefit the company. After all, some 150 smaller companies have happily offered their products up for scrutiny.

It must also be admitted that some concern has been expressed over the best way to 'vet' a company whose word, at the end of the day, has to be relied upon. In the UK, a five-year threshold on testing has been adopted by groups such as the BUAV. Body Shop operates along the same basis. This means that these companies pledge that products will not be made by them using ingredients tested on animals within the past five years. Theoretically, substances tested today could be used by 'cruelty-free' companies in five years' time – the 'goalposts', are mobile ones which move with the passage of time!

Critics of this system argue that it does not discourage the testing of new and, they would say, superfluous chemicals. They point to European consumer groups who have 'stopped the clock' and only approve companies who eschew ingredients after a set date – 1978, for example, in West Germany, where companies are given a rating, positive or negative. Those breaking the criterion are heavily fined (50,000 DM) and lose their right to the approved symbol. Some UK companies, notably Honesty and Beauty Without Cruelty, adhere to this stricter definition.

The situation in the UK at present is an encouraging one. High-profile campaigns have alerted the public to the issue and pressure is mounting on those still defending animal experiments. Realistically, the five-year guideline is helping companies switch their product lines over to cruelty-free and gives some leeway to them to check out suppliers of raw materials.

However, with so many ingredients available, and with the fast greening of companies, it would seem reasonable now to 'stop the clock' in the UK, and tighten things up so that consumers here are as assured as their West German counterparts. With the opening of the European market, 1992 would seem an ideal time.

When choosing products, it is wisest to assume that the company has tested if it isn't prepared to state that it hasn't. A cruelty-free declaration is a positive boon to sales. Because of rivalry and industrial secrecy, little or no information comes into the public domain unless it is obtained illegally or through the American Freedom of Information Act. In the UK we have no freedom of information to find out how animals are suffering and dying or where, even though the government licenses the companies who carry out the experiments.

But in the USA, companies who animal-test their products have to register the details with the relevant government departments. This is where multi-national companies, often with glamorous images, hang out their dirty washing. We know that Revlon, Avon, Rimmel, Estee Lauder, Elizabeth Arden, Benetton, Dunhill, and Johnson and Johnson, for instance, have all used animals.

Benetton, after testing their Colours of Benetton range on animals, pledged never to do it again after a well-orchestrated campaign in the USA and Britain. Pity they never considered it before they made animals suffer and die. Others turning over a supposedly new leaf are Revlon and Avon, who in 1989 publicly announced they would no longer animal-test. Whilst such genuine changes in company policy are to be welcomed, time will tell if they actually move toward a cruelty-free position. Avon's UK President, David Arnold, stated: '. . . suppliers to the cosmetics industry may have to continue to do some animal testing to substantiate the safety of their new ingredients' (which Avon will, presumably, then use). Yet such developments demonstrate that even big multi-national groups have to respond to the market forces that you, the consumer, ultimately dictate.

On pages 75–6 is a list of companies who have conducted animal experiments – either themselves, or in contract laboratories. Do you use their products? Do you wish to continue

TWIGGY

'Testing products like cosmetics and toiletries on animals is not only cruel, it's so unnecessary. I support the Living Without Cruelty campaign to end these barbaric tests. Let's have beauty products which live up to their beautiful images.'

giving your patronage to a corporation which causes needless suffering and death?

Making the Living Without Cruelty switch to beauty without cruelty couldn't be easier, and consumers can choose with confidence from the approved list of companies. But questioning shoppers could be forgiven for feeling confused. Manufacturers often claim to be pure, natural and so on, and a variety of 'pledges' appear on packaging, sometimes with vague or ambiguous wording; for example: 'produced and tested without cruelty to animals'. This sounds fine, but it *could* mean that those who carried out animal tests decreed that they weren't cruel, which is the stance taken by many laboratories who do these experiments!

Even so, the best course of action is to buy products where an actual pledge is given on the packaging, even if the wording might not be watertight. This means that, under the Trades Descriptions Act, the company are stating they are producing a product free from animal testing (and animal ingredients where stated). Companies would be foolish to compromise themselves by telling lies, so a published assurance does offer consumer protection.

But the most reliable avenue of information is to contact animal societies who have undertaken their own research and obtained concrete assurances from the companies themselves. Both Animal Aid and the BUAV do this, with the latter awarding a rabbit logo to companies who pass the vetting. This symbol is beginning to appear on packaging and is a helpful aid to the consumer. All the cosmetics used in this book are from approved companies and demonstrate the diversity and quality of the products.

It's difficult to understand, when so much cruelty-free choice exists, why companies still tarnish their images by resorting to animal experiments that are medieval in their barbarity. After all, there is no legislation which says they have to. The tests are so crude and unscientific, anyway, that it can hardly be argued any longer that they offer even an illusion of safety. If testing is needed, there are a host of alternative systems which actually produce results relevant to people – and more are being developed. Body Shop, for instance, have launched a project designed to simulate a testbed of human skin, and the company Cosmetics To Go have developed

the Assisi Test which they use to assess irritancy. Human volunteers are never lacking either – Animal Aid has its own panel of members which Body Shop regularly use to assess new products.

There are so many tried and tested ingredients available which have been proven safe after decades – sometimes centuries – of human use that there is simply no excuse for inventing any more. How many do we need? Go into any big store and the choice is already overwhelming, yet for every new formulation another batch of animals may suffer and die to produce what is, after all, a triviality.

Outrageous new EEC directives propose *mandatory* animal testing of *all* cosmetic ingredients – even safe, natural substances like honey. Freedom of choice is threatened by this lunacy because ethical companies will close rather than capitulate. Sign the Body Shop petition and protest to your MEP. Let's stop it now.

Companies who have tested on animals

Alberto-Culver Co. (make VO5 haircare range)
Almay
American Cyanamid Co. (make Breck and Ultra Swim shampoos/Old Spice, Blue Stratos, Mandate men's toiletries/Lady's Choice deodorant/La Prairie skincare/L'Air du Temps, Pierre Cardin perfumes)
Amway Corp.
Aramis Inc.
Avon Products Inc. ★
BeautiControl Cosmetics Inc.
Beecham Cosmetics Inc.
Benetton ★
Bristol-Myers Co.
Carter-Wallace Inc. (make Arrid antiperspirants/Nair depilatories)
Chanel Inc.
Charles of the Ritz Group Ltd
Chesebrough Ponds Inc.
Christian Dior Perfumes
Clairol Inc.
Clarins of Paris
Clinique Laboratories Inc.
Colgate-Palmolive Co.
Coty
Crabtree and Evelyn Ltd
Dana Perfumes Corp.
Dorothy Gray

Dow Chemical Co.
Drackett Products Co. (part of Bristol Myers)
Elizabeth Arden
Estee Lauder Inc.
Fabergé Inc.
Germaine Monteil Cosmetiques Corp.
Gillette Co.
Helena Rubenstein
Houbigant Inc. (makes Monsieur Houbigant aftershave etc./Chantilly and Quelques Fleurs eau de toilette)
Jean Patou Inc.
Johnson and Johnson
S. C. Johnson and Son Inc.
Johnson Products Co. Inc.
Jovan Inc.
Lamaur Inc.
Lancôme
Lever Bros Inc.
L'Oreal
Mary Kay Cosmetics Inc.
Max Factor and Co.
Maybelline
Merle Norman Cosmetics
Neutrogena
Nina Ricci
Noxell Corp. (Cover Girl)
Proctor and Gamble Co.
Quintessence Inc.
Rachael Perry Inc.
Redken Laboratories
Revlon Inc.★
Richardson-Vicks Inc. (part of Proctor and Gamble. Make Olay skincare/Vidal Sassoon, Pantene haircare/Saxon aftershave)
Rimmel★
Schering-Plough (Maybelline)
Sea and Ski Corp. (part of Carter-Wallace)
Shaklee Corp.
Shiseido Cosmetics
Shulton (part of American Cyanamid)
Squibb
Sterling Drug Inc. (part of Eastman-Kodak: Dorothy Gray, Tussey, Ogilvie)
Vidal Sassoon Inc.
Warner-Lambert Co.
Wella Corp.
Westwood Pharmaceuticals Inc. (part of Bristol Myers)
Zotos International Inc. (part of Shiseido Co., Japan)

★ indicates those companies who have announced during 1989–90 their intention to cease animal testing. In the case of Avon, it appears that animal testing may now be left to Avon's suppliers and no longer carried out on their own premises. As with Revlon, there is no indication of adopting any cruelty-free criteria for the future.

List compiled by People for the Ethical Treatment of Animals, USA. Additional information via EIRIS Services Ltd.

This list is not exhaustive. Information on companies is more easily obtained from the United States than in the UK. Here, secrecy and confidentiality make it virtually impossible to discover who the customers of contract laboratories are. Large companies often have in-house labs, and little is published in the public domain about this area for fear of product boycotts.

Where brand names are mentioned, this does not necessarily imply testing of individual products or ranges. Such verification is difficult to obtain. For most consumers, it is usually enough to know that a company has caused unnecessary suffering and death.

Marie Helvin

Marie grew up in Hawaii and learnt from an early age to appreciate nature and the beauty of a world filled with lush vegetation, golden beaches and the blue of the Pacific ocean. Her father made sure his children lived a healthy life. Meat was taboo, although being raised on an island meant that fish formed an important part of the family diet.

'Eating meat would seem so alien to me now. Dad was so serious about health. I just wouldn't have it in the house or prepare it for anyone – not even my cats! I don't actually think of myself as "a vegetarian" – to me it's just *good food*. It's important in my professional life to balance unhealthy aspects by having a good diet and trying to do the best for my body to keep it in tip-top condition – both inside and outside.'

Marie began her modelling career unexpectedly at fifteen when she was offered a contract whilst visiting Japan with her mother.

Four years later, and much travelled, she was invited to London for an important fashion show and her international career took off. In 1975 she met David Bailey and their relationship, now ended, was continually in the headlines.

Marie's modelling assignments have taken her around the world. The work is hard and demanding – not always the glamorous image portrayed in the pages of fashion and beauty magazines. She discovered Beauty Without Cruelty products after reading a magazine article, and helped publicize animal testing issues. Her own beauty routines are subtly simple.

'I've always used a good vegetable soap and water for cleansing. My skin type is fine for that, but during winter when my skin dries out in chill winds I use Flora sunflower oil for cleansing – oil first, then wash afterwards. That way my skin doesn't dry out. Sesame oil is good too. A big bottle goes a long way. Avoid olive, peanut or corn oils because they have a pungent smell. I use sunflower for bath oils as well and mix it with some strong aromatherapy oils or a perfume essence of flowers. My favourite is a mix of sunflower, musk rose essence, vitamin E oil, avocado oil and wheatgerm oil. It's easy to make your own blend and much cheaper than buying it! You can improve night creams, too, by adding a pierced capsule of vitamin E oil or a little almond oil. They go further and make your skin very supple. I try not to spend a lot on skincare products which I'll be using for the rest of my life, and as most are only based on simple oils, why not make your own?

I think that the Body Shop products are very good, and the colours and textures of Barbara Daly's cosmetics are great for everyday use. I wish there were more cruelty-free cosmetics available in the big stores, not just health shops. It's time the big companies stopped animal testing, but will they?

'I don't think it makes any sense to carry out animal experiments. They are so different from us. I wouldn't want to use cosmetics tested on animals. I'd prefer to know that the products had been properly tested in tests relevant to my skin, not some poor rabbit's or guinea pig's. They can also be tested by human volunteers. There are lots of tests now which could replace animals in this area.

'Something else I feel strongly about is the fur issue. I've always had a policy not to model fur. I find the idea of owning a fur just obscene, but more than that I find it weird – that a person would actually want to drape over their back the skins of dead animals. If you want fur, you can buy a fake which means you get something much nicer for a fraction of the cost.

'My work means I have to look good outside and I exercise regularly with a special work-out I really enjoy. To keep fit inside, I eat masses of fruits and vegetables. During summer I keep breakfasts light and enjoy yogurt and toast with cheese. My favourite is fresh fruit with cottage cheese. I only eat lunch if there's time, but then stick to pastas with fresh herbs and vegetable sauces, perhaps with a Mozzarella and tomato salad – everything as fresh as possible. I love cooking and make a mean aubergine lasagne, but I also think Thai and Lebanese food offer good things – most of their cuisine is without meat, and falafel and their chilli dishes are superb.

'I believe that a good diet and attention to your vitamins help to prevent illness and maintain a healthy and beautiful complexion from the inside. Make sure the beauty you put on the outside hasn't been bought at the price of animal suffering.'

Living Without Cruelty, beautifully!

Beauty Without Cruelty, founded by Muriel, Lady Dowding, was the first company to produce ethical cosmetics and is a familiar name to consumers. The range is extensive and the quality superb, appealing to all age groups. Most health stores stock BWC and other approved brands, and on high streets in most major towns you'll find a Body Shop with the Colorings range by Barbara Daly.

Anita Roddick, founder of Body Shop, broke the mould in cosmetic retailing by forsaking the department store and setting up an independent manufacturing and retailing empire, providing consumers with reasonably priced, quality body care products and bringing the animal testing issue right to the forefront of public thinking. There is no doubt that Body Shop's success is partially responsible for pressurizing other, previously intransigent, companies to think again over the animal issue.

There are also some very good mail order

Men's bathroom cupboard

Top: Carters Shaving Cream by Cosmetics To Go.

Non-animal hairbrush. John Lewis Partnership.

Echoes designer fragrance man's soap from L'Arome.

True Grit soap bars by Cosmetics To Go for heavy-duty hand cleansing.

Centre: Amun cream face protector by Cosmetics To Go.

Fleur aromatherapy massage oil.

Echoes designer fragrance man's talc from L'Arome.

Luxury Fizzer Bath Bomb by Cosmetics To Go.

Bottom: Echoes designer fragrance aftershave and matching cologne from L'Arome.

Sarakan toothpaste.

Weleda and Nelson's homoeopathic remedies.

No. 1 men's shaving cream from Body Shop.

Echoes designer fragrance matching deodorant from L'Arome.

Karayan hair gel from Cosmetics To Go.

companies which are well worth investigating. A new one, with a real get-up-and-go image, is Cosmetics To Go, who have an exciting range in innovative packaging. Quality is excellent and the products represent good value for money. Orders come back super-fast.

Most companies also cater for men, producing high-quality yet inexpensive toiletries. Cosmetics To Go and Body Shop both offer complete ranges. The L'Arome company offer a complete co-ordinated range of products with designer fragrances for both men and women.

CTG have also developed a super new range of baby products, Baby Revels, which includes soaps, shampoo, talc, nappy creams and sunscreen – all tested for irritancy on the only valid animal, humans (volunteers, of course!).

Bottled-up insides

One other area of concern, apart from the testing, is that of animal-derived ingredients. As most companies do not list product ingredients, consumers have no way of telling what is in the bottle. This is an area where legislation is urgently needed and is particularly vital for allergy sufferers who cannot identify products they should avoid.

Slaughterhouse by-products, particularly fats, are still widely used, although you'll avoid this by choosing cruelty-free companies who stipulate a vegetarian ethic. Most non-testing companies, ever aware of the growing movement away from animal products, are quickly replacing remaining doubtful ingredients with plant-derived alternatives, and ethical companies often list their ingredients or are happy to provide the information to customers.

A recent trend from the big cosmetic houses is the use of both animal and human placentas in expensive creams. But apart from all this, one product remains which continues to attract consumers, despite the terrible animal suffering which is involved in manufacture – perfume. As the extracts are very expensive to obtain, it is the top end of the market which usually contains them. Most women would shudder if they knew what was in the glitzy expensive bottle adorning their dressing-table.

Perfumery prices

Perfume/ Company	Eau de Parfum Price per 50 ml	
Coco (Chanel)	£30.00	Company animal-test
Chanel No. 5	£26.00	Company animal-test
Lou Lou (Cacharel)	£21.50	Testing unknown
Dioressence	£26.00	Company animal-test
Je Reviens (Worth)	£17.50	Testing unknown
Colours of Benetton★	£16.00	Product animal-tested

The above perfumes may contain animal ingredients.

Numero Quinze (Reform)	£5.95	Similar to Chanel No. 5. Cruelty-free.
Pas de Musque (Cosmetics To Go)	£4.75	30 ml bottle. Cruelty-free.
Gemina 3 (BWC)	£5.25	8 ml bottle. Cruelty-free.
Echoes designer fragrances (L'Arome)	£9.99	Fragrances akin to any brand names. Cruelty-free.

None of the cruelty-free perfumes contain animal ingredients nor are they animal-tested.

★Company has promised not to undertake further animal experiments after campaign aimed to boycott this product range.

Ambergris: a waxy sputum-like substance from the intestines of whales, which is often found floating on the surface. It is, however, more usually obtained when a whale is killed.

Castoreum: comes from the scent gland of a dead beaver and is a very lucrative by-product of the fur trade. Five hundred thousand beavers died in the USA and Canada in 1984, most in the barbaric leg-hold trap. Castoreum is used in oriental perfumes and men's aftershaves which have a 'leathery, sultry' fragrance.

Civet: extracted from the civet cat, which is snared or netted in Ethiopia or kept in the equivalent of the factory farm. Thousands live miserable existences to supply this demand.

Musk: from the little musk deer, is the most expensive animal product in the world. A traumatic procedure extracts the musk pod, which is scraped from a gland near the animal's reproductive organs. The extract is mixed with alcohol and used in many traditional, often French, 'high-class' perfumes. Hunting threatens the species' survival, with at least four thousand adult males killed annually. Just thirty thousand survive in an area capable of supporting two hundred thousand. A hundred animals are used to produce just 1 kg of musk. So much suffering, yet a synthetic musk, made from ambrette seeds, is just as good.

Spermaceti oil: taken from the endangered sperm whale and was formerly used in many preparations. Thankfully, jojoba has now largely replaced it.

Kate O'Mara

'I was born just before the war, and because of the rationing I just never got used to eating unhealthy things. I stopped eating meat when I was nineteen for health reasons, and felt very well on it. It was later that I found out about the animal connections, which truly appalled me. I read about pâté production in France and could hardly believe it. Then I discovered that animals were used to test cosmetics. In those days it was more difficult to find vegetable soaps and cruelty-free cosmetics. Beauty Without Cruelty were the only ones I could find.

'People who meet me for the first time always look for the Ferrari parked round the back, the swimming pool and the wardrobe full of furs and designer dresses, but that's my image – the *femme fatale*, the vamp, the sexy, sophisticated man-eater. It all started from a TV appearance in *Dangerman* as an Italian racing driver. Then in my big break, during a film with Peter O'Toole, I had to do publicity shots as part of the contract, some in the inevitable swimsuit. I didn't think about it at the time, but the pictures went into the papers and since then all the offers I've had for TV and film work have been for the seducing, wicked woman. At first I fought against it, but in the end it was work, so I decided to do those parts as well as I could. I've played all the women's meaty stage roles including Shakespeare

– Lady Macbeth, Cleopatra. This surprises people who only see me on the TV.

'The money I earned in *Dynasty* helped me finance my own theatrical company, to do the roles I really enjoy. During *Dynasty* they wanted me to wear a sable coat. I discovered, of course, that it wasn't sable, but fake. Everything was fake – furs, jewels and so on. If it were real they'd never afford the insurance. I made a film in Finland once and they asked me to model furs. When I refused, they couldn't understand why, but I'm just not the sort of person who wants to be seen in one. I was a beatnik, then came flower power and the hippy era. That's the real me.

'So people expect one thing and get something quite different. For instance, I live in a cottage surrounded by fields. There are heifers there at the moment and they gather around my garden gate in the morning. When I'm rehearsing, I recite Shakespeare to them. They look and listen and saunter off when it gets boring, and I look into their beautiful eyes and wonder how anybody can kill such sensitive and lovely creatures. We have pheasants, too. They come into my garden to hide from the guns. Somehow they know they won't get shot on my little piece of land. I feel that until we, as a human race, start treating our fellow animals on this planet as we'd like to be treated, there's no hope for us.

'All the things connected to the Living Without Cruelty lifestyle can be discovered by simply becoming aware of one aspect. I read *The Vegetarian* magazine and found out about cruelty-free cosmetics and a host of other related things to do with health. I think that each of us makes our own stand, and you change over the years. I'm always trying subtly to convert my fellows, and I'm sure I'm considered a deep eccentric in some ways. I'm living proof that you don't need meat. I'm fifty now and have energetically done without it for thirty years. Fifteen years ago I also stopped eating fish – quite happily, because I was ready to do so. I eat eggs (always free-range) and vegetarian cheese only very occasionally.

'I'm afraid I must have my cuppa in the morning, but I tend to cook very little – in fact, I only possess one saucepan. I make very good vegetable soups. Pea and lettuce is really delicious. And the rest of my diet consists of raw and uncooked foods like avocados, which I absolutely adore. I eat them with Protoveg Smokey Snaps in the middle, sprinkled with lemon juice – peculiar but absolutely divine. I love bananas and really good stoneground bread (Whole Earth bread is wonderful). I also eat lots of peanut butter. I've also given up alcohol completely. I drink Aqua Libra water, which helps get rid of headaches and tastes excellent.

'So what started as a health thing for me has progressed. Life is actually better for knowing about something – even if it's something horrible – and then being able to make up your mind to do something about it. For instance, choosing a delightful perfume or a new set of eye colours when you know they haven't caused pain and suffering, makes shopping to me a real pleasure.

Colour cosmetics – price comparisons

Company	Lipstick	Compact Powder	Single Eye Colour	Mascara	Blusher	How Tested?
Estee Lauder	£7.50	£12.50	£9.00	£8.50	£12.50	Company animal test
Revlon*	£4.95	£8.95	£2.95	£4.95	£8.50	Company animal test
Elizabeth Arden	£7.95	£8.95	£6.95	£7.95	£10.50	Company animal test
Helena Rubenstein	£6.50	£10.95	£6.95	£10.95	£11.50	Company animal test
John Lewis own brand†	£1.75	–	£1.95	£1.95	£2.95	Unknown
BWC	£1.80	£2.30	£1.80	£1.80	£1.75	Cruelty-free
Cosmetics To Go	£2.50	–	£1.75	£2.25	£3.75	Cruelty-free
Body Shop	£2.10	£2.75	£2.00	£1.75	£1.95	Cruelty-free
Body Reform	£2.50	£3.25	£3.95 for 2	£3.45	£3.95	Cruelty-free
Yvonne Gray Int.	£4.50	£7.95	£2.50	£4.95	£3.50	Cruelty-free

*Revlon products have been animal-tested, but in 1989 the company did announce its intention to cease animal experiments.
†John Lewis's Jonelle cosmetics were chosen simply to reflect the price range seen in most own brands. Unfortunately it is extremely difficult to find out who makes these cosmetics, or to ascertain how they are tested.

Living Without Cruelty, naturally!

Cruelty-free cosmetics contain natural substances mainly derived from plants. Here is a guide to some commonly used ingredients:

Almond: essential oil derived from the kernel of sweet almonds. Protects and softens skin. Rich, and particularly effective for face and neck. Used for centuries.

Aloe vera: from the leaves of the aloe plant. Has healing and water-retentive properties, especially effective for dry, tender and sunburnt skin. Cools, softens and protects.

Avocado: rich in vitamins A and B. Cleans, softens and makes skin supple.

Carrot: the oil contains beta-carotene and vitamins C, D and E plus B complex. A superb tonic for dry, scaly skins.

Chamomile: versatile cosmetic herb. Creates highlights in blonde hair; enriches dry, fine hair. Soothes sensitive skins when used in creams and lotions.

Cocoa butter: solid fat derived from roasted cocoa plant seeds. Lubricating properties soften and protect skin.

Coconut oil: aromatic, effective lubricant for hair and body preparations.

Elderflower: used for centuries to soften complexions and to refresh.

Honey: ancient ingredient. Natural antiseptic which softens and heals skin. Good for dry and mature skin.

Jojoba: oil obtained from the seeds of this shrub.

Orange flower: used as a skin hydrant, so effective on dry complexions.

Orchid: the oil has mild, gentle and moisturizing properties. Used for dry, mature or problem skin.

Peppermint: cooling, antiseptic herb.

Rosemary: hair conditioner, soothes sensitive scalps; the oil adds lustre to dark hair.

Rosewater: soothes and cools. Often used in toners.

Witch hazel: originally used medicinally by American Indians. Soothing astringent, reduces oiliness of greasy skin.

All of these ingredients and many more are skilfully utilized by approved companies in their products, without the need for animal experiments or having to use the leavings of the abattoir. After all, these products are going on to your face and every intimate area of your body!

A word too about price. Cruelty-free brands are often cheaper, but this does not reflect on the quality of the product – far from it. Ethical companies do not need to sustain the level of hype which others do. They often sell direct, which cuts out middlemen, either through mail order or their own outlets; and they have their own innovative approach to marketing which means they never have to get on the department store bandwagon. Some own brands and lower-end-of-the-market products such as Rimmel may be cheaper than some cruelty-free products, but the monetary savings are small. Buying cosmetics the Living Without Cruelty way does give a sense of well-being. As Linda McCartney commented, 'You really do feel a better person!' So next time you shop for cosmetics, toiletries or perfume – for yourself or for gifts, especially at Christmastime – show that you care and buy cruelty-free products. Remember, suffering is never beautiful.

Down to basics

Beauty professional Theresa Fairminer, from BBC TV's *The Clothes Show*, shares her beauty secrets to help you look your best by Living Without Cruelty. . . .

'The key to a healthy, youthful complexion really comes from within you. Some of the most beautiful faces I've seen have always drunk a glass of fresh water first thing in the morning and last thing at night. This helps cleanse the system and is very beneficial.

'Avoid chocolate, coffee and fatty foods as they will only irritate any skin problems. A healthy eating programme and your own basic and simple beauty regime will help you get the very best from your skin – a healthy, glowing complexion.

'I'm often asked "What skin-care products should I use?" The answer lies not in the brand name but in how you apply the different creams and lotions. The first thing to do is to diagnose your skin type.

(a) predominantly dry face – *dry skin type*.
(b) oily and prone to spots – *oily skin type*.
(c) combination – oily centre, dry at sides – *combination*.

(d) sensitive: apt to be sore, allergic and red – *sensitive*. This type can belong to either the dry, oily or combination groups.

'Buy or make a skin care range for your type to get the best results. How you cleanse is the most important part of your skin-care routine. Simple and often is the golden rule. Soap and water are fine if you don't use make-up, but all the older ladies I've met whose skin is in beautiful condition have used cleansers as opposed to soap and water. Both cleansing creams and fresheners are more effective in removing make-up.

'Apply lightly with clean hands, then tissue off gently. If I wear heavy make-up I tend to do this twice. Waterproof mascaras may need a special eye make-up remover to cleanse properly. Next apply a skin freshener. The strength of this will depend on your skin type, but only use an astringent containing alcohol if you have an excessively oily complexion. A simple 'wash' with a cotton wool pad and skin freshener should be all you need in the morning.

'Moisturizer is the next and final step before applying cosmetics, but only use it if you feel your skin needs it, or as a skin protective before foundation, and only apply it to the dry parts of your skin. The oily sections such as chin and nose areas will reject the cream, which will shine on the surface. Moisturizing *lotions* are best for young, dry and combination skins, whilst the *creams* are richer and better-suited for older, dry and combination skin types.

'Reject immediately any products which sting or irritate your face. I don't care for the facial peeling lotions now available and find them too abrasive. Your facial skin renews itself automatically.

'If you are prone to blackheads, apply a hot towel to your face, allowing the heat and steam to soften and open up the pores of your skin. Then *very gently*, using cotton wool, squeeze out the blackheads. Do not over-squeeze the area and make your face sore, or you will scar your face. Repeat this once a month until the appearance of your skin has improved. Meanwhile, give your diet some thought and make sure you cleanse these problem areas thoroughly.

'Nourishing and firming creams are used at night, but only start using them when you really find it necessary, otherwise they will not be so beneficial when your skin really starts drying out. I started using them at thirty.

'A face mask can be a weekly treat. It will invigorate your skin and help you relax and feel pampered. Try my two easy but special recipes, and next time you shop for skin care products choose natural beauty without animal cruelty.'

Theresa's face-mask recipes

CUCUMBER AND LEMON MASQUE

Useful for oily to combination skin types.

½ cucumber, peeled
½ teaspoon lemon juice
2 teaspoons witch hazel
1 egg white, whipped till peaky

Place the cucumber, lemon juice and witch hazel in a blender and whizz for 15 seconds. In a bowl carefully mix the egg white and the blended ingredients. Apply to the face, putting cucumber eye pads or sliced cucumber over your closed eyelids. Relax for 20 minutes, then wash off with water.

OATMEAL MASK

3 teaspoons rosewater
½ cup milk
3 teaspoons oatmeal

Cook the oatmeal and milk carefully over a very gentle heat until soft. Remove from the heat and add the rosewater. Mix well. Apply to your face when the mixture is just warm, or leave to cool completely. Leave for 20 minutes, then rinse off with water.

Note: See the colour pictures between pages 96 and 97, which show the results of the beauty treatments on these two pages.

Beautiful hands

Model: Janet Kay
Photographer: Bob Marchant

'Top hand model Janet has naturally beautiful hands. Her carefully thought out hand care programme ensures they stay that way. Here are some of her secrets for an at-home manicure.

'First shape the nails. It doesn't matter if they're short – as long as they're neatly filed they will look all the better. The rough side of the emery board is for shortening the nail, and the gentle side for shaping and smoothing. Don't file the nail to a pointed shape: this looks ugly and weakens the nail. Aim for as square a shape as possible, with the ends a gentle oval. Always file into the centre of the nail, and never take off too much at the sides.

'After shaping apply a rich cream to the cuticle. Massage around the nail base and cuticle, then soak your hands for a minute in warm water. Dry your hands carefully, then, using an orange stick, gently push back the cuticle. Only cut the cuticle with scissors if absolutely necessary, and then very carefully.

'Next give your hands a good massage with hand cream. Animal Aid have an excellent hand and body lotion for this. Regular hand massage will help revitalize tired skin, leaving hands soft and youthful-looking. Janet admits it's a bore, but she always wears gloves when doing housework.

'If you want to wear varnish, first apply a non-greasy remover over the nails to increase adherence. Apply the base coat, being careful not to cover the cuticle, which would cause harm to the nail. When the base has dried apply the top coat. Varnish should be applied in three deft movements. One to each side of the nail first, and the third down the centre. BWC nail colour Peach Dream was used in the photograph.

'Regardless of age or skin type, this simple manicure, carried out once a week, will bring about a definite improvement in your hands.'

T.F.

Making up is hard to do?

Make-up artists Theresa Fairminer and Susie Sutherland set to work to transform five faces using cruelty-free products: Elaine, a dark redhead; Helen, a brunette; Linda, with black skin; Elayne, a blonde; and Gwen, with greying hair. A fun day was had by all in the studio, and everyone with the exception of Linda, were total amateurs in front of the camera.

Although they all use some cosmetics every day, most were unsure how to highlight their best features. This exercise in looking good demonstrated just how a few deft touches of colour can do much to lift your confidence and your performance. Our 'before' pictures captured faces unsure of themselves . . . what would the camera reveal? Our 'after' shots speak for themselves. Confident, self-assured and no longer afraid of the dreaded lens. There's a little of the model in all of us!

Elaine

Make-up: Theresa Fairminer
Hair: Tony Collins for Michaeljohn
Photographer: Tim Bret-Day at Camilla Arthur

'Elaine had the perfect face for make-up, but was unsure how to use it. BWC 'Honey Beige' Foundation was applied with a damp, wedge-shaped cosmetic sponge for speed and ease. This was applied very lightly as I didn't want Elaine to look as though she was wearing any foundation. BWC translucent powder was then applied all over to help the make-up last. BWC 'Tawny Whisper' blusher, applied just under the cheekbones, both highlights and gives the face a slimmer shape.

'BWC navy blue pencil was used to outline her eyes, and BWC Koala and Tiger's Eye used for a natural hint of colour. I decided to use these very natural shades on the eyes, but emphasized the lashes by first curling them with eyelash curlers before applying BWC brown mascara.

'To emphasize a small mouth I showed her how to line her lips with a darker lipstick, BWC Red, then fill in with BWC Iced Melon. Colourings lip tint was used in the centre of the bottom lip and blended in, which makes the lips appear fuller.'

T.F.

Hair: Elaine washed her hair with Cosmetics To Go Sea Level shampoo, made with seaweed. No conditioner is needed unless your hair is over-processed. Tony used Michaeljohn Sculpture Lotion to add body and discipline, followed by Michaeljohn spray to keep the shape of Elaine's classic style.

Helen

Make-up: Susie Sutherland
Hair: Tony Collins for Michaeljohn
Photographer: Tim Bret-Day at Camilla Arthur

'Helen has a delicate and sophisticated bone structure and needs a careful choice of colour to emphasize this. Cosmetics To Go moisturizer was used, then BWC Cool Beige foundation, a good match for Helen's skin was applied with a damp sponge. The excellent concealer from Naturally Yours was used to tone down under-eye shadows and blemishes. The base was completed with a dusting of BWC translucent powder, applied with a fine powder brush. Her cheekbones were brushed lightly with Cosmetics To Go Cream Cocoa blusher.

'BWC Tiger's Eye shadow was applied from the inner to the middle eyelid and blended with BWC Timber Wolf on the outer lids. BWC Ginger Cat was used as highlighting on the outer brow-bone and the colours carefully blended into one another. Eye definition, close to top and lower lashes, was with a Body Shop grey eye pencil and BWC Olive crayon was smudged under the lower lashes for dramatic emphasis. BWC black mascara highlights Helen's long lashes. Brows were defined with Body Shop eye-brow make-up.

'Lips are BWC Koala.'

S.S.

Hair: Helen's hair was washed with Crimpers hypo-allergenic shampoo and treated with Crimpers conditioner. Tony used Michaeljohn City Sculpture Lotion for body and lift and held the style with Michaeljohn spray.

Linda

Make-up: Theresa Fairminer
Hair: Tony Collins for Michaeljohn
Photographer: Tim Bret-Day at Camilla Arthur
Linda Tolbert is with Max Presents.

'Linda Tolbert, a top fashion model, was visiting the photographer at the same time as our session. She enthusiastically volunteered to be included and was delighted with the results.

'Cosmetics To Go moisturizer was applied before Barry M foundation No. 10. BWC blusher Rosetta was used to highlight bone structure.

'Eyelids were done with BWC Timber Wolf on lids, with BWC Plum Crush in the crease. Eyes were outlined with black BWC definer, which also strengthened Linda's brow shape. Lashes were coloured with BWC Black mascara.

'Wonderful bright lips were achieved with Barry M. No. 2.'

T.F.

Hair: Tony used Michaeljohn City Slicker as a pomade, finishing with Michaeljohn spray.

Elayne

Make-up: Susie Sutherland
Hair: Elayne Maytum
Photographer: Tim Bret-Day

'Elayne's 'soft-rocker' look began with a moisturizing base from Cosmetics To Go and followed by their Ash Beige foundation blended with a damp cosmetics sponge to even out the skin tones, together with a little help

from the Naturally Yours cover stick. Body Shop translucent loose powder was dusted over lightly to set the foundation, using a powder brush.

'Brows were enhanced and balanced with Body Shop eyebrow make-up to make a frame for the soft eye shades: Body Shop shadow 02, across the lid; BWC Hot Chestnut in the socket line; with BWC Plum Crush on the outer brow-bone. Eye definer was a mix of BWC Black eyeliner and Plum Crush shadow. Lashes were finished with BWC Black Mascara.

'Two applications of the aptly named Rebel Rose by BWC was used for the lips. By using a strong lip shade only a hint of colour was needed on the cheeks – BWC Shanghai blusher, which gives just enough warmth to Elaine's face.'

S.S.

Hair: Elaine washed her fine blonde hair with Neal's Yard Chamomile and Orange Flower shampoo and then applied their Chamomile and Jojoba conditioner. Lift and body was achieved with Crimpers gel and hairspray.

Gwen

Make-up: Theresa Fairminer
Hair: Tony Collins for Michaeljohn
Photographer: Tim Bret-Day at Camilla Arthur

'Gwen's complexion was very dry and a good moisturizer was essential (Cosmetics To Go). BWC's Honey Beige foundation was applied with a damp cosmetic sponge. (Hint – always start from the centre of the face and work outwards down to the chin and blend in. Foundation should be the same colour as your face, otherwise you'll get a tide-mark between chin and neck. Always test new colours on the side of the face, just below the ear, to see if the colour is right. It's no good testing foundation on your hand.) BWC's translucent powder was then used, omitting the area under the eyes. BWC Sun Gold blusher highlights the cheekbones. (Hint – buy a good blusher brush for an even, natural coverage – obviously not badger hair! Large, synthetic cut-down artists' brushes work well. Look for Daler's Dalon range. Manufacturers please note this gap in the market.)

'To help make Gwen's eyes larger a grey BWC eye pencil was used to outline the eyelid close to the lashes. BWC Koala shadow coloured the lids and was highlighted with BWC Lovebird. Lashes were done with BWC Brown.

'BWC Cool Clover lipstick, applied with a brush, finished the look.'

T.F.

Hair: Gwen washed her hair with a chamomile shampoo by Simply Herbal, followed by calendula conditioner by Neals Yard. Tony simply used tongs to restyle Gwen's natural curls, and held the effect in place with Michaeljohn hairspray.

Colouring up with Barbara Daly

'Every woman, whether learning to use make-up for the first time or wanting a fresh new look, should feel comfortable, at ease and familiar with her face. Make-up can, and does, make you look and feel better. Understanding your face is more important than having a vast range of make-up at your disposal; and getting to know your best features, where to and where not to apply make-up, is essential. First, get to know yourself – your faults and your good points. Everybody has both!

'Many women are discouraged from experimenting with make-up simply because there is so much conflicting advice available and they find it very confusing when trying to deal with specific problem areas such as disguising wrinkles or hiding ugly blemishes, or simply the overall shape of their face. No face is flawless, and everyone has something they would like to change, conceal or emphasize. Careful use of make-up can help to achieve this.

'Not everyone needs *foundation*, but if you are going to wear some, apply that first and use concealer afterwards. To find the right shade of foundation for you, test by applying a little on the side of the cheek near the jawline. If it's a good match you won't get a tideline – it should be as close as possible to your natural skin tone. If you've picked the right colour, you won't need to take it all the way down your throat. A damp sponge will help you obtain a professional finish. Always start in the middle of the face and work outwards. Take care not to push foundation into your hairline.

'*Concealer* is an essential item in everyone's make-up kit. You can use it to cover broken veins, spots and minor skin discolorations, including eye 'shadow'. It can help to disguise a high colour in the cheeks. Don't apply a concealer to eye-bags; it will only highlight them. You can pat concealer on with your finger, but for best results apply with a lip or eyeshadow brush. However, if you suffer from acne, or if your skin has broken out badly, it is better not to wear any make-up and to seek medical attention. With minor skin blemishes a good tip is to use the rest of your make-up to take attention away from the outbreak area. For example, if the spots are on your forehead, choose a bright lipstick. If they're on your chin, make use of your eyes and play down your mouth with a neutral or muted lip shade.

'Always use *face powder* as it helps to hold your make-up in place and gives a more professional, finished look. It also takes away shine – especially important with oily skin. Always use powder sparingly around the eyes so as not to emphasize any fine lines.

'*Blushers* are used to make the face look alive and the skin glow, not to shape the face, but careful placing of blusher can be used to flatter your face shape. The effect should always be subtle. Remember, if you are using a cream blusher it should be applied before your powder, but a powder blusher should go on after your powder.

'A square face can be given more curves by emphasizing the centre of the cheeks and possibly highlighting the chin. Most square faces have very well-defined cheekbones, but as they are also wide it's a good idea to try and bring the cheek colour and emphasis towards the centre of the face. This is done by keeping cheekbone highlight high to the sides of the face, and the blusher well forward on the cheek. Although square faces often have a prominent chin, some don't, and if you wish to make your chin more pointed you can add *highlight* to the tip of it.

'People with round faces usually have smaller noses and often full lips. Round faces may look plump if blusher is in the wrong position, and the right combination of blusher and highlighter helps to slim and flatten the face. Blusher should be applied in a fine downward shape and smoothed carefully into the skin so there are no hard edges. A little highlighter can be used to emphasize the cheekbones and the chin, but be careful to blend these in very well so that they don't look like white patches.

'Long faces often have attractive, well-defined cheekbones. Make the most of them with clever use of one or two shades of blusher. A dot of blusher on the tip of the chin will help to shorten it, but don't overdo it. The correct placing of your blusher or blushers, if you decide to use more than one colour, can help make the face look shorter and emphasize the naturally high cheekbones. The cheek blusher is applied across the cheek, gently blending the edges; a darker blush can be applied below this to give some extra contour to the face and blended into the blusher above.

'Eyes can be divided into two basic categories of shape, depending on the size of the lid. The first is the deep-set or 'small' eye, where there isn't much lid showing. This kind of eye often has a narrow area between the line of the upper lashes and the eyebrow, and no well-defined socket. The second is the 'protruding' eye, which has a rather prominent upper lid. Apart from these differences eyes are all more or less the same almond shape, but set in different-shaped sockets.

'When considering what to do with your own eye make-up you need to assess how much lid you have to work with. If there isn't a lot of lid showing, keep darker eye shadows towards the outer edge of the eye and lighter colours from the centre of the eye inwards, towards the nose. If you think your eyes look too full or protruding, keep the colour stronger at the centre of the lid and gradually fade it away to the outer and inner corners of the eye. Keep shadows soft and matt on protruding eyes or very full eyelids – shiny eye shadows will only emphasize the problem. A good point to remember is that dark, matt colours make problem areas recede, and light, shiny colours emphasize your good points.

'Although you can, to some extent, give the impression of making your mouth larger or smaller by using your *lipstick* in a certain manner, it isn't a good idea to try to overpaint or underpaint more than a hair's breadth on either side of your natural lip line. If you do want to alter your lip shape, you must learn to draw a clean outline using either a lip brush or lip liner pencil. Remember, darker colours will tend to make your mouth look smaller, although they will also draw attention to it, and lighter colours can make the mouth look fuller. Using a lip pencil or lip brush will help prevent lipstick 'bleeding', and blotting your lipstick well, then lightly powdering the edges of the line before you add more lipstick or gloss to the centre of the mouth, is another safeguard against spidery lines.

'Not everyone has the features to be a model, but the right make-up correctly applied can draw attention away from your weakest features while making the most of your best ones. Even small changes can create a whole new appearance. Everyone has the potential to look

their best – you just have to concentrate on your best points, otherwise you're letting your best features go to waste.'

Barbara Daly

Annie Lennox

'I'm basically an honest person and like things to be out in the open, so I don't refer to myself as a vegetarian because I still eat and enjoy fish and I still wear leather. In the back of my mind my tendencies are towards vegetarianism, but I'm not ready to take these other steps yet.

'My ex-husband was a very strict vegetarian and influenced me greatly towards a different lifestyle. Part of my family are farmers, so I grew up aware of animals. Granny would go into the yard and kill a chicken to eat for dinner. Grandfather was a gamekeeper. This seemed fair enough at the time and was the way of things. My uncle fattens beef cows for a living. It's all he knows, so discussing vegetarianism wouldn't make any sense to him.

'I find something intrinsically ugly about the mass consumerism of animals. There's a terrible, brutal butchery which is governed by commercial greed. I find this awful. I always feel for the underdog and I identify with those who are suffering, so I could see things from the animals' point of view. Giving up meat eating wasn't difficult. I'm a natural pessimist I suppose, but I can see there's been a great movement during the past fifteen years towards a more conscious and compassionate way of life. I believe people are interested in healthier options, food without additives and natural things, but it's important that we know what's behind the food we're eating – what's in the meat and what its origins are.

'I don't believe in preaching any sort of doctrine about life, but if you're positive about your life and are yourself this is more likely to inspire people around you towards change. That's why I'm here in this book. Living Without Cruelty demands no absolutists. It's prepared to embrace people who are halfway or a quarter of the way there. It's important to be tolerant and open-minded because we all fall, we all make mistakes, and sometimes it's a slow process to change habits acquired over a lifetime.

'My dad died from cancer a while ago. During his illness I drew my parents' attention to diet. Even though this created difficulties, Mum has now virtually cut all meat out of her diet and since then has been surprised that the rheumatism in her hands has definitely improved. Her friends have also cut their meat consumption considerably. This is quite a shift for people brought up on a meat-based diet, but it shows that people are interested in their health. I'm just waiting for the day when the health food shops are the supermarkets – when good, healthy food is the norm, not the exception, and is available to everyone.

'I like cooking when time permits, and prefer light meals. I don't like stodgy foods. My favourite meals consist of good salads with Feta cheese and baked potatoes. In the winter I make lentil soups and noodle and pasta dishes, and I adore vegetable lasagne.

'There are alternatives available to virtually everything. It's not taking second-best. I get lots of fun from fake furs, for instance. And cruelty-free cosmetics just have to be better than products which cause so much suffering.'

Pretty potions – do-it-yourself natural beauty

Making up your own beauty preparations isn't the daunting task you might imagine, and inexpensive creams and lotions can be made in the kitchen using simple cooking utensils. Ingredients needed are usually easy to obtain – many just from the greengrocer, florist, or your own vegetable or herb garden! Waxes and other ingredients can be obtained from chemists. Making your own can be fun to do, and very economical. Save any small and attractive pots and jars so you can refill them with your favourite concoctions.

If you suffer from allergy problems caused by chemical preservatives or other substances which cause sensitivity, then making up your own cleansers and moisturizing creams may be the answer to your skin problems. In this way you can keep control over the ingredients and make small batches to keep in the fridge. Make

another fresh potful when needed. Try some of the DIY recipes below from Living Without Cruelty supporters Suzy Kendall and Pat Wellington (from their book *Natural Appeal*, published by Dent, 1980) and if you want to explore further there are books available with extensive recipe sections (see page 00).

DIY beauty recipes

STRAWBERRY CLEANSING CREAM
6 tablespoons petroleum jelly
Pinch of borax
1 tablespoon strained fresh strawberry juice

Melt the petroleum jelly over a very gentle heat. Dissolve the borax into the strawberry juice and beat thoroughly into the melted jelly until the consistency is creamy and the mixture cool. Pot and keep in the fridge.

Fresh strawberry pulp is also good on its own, acting as an astringent, removing oiliness and encouraging circulation. Strawberries also act as a skin whitener.

COCOA BUTTER CLEANSER
3 oz/75 g cocoa butter
1 oz/25 g almond oil
2 oz/50 g rosewater

Slowly melt the cocoa butter over gentle heat whilst warming the almond oil in another pan. Gradually, drop by drop, add the oil and the rosewater to the cocoa butter, beating all the time. Remove from the heat and continue beating until smooth. Leave to cool, then pot.

LETTUCE SKIN TONIC
¼ head lettuce (you can substitute carrots or celery)
1 glass water
½ teaspoon tincture of benzoin

Finely chop the lettuce and put it into a blender at high speed with the glass of water. Strain through a fine sieve or nylon stocking and refrigerate the liquid for a day. Strain twice more, add the tincture of benzoin, shake vigorously and use.

GRAPE, YOGURT AND HONEY FACE MASK

Equal parts of honey and plain yogurt
Handful of mashed grapes

Mix the ingredients together and apply to your freshly steamed face. The mask is soothing, penetrating and moisturizing. The grapes are beneficial to sun-dried skin and help to restore skin acidity. Yogurt helps greasy skin and also acts as a mild bleaching agent on winter-dingy complexions. Relax for 15–20 minutes with the mask on. Wash off with tepid water, then splash your face with cold. If you've any 'mask' left over – eat it!

GARDEN FRESH BATH OIL

Handful of rose petals or any other sweet-smelling
flower such as freesias or lavender
2 oz/50 g glycerine
2 drops pink vegetable food colouring (optional, but
makes it look pretty)

Steep the petals in the glycerine for about a week. Strain off the petals, add the other ingredients and shake well. Decant into a pretty bottle and drip into your bath when required. Can also be used after the bath instead of a body lotion.

AVOCADO BASIC MOISTURIZER

2 teaspoons beeswax
1 teaspoon emulsifying wax
2 teaspoons almond oil
3 teaspoons avocado oil
4 tablespoons rosewater

Melt the waxes in a bowl which is standing in a saucepan of hot water so that the heat source is indirect. When ready add the two oils to the melted waxes. In another bowl heat the rosewater in the same way until the contents of both bowls are the same temperature. Drop by drop, add the rosewater to the oil and wax mixture, constantly stirring with a wooden spoon. Remove the complete mixture from the heat and keep stirring until it sets. Pot.

Living Without Cruelty – your guide to approved companies

Choose with confidence from these companies keyed as follows, all of which do not test on animals.

(V) = all products free from slaughterhouse ingredients. Many products made by these companies are also free from other animal ingredients such as lanolin and honey and are therefore suitable for vegans and those allergic to any animal product.

(V–) = products free from slaughterhouse ingredients except those listed in italics.

(Vx) = companies do not test, but products do contain some slaughterhouse ingredients.

Oils = aromatherapy products.

H = home sales (contact company for details).

Useful addresses

Aethera Products (V)
4 Felindre
Lon Hendre
Waun Fawr
Aberystwyth
Dyfed
SY23 3PY
0970 611112
Skincare, bath and sun products sold through health stores and mail order.

Alan Paul PLC (V)
164 New Chester Rd
Birkenhead
L41 9BG
051-666 1060
Hair products sold through own salons.

Angela Wall (V)
Deans Bank Farm
Bredgar
Sittingbourne
Kent
ME9 8BG
062784 394
Skincare products sold through mail order. H.

Animal Aid (V)
7 Castle St
Tonbridge
Kent
TN9 1BH
Skincare, hair, bath, sun and men's products sold through mail order. Profits fund compassion campaigns and school educational materials. Exceptionally good value. Mail order. Recommended.

Anita Phillips Aromatherapy Ltd (V)
Sarnett House
Repton Drive
Gidea Park
Essex
RM2 5LP
0708 20289
Skincare, hair and bath products and aromatherapy through mail order, health stores and Harrods. H.

Aqua Natural Ltd (V)
50 Lawrence-Leyland Industrial Estate
Irthlingborough Rd
Wellingborough
Northants
NN8 1RT
0933 441818
Depilatory for professional salon use.

Aroma Therapy Supplies Ltd (V)
The Knoll Business Centre
Old Shoreham Rd
Hove
Sussex
BN3 7GS
0273 412139
Skincare, hair and bath products, fragrances, aromatherapy sold through health stores, mail order and chemists.

Austrian Moor Products Ltd (V)
Whiteladies
Maresfield
East Sussex
TN22 2HH
0825 2658
Skincare, hair, bath, dental, men's, sun and baby products sold through health stores, mail order, chemists, clinics and salons. H.

B Pure Ltd (V)
5 Brooks Court
Cringle St
London SW8 5BX
01-498 0902/3
Skincare, hair, bath, men's and sun products sold through mail order, health stores, chemists and department stores such as Fenwicks and Harrods.

Back to Nature (V)
PO Box 38
Flitwick
Bedford
MK45 5NT
0525 713065
Skincare, hair and aftershave products sold through mail order.

Bare Necessities (V)
The Village Arcade
10 Brook St
Tavistock
Devon
0822 617814
Skincare, hair, bath, fragrances, men's, sun and baby products sold through own store and mail order.

Barrier Reef Aloe Vera Enterprises (V)
The Body Place
5 Castlegate
Clitheroe
Lancashire
BB7 1AZ
0200 24550
Skincare and sun products sold through own shop, mail order and events. H.

Barry M Cosmetics (V–) *bath pearls/fruit soaps*
Unit 1
Bittacy Business Centre
Bittacy Hill
Mill Hill East
London NW7 1BA
01-349 2992
Skincare, hair, bath, fragrances, men's and colours sold through health stores, department stores, salons, chemists and boutiques, plus own stores. Bright and bouncy colour ranges especially good for the young and also ideal for stage use, with black, green, blue lipsticks etc., hair streaks and brilliant dazzle pots to choose from. Good value.

Beauty By Post (V)
14 Sefton Pk Rd
Bristol
BS7 9AJ
0272 423403
Skincare, fragrances and aromatherapy by mail order. H.

Beauty Without Cruelty (V)
Avebury Avenue
Tonbridge
Kent
TN9 1TL
0732 365291
The originators of cruelty-free beauty, founded twenty-five years ago by Lady Dowding. Skin, hair, bath, sun, perfume and men's products, soap and colours, sold through health stores, department stores, chemists, some Tesco stores and mail-order. Good quality, with special appeal for older women wanting to change brand allegiance. Bright colours too for the more experimental approach. Foundations and compact powders especially fine. Recommended.

Bermar (V)
Dart Sales and Promotions
Clitheroe House
35 Clitheroe Rd
Brierfield
Lancs
BB9 5QH
0282 603589
Hair products sold through mail order and health stores. H.

Blackmores (V)
Unit 7
Poyle Technical Centre
Willow Rd
Poyle
Colnbrook
Bucks
SL3 0PD
0753 683815
Skincare, hair and dental products, sold through health stores and chemists.

The Body and Face Place Ltd (V–) *bath pearls/ fruit & novelty soaps*
164 New Chester Rd
Birkenhead
Wirral
L41 9BG
051 666 1496
Skincare, hair, bath, fragrances, men's, sun, aromatherapy and household products and colours sold through own outlets and mail order.

Body Basics (V)
Kent House
The Street
Old Costessey
Norwich
NR8 5DB
0603 745258
Skincare, hair, sun and bath products and fragrances sold through mail order and in selected shops. H.

Body Care (V)
50 High St
Ide
Exeter
Devon
EX2 9RW
0392 217628
Skincare, Mellow soaps and Kobashi aromatherapy oils, sun and hair products sold through health stores and mail-order.

The Body Care Company (V)
Churchgate Buildings
Lavenders Brow
Churchgate
Stockport
Cheshire
SK1 1YW
061-480 3700
Skincare, hair and bath products sold through mail order, chemists, various retail outlets. H.

Body Centre Scotland (V–) *bath pearls/fruit & novelty soaps*
17 Kingsgate Centre
Dunfermline
Fife
KY12 7QU
0383 730871
Skincare, hair, bath, fragrances, men's, sun and aromatherapy products sold through mail order and own stores.

Body Language (V–) *bath pearls/fruit & novelty soaps*
10 Cambridge Rd
Hastings
East Sussex
TN34 1DJ
0424 424237
Skincare, hair, bath, fragrances, men's and baby products sold through own store.

Bodyline Cosmetics Ltd (V)
Units 4/5
Alders Way
Yalberton Industrial Estate
Paignton
TQ4 7QL
0803 555582
Skincare, hair, oils, men's, fragrances and bath products sold through own shops, mail order and stockists, Friends of the Earth. Well-presented quality products with some unusual ideas such as huge glass jars filled with bath salts. Good value. H.

Body Natural Ltd (V)
Telford Industrial Centre
Stafford Park 4
Telford
Shropshire
TF3 3BA
0952 290164
Skincare, hair, bath, men's, sun, fragrances and baby products, also oils, sold through own stores. H.

Body Potions (V)
7 Pavilion Square
Scarborough
North Yorks
YO11 2JN
0723 354007
Skincare, hair, bath, dental and sun products and oils, sold through mail order and own store. H.

The Body Shop International PLC (V–)
  Elizabethan washballs/bath pearls/fruit soaps
Hawthorn Rd
Wick
Littlehampton
West Sussex
BN17 7LR
0903 717107
Skincare, hair, bath, sun and men's products, oils, fragrances and colours (Colourings make-up by Barbara Daly), sold through own stores throughout UK and overseas. Excellent quality and value. Treat yourself to an hour's browsing and take your chequebook!

Bodywise Ltd (V)
The Arches
Richmond Bridge
Richmond Rd
Twickenham
TW1 2EF
01-891 1485
Fragrances, men's products and oils, sold through mail order.

Bonita Skin Care (V)
23 Archers Close
Droitwich
Hereford and Worcester
WR9 9LH
0905 771908
Skincare and bath products and oils sold through mail order.

Camilla Hepper Ltd (V–) *bath pearls/fruit and novelty soaps*
18–19 Mountbatten Way
Tiverton
Devon
EX16 6SW
0884 258673
Skincare, hair, bath and dental products, fragrances, men's and sun products and oils, sold through mail order, own stores and exclusive stockists.

Cara Collection (V)
MCV Formulae Ltd
Unit 25
Mountbatten Rd
Kennedy Way
Tiverton
Devon
EX16 6SW
0884 275612
Skincare, hair, bath, men's, sun and baby products and fragrances, sold through health stores and chemists.

Carmela (V)
Kuni House
8 West Rd
Emsworth
Hants
PO10 7JT
0243 373639
Skincare, hair and bath products, sold through health stores, mail order and chemists.

Caurnie Soap Company (V)
The Soaperie
Canal St
Kirkintilloch
Glasgow
G66 1QZ
041-776 1218
Skincare, hair and household products and soaps, sold through mail order, health stores and chemists.

Cherish Natural Skincare (V)
34 Woodlands Ave
West Byfleet
Surrey
KT14 6AT
09323 40650
Skincare, bath and men's products and fragrances, sold through health stores and mail order. H.

Clare Maxwell-Hudson Ltd (V)
87 Dartmouth Rd
London NW2 4ER
01-450 6494
Skincare products sold through mail order, health stores and department stores. H.

Colourflair Studios (Vx)
25 Old Steine
Brighton
East Sussex
BN1 1EL
0273 571788
Skincare, hair, bath, colours, men's and sun products and oils, sold through mail order and beauty professionals. H.

Colourings Ltd (V)
4 Albion Place
Off Galena Rd
London W6 0LT
01-741 8090
Make-up sold through mail order and Body Shops. Professional quality well presented and designed by top make-up artist Barbara Daly. Recommended.

Cornish Gold Aromatics (V)
PO Box 2
Lostwithiel
Cornwall
PL22 0YY
0208 872073
Skincare and oils sold through mail order. H.

Cornucopia (V)
50 The Half Croft
Syston
Leicester
LE7 8LD
0533 602690
Skincare, hair and bath products, sold through health stores and mail order.

Corvic Marketing Ltd (V)
1 Priors Court
Priors Haw Rd
Weldon
Northants
NN17 1YG
0536 401070
Skincare, bath, colours, fragrances and men's products, sold through mail order, chemists, department stores, supermarkets and Boots. H.

Cosmetics To Go (V)
Constantine and Weir Ltd
29 High St
Poole
Dorset
BH15 1AB
0800 373366 – Freephone orders by credit card with 24-hour turn-around
0800 373335 – Advice line and product information. Mail order and own shop.
CTG will send gift parcels anywhere in the world, wrapped with brown paper, string and sealing wax, complete with message 'This is your present from . . . . do not open until . . . .' If within UK, it's post-free.
Colours, soaps, hair, skin, perfume, men's, babies, tropical and ski preparations, gifts and real fun items such as Liquid Stockings, a product idea from the days of wartime rationing when women painted the 'seams' on to their legs because stockings were in short supply! Great fun and good quality, although some of the packaging needs rethinking. Liptins brilliant – stay on all day. Catalogue full of clever ideas. Recommended.

Country Cosmetics (V–) *bath pearls/fruit and novelty soaps*
39 Sir Isaacs Walk
Colchester
Essex
CO1 1JJ
0206 762161
Skincare, hair, bath and sun products, fragrances and oils, sold through own stores.

Creighton Laboratories PLC (V)
Water Lane
Storrington
West Sussex
RH20 3DP
09066 5611
Skincare, hair, bath, sun and men's products, sold through mail order, health stores, department stores, chemists and supermarkets.

Crescent Preparations (V)
Tyler Hill
Canterbury
Kent
CT2 9NG
0227 472422
Skincare, hair, bath, men's and sun products, sold through mail order.

Crimpers Pure Products (V)
63–67 Heath St
London NW3 6UG
01-794 8625
Hair products, sold through mail order, health stores, department stores, chemists, own salons and some products through Animal Aid. Recommended, especially lacquer and gels.

Culpeper Ltd (V–) *some soap*
Hadstock Rd
Linton
Cambridge
CB1 6NJ
0223 891196
Skincare, bath, hair, fragrances, men's and baby products and oils, sold through mail order and own stores.

Daniel Field Retail Ltd (V)
23 Topsfield Parade
Crouch End
London N8 8PP
01-348 2514
Hair products sold through mail order, own salons and Boots.

Denise Wynne Herbal Cosmetics Ltd (V)
Unit 3
Morrison Yard
551a High Rd
Tottenham
London N17 6SB
01-808 8973
Skincare, hair, bath and men's products, sold through mail order, health stores and chemists. H.

Dolma (V)
19 Royce Ave
Hucknell
Nottingham NG15 6FU
0602 634237
Skincare, hair and bath products, oils and fragrances, sold through mail order and health stores.

East of Eden Ltd (V)
Crosscroft Industrial Estate
Appleby
Cumbria
CA16 6HD
Skincare, hair, bath, dental, fragrances, men's, baby and household products, and oils, sold through mail order, health stores, chemists and other retail outlets.

English Country Garden Skincare (V)
17 Hanover Place
Worcester Rd
Bromsgrove
Hereford and Worcester
B61 7DT
0527 33226/0905 778424
Skincare, hair, bath and sun products, fragrance, sold through own store, chemists, gift shops and mail order. H.

Exmoor Natural Beauty Collection (V)
Kingsmede Farm
Stoodleigh
Tiverton
Devon
EX16 9PQ
03985 263
Skincare, bath and sun products, sold through mail order. H.

Faith Products Ltd (V)
Unit 5
Bury Industrial Estate
Kay St
Bury
BL9 6BU
061-764 2555
Skincare, hair, bath and household products, sold through mail order, health stores and department stores.

Fantome Cosmetics (V)
Reed Bond (Yorkshire) Ltd
Springfield House
49 Springfield St
Barnsley
South Yorks
S70 6HH
0226 296034
Skincare, hair and bath products and fragrances, sold through mail order and health stores.

Farrow and Humphreys Ltd (V–) *some soaps*
24–26 Towerfield Rd
Shoeburyness
Essex
SS3 9QE
0702 298000
Skincare, hair, bath and men's products, sold through departments stores and gift shops.

Fleur Aromatherapy (V)
8 Baden Rd
London N8 7RJ
01-340 4097/1826
Skincare and bath products, fragrances and oils, sold through health stores, chemists, clinics, health clubs and mail order. H. Beautiful hand-made skin creams and wonderful strong aromatic oils for bath/massage. The rose moisturizer, which contains real oil of roses, is excellent. Recommended.

Fleur Naturelle (V)
Unit A
Mark Grove House
Allen Rd
Rushden
Northants
NN10 0DU
0933 311229/57179
Skincare, hair, bath, men's and sun products, oils and fragrances, sold through mail order, chemists and health stores. H.

Frangipani (Vx)
Face Place
28 The Arcade
Broadmead
Bristol
BS1 3JD
0272 262969
Skincare, hair and bath products, sold through mail order, health stores and own shops.

The Garden of England (V)
Berenger Jeune
Malthouse
Sandhurst
Kent
TN18 5HR
058 085 371
Bath and men's products and fragrances, sold through mail order.

Garland Skin Care (V)
Borrowdale
Storeton Lane
Barnston
Wirral
L61 1BU
051-648 2027
Skincare, hair and bath products and fragrances, sold through mail order.

Geneve (V)
Customer Services Dept
North Tyne Industrial Estate
Newcastle-upon-Tyne
NE12 9SZ
091-2700807
Skincare, hair, bath, men's and sun products, oils and fragrances, sold through mail order. H.

Gina Cosmetics (V)
Box 100
Cowbridge
South Glamorgan
CF7 7XA
04463 5465
Skincare, fragrances and colours, sold through chemists, outlets and mail order. H.

Goodebodies (V)
Osbourne House
20 Victoria Avenue
Harrogate
North Yorks
HG1 5QY
0423 500206
Skincare, hair, bath, dental, fragrances, men's, oils, sun and household products, sold through mail order and own stores.

ANNIE LENNOX
'I don't believe we humans are particularly
civilized. It's the mass mobilization of
animals for profit which really upsets me.
There's something so ugly about industries
that are sustained by the suffering of others.'

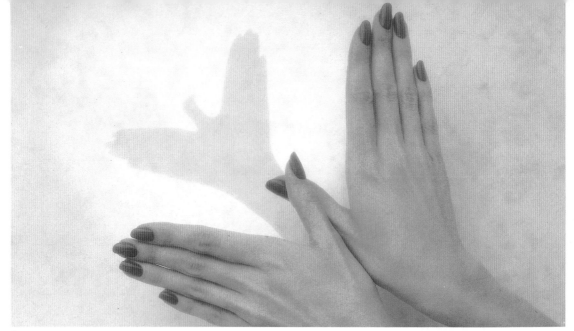

Beautiful hands

ELAINE MINTO

HELEN CRUDDAS

Makeovers – see pages 84–5 for details of how they were achieved.

LINDA TOLBERT

GWEN TREADWELL

ELAYNE MAYTUM

VIRGINIA McKENNA
'When Pole Pole died in that concrete cell, a disturbed, pitiful and lonely prisoner, we knew we had to do something, and almost overnight Zoocheck came into being.'

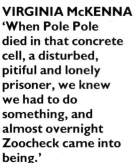

KATE O'MARA
'How can anybody kill these animals? They are just as entitled to be here as we are, to live their lives through with dignity. Making animals suffer and die, especially for reasons of vanity, is simply appalling.'

TOYAH WILCOX
'There's no pride in wearing something an animal's suffered for. I'm not impressed by fur wearers – I think they're absolute prannies.'

SUSANNAH YORK
'I want to look good and at the same time feel good about the cosmetics I wear.'

HAYLEY MILLS
'More people are becoming aware and are screaming out for change. We have it within our power to make this a much healthier, happier world. Let's do it!'

LYSETTE ANTHONY
'Buying fur is like purchasing a piece of the
world's misery.'

SIR JOHN GIELGUD
'I've always thought the idea of vivisection horrible. Such wonderful scientific discoveries are supposed to result – so they tell us! We don't seem to be very much better off as a result. . . .'

PETER CUSHING
'Let a dear chicken be free-range and enjoy its life as God intended. And if it has a mind to, it can lay a lovely egg for your tea which you can give thanks for, but to put them in those horrendous cages is such an offence. Factory farming is a disgrace to God and to mankind and should be stamped out.'

Green Farm Catalogue (V)
Green Farm Nutrition Centre
Burwash Common
East Sussex
TN19 7LX
0435 882482/883457
Skincare and oils, sold through mail order, health stores and chemists.

Green Things (V)
PO Box 59
Tunbridge Wells
Kent
TN3 9PT
0892 864668
Skincare, hair, bath and sun products and oils, sold through mail order, health stores and National Trust Shops.

Green Valley by Mountan Breeze (V)
6 Priorswood Place
Skelmersdale
Lancs
WN8 9QB
0695 21155
Skincare and hair products, sold through mail order and health stores.

The Hair Company (Vx)
5 Oswald St
Glasgow
G1 4QR
041-221 7412
Skincare, hair, bath, men's and sun products, oils and fragrances, sold through department stores and own shops. H.

Helena Harnic Clinic (V)
19 Upper Berkeley St
London W1
01-724 1518/258 3674
Skincare and oils, sold through mail order, own clinic and shop.

The Herbarium (V)
11 Oxford Rd
Altrincham
Cheshire
WA14 2DY
061-941 6618
Skincare, hair, bath, dental, fragrances, oils, men's, baby and sun products, sold through mail order and own shop.

Herbs From The Hedgerow Ltd (V)
Unit 32
Garden City Industrial Park
Deeside
Clwyd
CH5 2HW
0244 830440
Skincare and hair products and oils, sold through mail order, health and gift stores and chemists.

Holland and Barrett (V)
Canada Rd
Byfleet
Surrey
KT14 7JL
0932 336022
Skincare, hair, bath, men's and sun products and oils, sold through own health stores.

Hollytrees Products (V)
J. and D. Black Ltd
26 Hudson Rd
Bexleyheath
Kent
DA7 4PQ
01-303 2275
Skincare and dental products, sold through mail order, natural health centres and clinics. H.

Honesty Cosmetics (V)
33 Markham Rd
Chesterfield
Derbyshire
S40 1TA
0246 211269
Skincare, hair, bath, dental, fragrances, men's, sun and household products, sold through mail order and health stores. H. Excellent value products by this highly principled workers' co-operative. Discounts for fund-raising groups who promote the Living Without Cruelty ethic. Recommended.

Hymosa of London (V)
Admail 23
London W3 8XE
0482 75234
Skincare and hair products, sold through mail order, health stores and chemists.

Innoxa (England) Ltd (V–) *soap/One and All handcream*
Beauty House
Hawthorn Rd
Eastbourne
BN20 7BJ
0323 641244
Skincare and colours, sold through department stores, chemists and Boots.

Isis Cosmetics Ltd (V)
21 Clarence Rd
Kew Gardens
Richmond
Surrey
TW9 3NL
01-940 7530
Skincare, colours and fragrances, sold through salons. H.

James Bodenham and Co. (V–) novelty soaps
88 Jermyn St
London SW1
01-930 5340
Skincare, hair, bath and men's products and oils, sold through own shop and department stores.

Jeunique Cosmetics (V)
Yvonne Gray Cosmetics International Ltd
Jeunique House
Spinfield Lodge
Spinfield Lane
Marlow
Bucks
SL7 2LD
06824 72727
Skincare, hair and bath products, colours and oils, sold through mail order and salons. The formulations mostly include royal jelly. Magnetic compacts enable you to choose your own colour schemes. Nicely packaged, quality products ideal for the sophisticated, professional woman.

Julius Roth Ltd (V)
Tintagel House
Western Rd
Cheltenham Spa
Glos.
GL50 3RN
0242 221708
Skincare, hair and bath products, sold through mail order.

Kingfisher (V)
12 St Marys Works
Duke St
Norwich
NR3 1QA
Dental products sold through health stores, homoeopaths and supermarkets including Sainsburys.

Kittywake Perfumes (V)
'Cae Kitty'
Taliaris
Llandeilo
Dyfed
SA19 7DP
055 83619
Fragrances, oils and men's products, sold through mail order, health and gift stores.

Landarome Services (V)
24 Armston Rd
Barnwell
Oundle
Peterborough
PE8 5PP
0832 74244
Fragrances and men's products, sold through mail order and events.

Le Petite Parfumerie (V)
Wellfield Ct
Bangor
Gwynedd
0248 355439
Skincare, hair, bath, men's, baby and sun products and fragrances, sold through mail order and own shop.

L'Arome (UK) Ltd (V)
28 Parkway
Deeside Industrial Park
Deeside
Clwyd
CH5 2NS
0224 830220
Hair, bath and men's and designer fragrances, sold through independent distributors. Excellent quality. Recommended.

Laura Paige Cosmetics (Vx)
Bradgate Products Ltd
The Barracks
Barwell
Leicester
LE9 8EF
0455 42951
Colours, sold through chemists.

Leichner (V−) *Eau de Lys Body make-up/blood capsules*
Beauty House
Hawthorn Rd
Eastbourne
East Sussex
BN23 6QX
0323 641244
Colours and theatrical cosmetics, sold through department stores and chemists.

Little Green Shop (V)
Rolith International Ltd
8 St George's Place
Brighton
BN1 4GB
0273 571221
Skincare, hair, bath and household products, sold through mail order, chemists, health stores and department stores.

The Little Shop (V)
Rambledown Ltd
12 West St
Storrington
West Sussex
RH20 4EE
09066 2522
Skincare, hair, bath and men's products, oils and fragrances, sold through mail order and own shop.

Madame de Paris (V)
Unit G
Arnos Castle Trading Estate
Junction Rd
Brislington
Bristol
BS4 3ZE
0272 699387
Skincare, bath, colours, men's and sun products, oils and fragrances. H.

Magic Meadow Body Care Selection (V−) *bath pearls/fruit and novelty soaps*
Lower Rubhay
Tedburn St Mary
Exeter
EX6 6BJ
0647 61264
Skincare, hair, bath and men's products, sold through mail order and outlets. H.

Mandala Ayurvedic Imports (V)
Zetland Studios
7 Zetland Rd
Redland
Bristol
BS6 7AG
0272 427124
Skincare, hair and dental products, sold through mail order and health stores.

Martha Hill Ltd (V)
The Old Vicarage
Laxton
Corby
Northants
NN17 3AT
078085 259
Skincare, hair, bath, men's and sun products and fragrances, sold through mail order.

Maxim Pharmaceuticals (V)
4 Allison Rd
London W3 6JE
01-993 2528
Dental products, sold through health stores, chemists and outlets.

Micheline Arcier Aromatherapy (V)
7 William St
London SW1X 9HL
01-235 3545
Skincare, hair, bath, men's, baby and sun products, oils and fragrances, sold through mail-order and own store.

Michaeljohn (V)
23a Albemarle St
London W1X 3HA
01-491 4401
Michaeljohn Original and City hair care ranges, sold through own salons, mail order and selected retail outlets.

Miranda Natural Skin Care Ltd (V)
Advance Park
Rhosymedre
Wrexham
Clwyd
LL14 3YP
0978 810969
Skincare products, sold through mail order, health and own stores, chemists and events. H.

Miss Mary of Sweden (V–) *mascara/Beauty Bronze*
Radula Ltd
7–9 Tudor Rd
Broadheath Industrial Estate
Altrincham
Cheshire
WA14 5RZ
061-928 5050
Skincare, hair and bath products, fragrances and colours, sold through mail order.

Montagne Jeunesse (V)
Fragrance House of St George
London Production Centre
Broomhill Rd
London SW18 4JQ
01-871 5080
Skincare, hair, bath and sun products and soap, sold through health and department stores, chemists, mail order and supermarkets. Beautifully presented gift packs.

Mulcea Cosmetics Ltd (V)
304 Oyston Mill
Strand Rd
Preston
PR1 8UR
0772 721231
Skincare, hair, bath, baby and sun products, sold through mail order, health stores and chemists.

The National Trust (V–) *some soaps*
Heywood House
Westbury
Wilts
BA13 4NA
0373 826826
Skincare, hair, bath and men's products and fragrances, sold through own shops and concession outlets, and mail order.

Natural Beauty Products Ltd (V–) *bath pearls*
Western Avenue
Bridgend Industrial Estate
Mid Glamorgan
CF31 3RT
0656 766566
Skincare, hair, bath, men's and sun products, oils and colours, sold through mail order, chemists, own stores and Asda Body Centres. H.

Nature Care (V)
1 West St
Ware
Herts
SG12 9EE
0920 464054
Skincare, hair, bath, men's and baby products and oils, sold through mail order, health stores and own shop. H.

Naturally Yours Cosmetics Ltd (V)
1 Hanover Rd
Hanover Business Park
Altrincham
Cheshire
WA14 5TL
061-941 2251
Skincare, hair, bath, colours, fragrances, men's and sun products. Colour palettes good for teenagers. H.

Natures Ltd (V)
212 Watford Way
London NW4 4UA
01-203 1738
Dental products sold through mail order.

Nature's Secrets Cosmetics Ltd (V)
Unit 6
Link Industrial Estate
Howsell Rd
Malvern
Hereford and Worcester
WR14 1TF
0684 892825
Skincare, hair, bath and men's products, oils and fragrances, sold through mail order, health stores, department stores and chemists.

Neal's Yard Remedies (V)
2 Neal's Yard
Covent Garden
London WC2
01-379 7222
Skincare, hair, bath, dental, men's, baby and sun products, oils, herbs and powders, sold through mail order, own shop, health stores and department stores. Beautifully packaged in distinctive blue glass bottles, so great for giving. Soaps especially good. Quality superb, and if you can bear to part with them the bottles are returnable.

Nectar Beauty Shops (V–) *bath pearls*
Carrickfergus Industrial Estate
Belfast Rd
Carrickfergus
Co. Antrim
N. Ireland
BT38 8PH
09603 69133
Skincare, hair, bath, fragrances, men's, colours, sun and baby products and oils, sold through mail order and own stores.

New Mood (V)
33 Alva St
Edinburgh
EH2 4PS
031-225 2782
Skincare, hair, bath, dental, fragrances, men's and sun products and oils, sold through mail order, health and own stores.

Night and Day Natural Skin Care (V)
Parsons Green Ltd
PO Box 12 (South PDO)
Manchester
M14 6LW
061-225 9407
Skincare products sold through mail order.

Norfolk Lavender Ltd (Vx)
Caley Mill
Heacham
King's Lynn
Norfolk
PE31 7JE
0485 70384
Skincare, hair and bath products and fragrances, sold through mail order and department stores (John Lewis).

Nutri-Metics International (UK) (V)
15 Erica Rd
Stacey Bushes
Milton Keynes
MK12 6HS
0908 317033
Skincare, hair, bath, colours, fragrances, men's, sun and household products, sold through mail order. H.

Only Natural Ltd (V)
14 Pepper St
Nantwich
Cheshire
CW5 5AB
0270 627233
Skincare, hair, bath, men's and sun products, fragrances and oils, sold through mail order and own store.

Oriflame UK Ltd (Vx)
Tilers Rd
Kiln Farm
Milton Keynes
MK11 3EH
0908 261126
Skincare, hair, bath, men's and sun products and fragrances, sold through magazine promotions. H.

Pacific Isle (V)
PO Box 10
Ryde
Isle of Wight
PO33 1JX
0983 616980
Soap, sold through mail order and health stores.

Peaches & Cream (V)
22 Bedford Rd
Letchworth
Herts
SG6 4DJ
0462 679078
Skincare, hair, bath and sun products, sold through mail order, own shop and health stores.

Pecksniffs (V)
45–46 Meeting House Lane
Brighton
East Sussex
0273 28904
Skincare, hair, bath and men's products and fragrances, sold through mail order and own stores.

The Perfumers Guild Ltd (V)
61 Abbots Rd
Abbots Langley
Herts
WD5 0BJ
09277 63139
Bath products, fragrances and oils, sold through mail order and selected shops. H.

Perfumes by Renaissance (V)
Unit 1181
Skillion Mini Warehouse
Regent St
Leeds
LS2 7QA
0532 426212
Skincare, hair and men's products and fragrances, sold through independent distributors.

Phoenix Products (V)
2 Gothic Place
Marshall Rd
Godalming
Surrey
GU7 3AR
04868 28157
Skincare and bath products and oils, sold through mail order, health stores and events. H.

Plenty of Scents Ltd (V)
Unit J2
Blackpole Trading Estate East
Worcester
WR3 8SE
0905 57477
Skincare, hair, bath, fragrances, sun and men's products and oils, sold through mail order, health stores and department stores.

Profile (V)
27 St Cross Rd
Winchester
Hants
SO23 9JA
0962 61216
Skincare, hair and bath products, sold through mail order. H.

Pure Essentials (V)
The Willows
Main St
North Muskham
Newark
Notts
NG23 6EZ
0636 700313
Skincare, hair, bath and men's products, oils and fragrances, sold through mail order and own shop. H.

Pure Plant Products (V)
Health and Diet Food Co. Ltd
Seymour House
South St
Godalming
Surrey
GU7 1BZ
0483 426666
Skincare, hair and bath products, sold through mail order, health stores and chemists.

Richfield Fine Natural Body Care (V)
3b St George's Place
Brighton
East Sussex
BN1 4GA
0273 681206/773182
Skincare, hair, bath, men's, fragrances, baby and sun products and oils, sold through mail order, health stores, department stores and chemists.

Romany Herb Products (V)
Power Health Products
10 Central Avenue
Airfield Estate
Pocklington
York
YO4 2NR
0759 304698/302595
Skincare, hair, bath and sun products and oils,

sold through mail order, health stores, department stores, chemists and supermarkets. H.

Sarakan Ltd (V–) *cochineal in toothpaste*
106 High St
Beckenham
Kent
BR3 1EB
01-650 3476
Dental products, sold through health stores and chemists. Recommended.

The Secret Garden (V)
153 Regent St
London W1R 8HQ
01-439 3101
Skincare, hair, bath, fragrances, men's and sun products and oils, sold through mail order, own stores and Gleneagles Hotel.

Shanti Herbal Health and Beauty Products (V)
148 London Rd
Temple Ewell
Dover
Kent
CT16 3DE
0304 820129
Skincare, hair, bath, dental, fragrances, men's, baby and sun products and oils, sold through mail order, health stores, own shop and clinic. H.

Shirley Price Aromatherapy Ltd (V)
Wesley House
Stockwell Head
Hinckley
Leics
LE10 1RD
0455 615466/615436
Skincare, hair, bath, men's, oils, fragrances, baby and sun products, sold through mail order, health stores and natural health clinics.

Simply Herbal (V)
19 West St
Wilton
Wiltshire
SP2 0DL
0722 743995
Skincare, hair, bath, men's and household products, sold through mail order and own stores.

Specialist skin care creams, tonics, especially good for troubled skins. Recommended.

Skin and Tonic (V)
14 South Clerk St
Edinburgh
EH8 9PR
031-668 4240
Skincare, hair, bath, men's and sun products, sold through own store.

Slim and Tonic (V–) *bath pearls*
104 St Helens St
Ipswich
IP4 2LB
0473 231134
Skincare, hair, bath, men's and sun products and fragrances, sold through mail order and own store.

The Soap Shop Ltd (V–) *soap flakes*
44 Sidwell St
Exeter
Devon
EX4 6NS
0392 215682
Skincare, hair, bath and household products, sold through mail order and own shop.

Star Gazer Products (V)
PO Box 609
London SW3 4NS
01-733 3166
Skincare and hair products and colours, sold through mail order, department stores and own shops. H.

Supernatural Perfumes and Skin Care (V)
PO Box 989
London SE1 0LZ
01-633 9046
Skincare products and fragrances, sold through mail order, health stores and department stores.

Tiki (V)
G. R. Lane Health Products Ltd
Sisson Rd
Gloucester
GL1 3QB
0452 24012
Skincare, hair and bath products, sold through mail order and health stores.

Ultra Glow Ltd (V–) *some powders*
1–3 North Rd
London N7 9HA
01-607 9983
Skincare products and colours, sold through department stores and chemists.

Verde (V)
4a at No. 11 Long St
London E2 8HJ
01-739 3612
Skincare, bath and hair products and oils, sold through mail order, salons and gift shops. H.

Vevay (Vx)
Atcham
Shrewsbury
Shropshire
SY4 4UG
0743 75864
Skincare, hair, bath and sun products, colours and fragrances, sold through mail order.

Weleda (UK) Ltd (V)
Heanor Rd
Ilkeston
Derbyshire
DE7 8DR
0602 309319
Skincare, hair, bath, dental and baby products, sold through health stores, mail order and chemists. H. Besides making homoeopathic and anthroposophic medicines, Weleda also manufacture beauty products based on the same natural principles.

Witchwood Herbs (V)
Oldfield Rd
Bromley
Kent
Skincare, hair and bath products and oils, sold through mail order.

Woods of Windsor (V–) *soaps/bath pearls*
Queen Charlotte St
Windsor
Berks
SL4 1LZ
0753 855777
Skincare, hair, bath, fragrances, men's and household products, sold through mail order, department and gift stores, own shop and chemists.

Yin Yang Beauty Care (V)
Unit C1
New Yatt Business Centre
New Yatt
Witney
Oxon
0993 868881
Skincare products, sold through mail order, health stores and department stores.

Zohar (V)
Broom Lane Enterprises
Quality House
73 Windsor Rd
Prestwich
Manchester
M25 8DB
061-721 4418
Dental and household products, sold through mail order, chemists, department stores, supermarkets and kosher shops.

'Recommended' and other comments are those of the author; they represent a personal testing assessment only and are in no way a reflection on any other unmentioned products. Because of the ever-increasing number of companies, it was decided to concentrate on featuring those deemed most accessible to consumers, and it is these who largely appear in the photography. These products were chosen independently by professional make-up artists and body care experts and selected to suit the needs, colouring and so on of the people being photographed.

FURTHER READING
Herbal Cosmetics, Camilla Hepper, Thorsons.
Natural Appeal, Suzy Kendall and Pat Wellington, Dent.
Cover Up, Penny Chorlton, Thorsons Grapevine.

3 Dressed to Kill

Her high-heeled shoes were of python skin,
Her gloves of the gentle reindeer's hide,
And to make her card-case a lizard died.

From 'Coverings' by Stella Gibbons

Go into any major department store and look around at the extensive selection of clothing available to you as a consumer. The choice is overwhelming. You can keep warm; look smart and business-like; be sporty and casual, glamorous, frivolous, trendy, elegant or sexy. Whether you shop haute-couture, Marks and Spencer or Oxfam, looking good and Living Without Cruelty presents few problems.

Given the choice available, it's astounding that anyone should consider choosing a garment whose price is higher than any other. What price a life . . . if you choose real fur?

A recent survey revealed that 71 per cent of the British public believe it wrong to kill animals for their fur. Only two out of ten women had a fur in their possession, and of those who didn't only a tiny handful, a mere 8 per cent, expressed any desire to purchase one. So it is therefore astonishing that, worldwide, some 100 million animals die annually to satisfy this particular consumer demand.

Cheap labour and the growth of intensive fur factory farms have resulted in cheaper 'bargain' garments coming on to the market. The biggest fur consumers are the USA, Japan, Italy, Spain and West Germany. The latter was once the largest consumer worldwide, but since 1981 that market has spiralled downwards due to increasingly vigorous educational campaigns by animal groups. In America, fur income steadily increased throughout the sixties to an all-time high of $1.8 billion in 1987. Since then, with the welcome growth of animal protection activities, sales have started to slip.

Sales figures for the UK are difficult to obtain, but Great Britain is something of a special case, given the impetus of the anti-fur campaigns of recent years which have highlighted this controversial industry. This has led to a welcome depression in the UK fur markets.

Debenhams closed their famous fur departments, and other fur salons within major retailers have also been shut down. Numerous smaller establishments have also ceased trading within the past ten years. The most significant collapse was the withdrawal of the Hudson's Bay Company from Britain in December 1989, after three hundred years of trading in animal exploitive products – their first fur auction took place in 1670 in London and realized £1378.

Perhaps this explains why the Fur Institute of Canada, created to project a Mr Nice-Guy image for the trade, perceive the UK lobby to be the biggest threat to its activities and has allocated some $2 million to bolster its UK image . . . an image which offers glamour and seduction, whilst hiding the suffering and cruelty of fur production.

More than 38 million mink and foxes live out their miserable lives in row upon row of cages in the animal equivalent of the concentration camp – the fur farm or 'ranch'. Unable to fulfil their natural instincts of territory, nocturnal habit, social or family behaviour, they end their lives gassed, lethally injected or electrocuted – this being via a mouth clamp or by a rod inserted into the anus of the fox, through which 200 volts are passed.

Such is the degradation and confinement in the fur farms that many animals simply go insane, fighting and cannibalizing each other in their frenzied attempts to escape. From their birth on to cold wire in the spring, the only diversion is the daily feed – a blob of slaughterhouse offal thrown on to the cage top, which they must eat through the mesh. As winter comes, both foxes and mink near the end of their hell on earth. In Canada, where the winters are severe, the animals' tongues often freeze solid on to the metal and are ripped from their mouths as they attempt to free themselves.

In Alaska, animal activists Kristine Breck, fourteen, and her mother Betty attended an auction of live fur farm foxes destined for the fur trade. Prior to the sale, Kristine made friends with a frightened vixen. She wrote:

LIVING WITHOUT CRUELTY

'The men carried her, dangling from the neck, to the auction block and stretched her out for the crowd to view. The auctioneer bellowed and I could see her body shaking. I just had to rescue her from this. I got a bidding card and raised it again and again, to defeat a determined furrier. Finally, at $105, we won. At home we spent the next five days building a large outdoor enclosure with logs, a den and lots of toys. When she saw it that first time she explored till she was exhausted – she seemed awed by her freedom. After two months' gentle coaxing, she realized we weren't going to kill her. Now she comes into the house and curls up with the other animals. They wash each other. Her life means a lot to her. She is so soft, just over 1 foot tall, dainty, graceful and intelligent. Her tail is her banner and she carries it as if it had a life of its own. My heart aches for those who were killed at the auction – each as special as Lady. I hope that seeing her will convince others not to buy fur, to hasten the day when innocent animals will no longer be tortured and killed for their beautiful coats . . . their curse.'

Trapping accounts for between 25 and 30 million animals each year, with the main offenders being the USA, USSR and Canada. This has led to the near-extinction of some species. The main method used is still the barbaric steel-jawed leg hold trap, outlawed in Britain for almost thirty years. One observer quoted by Charles Darwin in an appeal against trapping in 1863, summed up the practise in words, shamefully, as relevant today:

'I know of no sight more sorrowful than that of these unoffending animals as they are seen in the torture grip of these traps. They sit drawn up into a little heap, as if collecting all their force of endurance to support agony; some sit in a half torpid state induced by intense suffering. Most young ones are found dead after some hours of it, but others as you approach, start up, struggle violently to escape, and shriek pitiably, from terror and the pangs occasioned by their struggles.'

In Great Britain alone a hundred thousand foxes annually are snared or illegally caught in gin-traps to provide the characteristic red fox furs which, sadly, some people seem to find so attractive. Why does it seem glamorous or appealing to wrap oneself in the skins of sad and innocent victims? Do the wearers not feel at least

a shade uncomfortable, knowing that their vanity, their desire for a mere status symbol, their obviously thoughtless purchase, has led to more needless suffering to fill that now vacant coat-hanger?

Quite simply, no one *needs* a fur coat. If, for some reason, you really like the look and the feel of fur, there are so many quality fakes available it's easy to say no to the products of suffering. Barbara Bush, America's First Lady, did just that when offered a fox fur coat to wear at the presidential inauguration. As the President and his wife stepped from their limo for the inaugural party, they waved and smiled at animal activists who held aloft the message 'Thank you, Barbara, for *not* wearing fur!' Such is the feeling aroused by mounting public opinion that on her US trip Raisa Gorbachev left behind her collection of furs 'to avoid offending' the Americans.

Worldwide, celebrities are refusing to wear fur, top designers are announcing they will no longer fashion garments made of fur, and models are refusing to pose in them. A growing number of newspapers and magazines such as *Cosmopolitan*, *Elle* and *She* no longer accept fur advertising. As one local campaign leaflet stated: 'Just remember, there's no such thing as a *new* fur coat – they all come second-hand via hell.'

As technology has advanced, helped by consumer demand, alternatives have become available for virtually all products once derived from animals and used by the fashion industry. The rest – bird plumage, for example – can simply be avoided. The millinery trade has a lot to answer for in causing the demise of many rare and exotic birds who were murdered for their colourful wings and tails to adorn ladies' hats in the past. Hopefully, fashion will not revive this particularly cruel extravagance.

Other animals who are trapped, slaughtered or 'farmed' for their skins include the well-publicized seal, where the fight to end the killing still goes on; the unloved crocodile and alligator, who die needlessly to become pathetic fashion accessories in the form of shoes, handbags, watch-straps and executive cases, and of course, snakes and lizards – much maligned and some now endangered, whose skin is coveted for similarly pointless trivialities. In Asia, snakes are often salted and skinned alive – they take up to four days to die. Other unfortunate species include wild cats, elephants, zebras, land and water buffaloes, deer, boar, kangaroos, turtles, sharks, ostriches and dolphins. So called 'fun' furs (from rabbits) and sheepskins come on to the market via the slaughterhouse, as does cow and calf, goat and pigskin. In some areas, kid goats are boiled alive to make gloves. The curly fur known as astrakan or karakul is from the purposely aborted body of an unborn baby lamb. This, apparently, is considered 'luxurious'.

Apart from the animal suffering, there is, inevitably, both a human and an environmental cost. Tanneries use dangerous substances, many of which are released in effluent into the environment. These include mineral salts such as chromium, aluminium, iron and zirconium. Other chemicals used and discharged are formaldehyde; coal tar products such as phenol, cresol and naphthalene; and various oils, dyes and finishes. Some of those used are cyanide-based. As well as all this, effluent also contains large amounts of proteins, hair, salt, lime, sulphides and acids. Elevated levels of lead, cyanide and formaldehyde have been found in ground water adjacent to tanneries, and this in turn poses a threat to human health, apart from the noxious soup described above. In one area surrounding a tannery in Kentucky the incidence of leukaemia among residents was five times the national average. The tannery process exposes workers to many cancer-causing substances, and many die from forms of the disease associated with the industry. A New York State Health Department study found that half of all testicular cancer victims worked in tanneries.

For those of us trying to avoid animal skin products, all that is needed is a little judicious shopping in order to discover the many alternatives that exist. For those beginning to incorporate vegetarian principles into their lifestyle, the wearing of leather items may seem hypocritical and therefore no longer acceptable. Individuals need to consider what fits comfortably into their thinking. Living Without Cruelty usually involves a gradual 'awakening' to the issues involved, and you should determine your own pace. Some people, in a fit of enthusiasm, go through their wardrobes and take every leather item to the nearest charity shop, but most of us, with finances to bear in mind, may find it more

sensible gradually to replace boots and shoes as they wear out, or when we see a new and fashionable alternative in the shops.

Five or six years ago, plastic shoes were indeed pretty horrible. They made your feet ache and perspire and the materials were hard and unyielding. New technology has changed all that, and footwear is now available in a huge range of soft, breathable materials which are light, comfortable and fashionable, with man-made leather, suede and snakeskin look-alikes. A good selection can usually be found in the more reasonably priced shoe stores such as Freeman, Hardy and Willis, Olivers, Barratts and Curtess, as well as many chain store outlets such as C&A, who offer very good sports shoes in synthetic materials. Hi-tec, Olympus and Nike are others in this field who also make man-made styles in sport shoes. Look out for the many localized specialist shops now beginning to cater for the growing demand in non-leather items.

Apart from leather-look materials, fabrics, rubber and a varied range of both natural and synthetic components are now being utilized to make jackets, skirts, shoes, belts, bags and cases. It pays to shop around and look for the man-made label. Prices are usually a bonus, too – being cheaper than their animal-derived counterparts. Although choice is now improving in this area, there is still a great deal of room for improvement. Designers and shoe manufacturers please take note!

Animal products are also used in fabrics such as wool, pure silk and other animal-based cloths such as vicuna, alpaca and mohair. Although the animal ingredients they contain do not necessarily connect directly to the slaughterhouse, the links to suffering are, in most cases, fairly obvious and many people may ultimately wish to avoid these products. In any event, the alternative man-made or plant-based cloths and yarns, available everywhere, usually wear, wash and keep their shape as well, if not better, without the need for fussy or expensive cleaning or laundering.

Eighty per cent of wool used worldwide comes from Australia, where 158 million sheep are raised for their wool and meat. They are Merinos, purposely bred to be hampered by excessive folds of skin which mean more wool for the farmer. In the fierce heat of the Australian summer many die from heat exhaustion or perish from the cold when shearing is done late. A 1967 estimate by Australia's Bureau of Agriculture Economics cited that 6.3 million sheep had died on Australian sheep farms, an apparently acceptable loss.

Because of their wrinkles, 'mulesling' is carried out on these animals. This process slices off a large section of flesh and wool around the backside to prevent blowflies from laying eggs in the folds of skin. The bloody wound, inflicted without anaesthetic, takes three to five weeks to heal – if infection doesn't set in. In their distress the animals lie immobile for days, falling down or stumbling pitifully on their knees.

Shearing brings more trauma, and wounds are commonplace and inevitable when speed means money. On computerized farms, the mechanically controlled equipment often fails to recognize teats and other protrusions before the cutter reaches them. Old sheep with feeding problems often have their teeth cut flat with a mechanical grinder or disc which cuts through at gum level, exposing the sensitive inner cavities, without any anaesthetic.

Every year, 18 per cent of all Australian sheep die on their way to the Middle East, where millions are ritually slaughtered. Packed into factory ships, 120,000 at a time, they are forced to stand in their own excrement for the entire three-week journey by sea before slaughter in Bahrain. This is part and parcel of the modern wool industry.

The silk industry spins the fibre which silkworms make to form their cocoons, but the production methods steam or boil alive thousands of silkworms in the process. As it is known that these creatures feel pain, silk can hardly be classed as a benign product. Some people may wish to avoid real silk and buy products made from the very beautiful synthetics widely available.

Richard Adams

The son of a doctor, Richard Adams grew up in the country and quickly developed an affinity with wildlife. After a public school education his studies at Oxford were interrupted by the war, and after five and a half years abroad in the army he returned to university, obtaining his degree in 1948. For the next twenty-five years he was a 'Whitehall warrior' and whilst still a civil servant wrote *Watership Down* – 'for fun, and to entertain my daughters then nine and seven'. He was astonished by the book's success and quickly followed it with *Shardik*, also a bestseller. 'After that I thought perhaps I was meant to write instead of being a public servant.'

He resigned in 1974 and has been writing ever since. It was after publication of *The Plague Dogs* – the story of two dogs on the run from a vivisection laboratory – that IFAW (International Fund for Animal Welfare) contacted him: would he be prepared to help campaign against the seal slaughter? 'I remember saying to my wife, "Do they really batter these baby seals to death on the ice?" She said, "Yes, didn't you know?" I couldn't believe it, but when IFAW sent the information I discovered it to be true enough. That was in 1977, and that was how I joined the animal movement.'

The campaign bore fruit – the EEC placed a ban on the import of harp and hooded seal fur, and later the Canadian government banned all commercial sealing. Richard asked IFAW what he could usefully involve himself with next. The fur trade, the killing of kangaroos and the illegal import of animals were suggested areas.

'I thought about it, and the cruellest, vilest and least justified was the fur trade. I've been campaigning against it now since 1984 and see it as a public moral issue, like black slavery or child labour in factories. I'm in no doubt whatever that the fur industry is very wicked and evil and we ought not to rest until it's been eradicated. Furs are still a status symbol, especially in the USA. If a furrier sells just one or two coats at £50,000 each he can keep going, so we must also reach out to those affluent enough to keep that market in business. We need the backing of influential people from all walks of life, especially MPs. The fur issue has all-party support, but there's still a lot of parliamentary work to be done.'

He teamed up with the LYNX organization and was soon involved in lecture tours, debates and media appearances. Visiting schools is something he particularly enjoys: 'Kids are great. They organize all sorts of events for animals – it's very heartening. These young people will be the

RICHARD ADAMS
'I'm in no doubt whatever that the fur trade
is very wicked and evil and we ought not to
rest until it's been eradicated.'

prosperous and influential adults of tomorrow. By the twenty-first century, I believe we will have people in power who will care enough to stop dirty tricks like the fur trade. Right now, the battle is really for people's hearts and minds.'

Hayley Mills

'I was brought up on a beef and dairy farm in Sussex. I remember those beautiful little calves stumbling up the ramp away from their mothers, and the cows left roaring in their pens at night at the loss of their offspring. It always made me feel sad.

'As children, my sister and I used to creep ahead of the guns at weekend shooting parties – we could have had our heads blown off – and we'd shoo away the birds to save them. Often I'd walk home crying, carrying a dead pheasant. Later, it would appear on the table and I'd eat it with relish. It's how things were. Then some years ago two things happened . . .

'My youngest son, Ace, developed a rapidly deteriorating hearing problem. The specialist said he needed surgery. We went to a naturopathic doctor who prescribed an unrefined meat-free diet for two months. His hearing returned to normal. We'd supported Ace and had also given up meat, which helped break our conventional eating pattern.

'It was *The Animals Film* on TV, though, which provided the impetus. I sat through it that night. Three hours of torture and torment of such horrendous proportions, the most ghastly vision of hell and what human beings do to animals. I cried and cried all night. What had happened to us? How could we accept it, condone it? For weeks I was a fanatic – enraged, upset and unhappy. I could talk about nothing else. I rang all my friends to see if they'd watched it. Ninety-nine per cent had switched off, not wanting to upset themselves. That shocked me – that people wouldn't confront it or want to have to do anything about it. But once you've looked certain truths in the face, you can never pretend you haven't, or that the knowledge hasn't changed your life forever.

'Initially, though, even I found excuses for myself. Perhaps we needed a weekly chicken for nutritional value? Perhaps fish was all right – they weren't as intelligent as cows, and weren't they immune to pain? But I knew these were poor excuses. And there's that awful comfort which stems from conformity, habit and tradition. The Sunday roast, Christmas dinner, the family, the conditioning, the indoctrination. Suddenly, you're in a different world of your own making. It feels a bit strange at first, if you're the only one – a bit lonely.

'I told the family very plainly and graphically why I'd gone vegetarian. The children looked glum – they loved meat. Crispian, eleven, was a real gourmet and would ask for frog's legs and snails – all those disgusting things. Ace, eight, was a child who'd refuse the veg and the salad, but eat the meat!

'So I said, "No meat at home – I won't cook it. Outside you can have what you like, your burgers and bacon sandwiches, but you're not getting it here." And to my eternal pride and delight they both gave it up themselves: Crispian gradually ("I don't like pork any more, Mummy", then beef, then sausages, etc.) and Ace suddenly. Collecting him after tea from a friend's house I'd discovered he hadn't eaten a thing, and they were his favourites, too – sausages and bacon. In the car home I said, "Ace, why didn't you eat your tea?" "Mummy," he said, "I couldn't. I just couldn't eat it. I want to be a vegetarian."

'We blind ourselves to reality – our excuses being that we like the taste, or the look of ourselves in fur – but why choose cruelty when alternatives exist everywhere? My purple coat couldn't be fakier, yet it feels luxurious, glamorous and warm. More people are becoming aware and are screaming out for change. We have it within our power to make this a much healthier, happier world. Let's do it!'

Lysette Anthony

With both parents working actors, Lysette learnt to work hard from an early age. Drama class, she says, was the highlight of the school week. She hasn't stopped working since. An early modelling career began after 'O' levels and suddenly took off after she did a cover for *Ritz* magazine. Offers of work, including film and TV, began to come in. She has appeared in many period roles, including

Dombey and Son, but audiences know her best from the comedy TV series, *Three Up, Two Down*. Recent film roles were in *Dangerous Love* and *Jack the Ripper* with Michael Caine.

'I had to grow up fast because there's a lot of hype and you have to cling to your sanity. Suddenly, at seventeen, I was inundated with offers and earning lots of money, but I sharpened up – the fame game isn't a problem to me. However, I lead a very unnatural and potentially unhealthy life, often up at 5 a.m. and working till very late. There's constant travel too.

'I hadn't really thought about animal abuse until the Beauty Without Cruelty company approached me. I began to examine my life as a result of learning about the animal testing issue. Now, I can't contemplate eating meat. I find the whole business gluttonous and horrid because people are making megabucks out of animal suffering.

'When I started living alone I never ate meat, partly because I just couldn't be bothered with it, but I didn't consider myself vegetarian. Then for my twenty-first birthday my sister cooked a rich celebration meal – quail, quail's eggs and champagne. I was violently sick – my body reacted against the sudden influx of cooked meats.

'I'm not obsessive about my vegetarianism. It's my personal preference, but it's only when you're educated about what you're eating that you can make an informed choice. Sometimes, with my precarious lifestyle, things can be difficult, especially in certain countries when you're miles from anywhere. Then I choose fish, but my favourite foods are very simple: baked potatoes; big, fresh-cut, colourful salads; goat's yogurt; tofu and stir-fried vegetables (the wok is a busy person's best friend). With a bottle of good wine and good bread I can't think of anything better. I drink lots of water to cleanse the body. My diet keeps me healthy, despite my chaotic timetable.

'I use BWC cosmetics for daytime and wherever possible on stage and film sets. Their fine compact powders and lipsticks are wonderful quality. There's absolutely no reason why cosmetics and toiletries should be tested on animals, and I hope consumers will switch allegiance to support humane companies.

'I wouldn't be seen dead in a fur coat, but I agreed to wear one for this book. It felt awful, and when I put my hand into the trap I realized what suffering these creatures must endure – all for a totally unnecessary piece of vulgarity. Buying fur is like purchasing a piece of the world's misery.'

Useful addresses

Westsports
18–19 Fleet St
Swindon
Wilts
SN7 1RQ
0793 32588
Make Fellwalka fully synthetic walking boots.

Burton McCall Ltd
Samuel St
Leicester
LE1 1RU
0533 538781
Gardening and walking boots.

Bridgedale Boots
Bridgedale
Samuel St
Leicester
LE1 1RU
Dryboots synthetic footwear. Send for catalogue.

Fake furs and leathers
Most department stores hold stocks during the season or you could buy some obviously fake fur fabric and make your own. For top-of-the-range garments look for labels such as: Jean Louis (Paris), Ramo Sport (Paris) and Babylon (Italy). Harrods and other top stores stock these makes.

Fake suede is also available through some outlets. It is known in the UK as Alcantara and in the USA as Ultrasuede.

British Home Stores are particularly good for non-leather purses, wallets and bags. Chain stores usually have a choice, although Marks and Spencer's still lag behind with their all-leather offerings.

Mocaton
Ashton House
67 Compton Rd
Wolverhampton WV3 9QZ
0902 26635/311200
Designers and manufacturers of exciting fake leathers, suedes, bikers jackets, bags, suits, and shoes. Commissions welcomed. Mail order and selected retailers. Excellent value. S.a.e. for catalogue.

Wallets are available from Animal Aid and BUAV, each with the organization's distinctive logo. See page 75.

Further information
Beauty Without Cruelty
(Registered Charity)
11 Lime Hill Rd
Tunbridge Wells
Kent
TN1 1LJ
0892 25587

LYNX
PO Box 509
Dunmow
Essex
CM6 1UH
0371 2016
The only campaigning group dealing specifically with the fur trade.

Compassion in World Farming
20 Lavant St
Petersfield
Hampshire
GU32 3EW
0730 64208
Against all factory farming, CIWF campaigns against this particular element of the fur industry.

International Fund for Animal Welfare
Tubwell House
New Rd
Crowborough
East Sussex
TN6 2HQ
0892 663374
Prominent in anti-sealing campaign and other worldwide initiatives.
 Designer T-shirts are available from most pressure groups listed in this book, but especially from LYNX at the above address or from their shop at:

LYNX
79 Long Acre
Covent Garden
London WC2
01-836 9702

Further reading
Killing for Luxury, Michael Bright, Franklin Watts, £5.95.

4 An Apple a Day

A Black Rabbit Dies for its Country

Born in the lab, I never saw the grass
or felt the direct touch of wind or sun
and if a rabbit's nature is to run
free on the earth, I missed it; though the glass
never let shot or eager predators pass,

while I was warm against my mother's side
something was waiting in the centrifuge
(the world's a cage, although that cage is huge)
and separate I lived until I died –
watered and fed, I didn't fret, inside,

and all the time was waiting for the paste
scooped with a spatula from the metal rim,
and concentrated bacillus at the brim,
and lived the life of feeling and of taste.
I didn't know it. Knowing would be waste

in any case, and anthrax is the hard
stuff that knocks out the mice, the dogs, the men,
you haven't any chance at all and when
they've finished with you, you're down on a card.
How could I know, to be upon my guard

when they pushed my container into line
with the infected airstream? Breath is life:
though something there more deadly than a knife
cut into me, I was still feeling fine
and never guessed the next death would be mine,

how many minutes later lungs would choke
as feet beat out the seconds like a drum,
hands held me on the table; this was a sum
with the predictable ending of a joke.
Fighting I died, and no god even spoke.

Gavin Ewart

Health – a new prescription

Driving into a brick wall, stepping under a bus or putting a plastic bag over your head are obvious ways to kill or seriously injure yourself, all fairly immediate, and no sane person would put themselves at risk in this way. Yet millions of people annually erode their own and their children's health through a lifestyle which promotes sickness and, ultimately, premature death. These diseases, mainly coronary heart disease, strokes, cancers, digestive complaints, respiratory disease, obesity and diabetes, are largely preventable, but the knowledge needed to help us avoid these illnesses is largely denied us because this would conflict with the powerful vested interests who profit from our ill health.

Also, the majority of us no longer accept responsibility for our own health. The doctor is expected to remedy matters with a magic prescription when illness strikes. The fault lies not so much with the patient, but with the medical and research professions, who present an image of godlike infallibility – health technocrats dispensing wisdom as well as wonder-drugs for the ever-grateful and unquestioning 'layman'.

But there are visible cracks in this medical machine. Many 'wonder-drugs' were not so wonderful as first thought and were withdrawn; drug side-effects have reached epidemic proportions; a large number of treatments merely gloss over symptoms temporarily, leaving patients dissatisfied. Plenty of claims are made on behalf of medical technology, but what is it achieving in terms of real health benefits?

Heart disease kills over 160,000 people (28 per cent of total deaths) annually in Britain alone. Major risk factors are bad diet, smoking and high blood pressure. Cancer claims some 140,000 UK deaths (24 per cent) with smoking the main risk factor together with diet, alcohol and cancer-causing chemicals in the environment which we must campaign to have removed. The World Health Organization estimates that at least 80 per cent of cancer is preventable! Another 73,000 people die through strokes (12 per cent) and 65,000 (11 per cent), through respiratory disease (smoking again). Thirteen thousand more perish in accidents where alcohol is the major preventable factor. Gloomy, isn't it?

But we aren't doing much to change things. Our National Sickness Service (Health?) has stretched its resources to the limit, with staff working ridiculous hours. Apparently, more patients than ever are being treated! Yet surely we should be aiming to treat fewer patients – not because of waiting lists or lack of money, but because more of us are healthier. This seems common sense, so why aren't we going down the road to health? A cynical look reveals that:

(1) The major cancer research charities spend very little on preventive cancer education – often less than 2 per cent – for a disease which is largely preventable. Overall, public donations exceed £1 million per week and the Imperial Cancer Research Fund, for example, has assets topping £65 million.

(2) More people living longer, active lives would mean that governments need extra billions for state pensions.

(3) The pharmaceutical industry would be threatened as product consumption dwindled. There are no profits in health – but plenty in sickness. Figures from 1983 revealed that drug sales for the top twenty-five companies were £35 billion. In 1985, the world's twelve best-selling drugs alone made over £6 billion for their makers.

(4) Other major industries would be affected. Proper health recommendations would drastically reduce consumption of meat and dairy produce; cheap, adulterated and over-refined foods would be replaced by more wholesome ones, thus avoiding many factory processes and use of additives; the tobacco industry would decline further; and alcohol consumption would fall to more moderate levels.

(5) A healthy population and environment would upset those who profit by its exploitation: for instance in agrochemicals, pesticides, chemical waste, factory farming and agriculture. Academic life and research itself would be affected, some areas becoming invalid and redundant. We don't have to spend millions to overcome stress, vices and disease in factory farming (as we currently do), for example, if we get rid of factory farming.

People need unbiased, easily obtainable health information which is untainted by commercial pressures. They are unlikely to get this from government departments. MAFF (the Ministry for Agriculture, Fisheries and Food)

for example, represents the interests of the powerful farming and agrochemical lobbies. It is also responsible for standards of food hygiene. The salmonella bacteria in egg production has been cited as indicative of this clash of interests, with producers given priority over consumers and health considerations. The salmonella problem had been monitored by anti-factory farming groups for years, but nobody took any notice. Much effort is made to prevent the public making links between the consumption of meat, dairy – and particularly factory farmed produce – and disease.

Similarly, the drug industry rarely admits liability for its products when they damage consumers – products proclaimed 'safe' after misleading animal experiments which deliver many useless and dangerous products on to the marketplace. Parents also seldom receive unbiased information about vaccination, which would enable them to make an informed decision for their child.

The job of a pressure group is to question and investigate 'facts' which are presented to us as correct, often by government. Such 'facts' can be manipulated and do not always hold up to scrutiny. Here's a hypothetical example: butter manufacturers initiate 'research' which 'proves' that margarine gives cancer to rats who are fed pounds of the stuff to get the result the butter manufacturers want. Dr X, who undertakes this 'impartial' investigation, publishes his findings. The media get in on the act and thousands of people stop eating margarine. Alternatively, the margarine manufacturers could get one of their scientists to give the rats butter and get a similar result. Scientifically meaningless, but so good for business!

Repeat the above scenario for any two competing products or for a product whose consumption is falling after adverse publicity. (Research proves . . . these crispy, fat-laden snacks are a healthy addition to your child's diet). Get the picture?

Taking back responsibility for our own health means we'll benefit. Healthy people make fewer demands on health services and consume fewer drugs, lessening the risk of extra illness through unwanted side-effects. By so doing we would be helping millions of laboratory animals who currently suffer and die to produce hundreds of duplicate 'me-too' drugs which serve no real therapeutic need, but boost drug company profits.

'Me-toos' are basically drugs with a slightly altered chemical formula to an existing product. This allows a separate patent to be issued, and the drug then competes for its market share under its own brand name. Sometimes claims are made for an improved effect over competitors. But these drugs basically do the same job as one another. For example: there are around twenty-three non-steroidal anti-inflammatory drugs, or NSAIDs, all competing for a slice of the £150 million British market in anti-arthritis pills. They all tend to do the same job as one very well-known anti-inflammatory drug – aspirin. One doctor, writing in *The Lancet*, therefore suggested a different label – 'New Sorts of Aspirin In Disguise!'

Generic drugs are identical chemically to brand names, but might look a bit different. They work the same way but are a lot cheaper. For example: 1000 5 mg tablets of Valium (brand name) costs the NHS £13.62. The generic, diazepam (the chemical name) costs £1.50! In 1984 the NHS drugs bill stood at £1.4 billion.

As there are so many irrelevant medicines around which add nothing therapeutically in the fight against disease, it makes sense to get rid of the useless, duplicated or dangerous ones. This is called a 'limited list'. Many hospitals operate a voluntary one and the World Health Organization lists just over two hundred on its list of essential drugs. New medicines would only be introduced if there is a medical need for them, as in Norway, whose list contains 1900 formulations. A limited list benefits patients, as doctors have only to familiarize themselves with the drugs on the list; this leads to safer prescribing habits and a greater knowledge of adverse effects because monitoring is easier.

In Britain we have eighteen thousand licensed drugs. As might be imagined, any attempt to introduce a national list here has been met with general hysteria from the pharmaceutical industry, who see their profits threatened. As all new drugs are tested on animals, a limited list would be good news for them as well as patients and the Health Service, because we could then cut out the 'me-toos' and start to put patients ahead of drug company profits. A 1986 survey by Health Action International stated: 'Most of the tens of thousands of drugs on the world market are either unsafe, ineffective, unnecessary or a waste of money.'

Living Without Cruelty offers the compassionate pathway to health by providing *you* with the tools to prevent disease – a healthy and caring diet and the means to eliminate harmful substances from your home environment. By taking back responsibility for your own health you'll find you will probably suffer less from irritating colds and other minor ailments and have a general feeling of well-being, both mentally and physically. A healthy body will improve your resistance to disease and assist in a quicker recovery should you happen to fall ill. If you suffer from debilitating illness and allergy problems you may well discover that alternative healing systems, coupled with a switch to a Living Without Cruelty diet, are just what's needed to help alleviate your problems or eliminate them completely. Many patients who have endured long-term and often hazardous drug treatments have found they've been able to throw away their pills forever simply by changing their lifestyle.

Vivisection – the sick science

Preventive medical approaches, coupled with a sensible health policy, could achieve a huge reduction in disease, suffering and death, but we shall still need research to help overcome remaining problems. Much current research involves living animals. During 1988 3,480,252 animals suffered and died in UK labs – 61 per cent in commercial concerns, primarily the drug industry, the biggest user of animals. Yet we can see that a great deal of their work is aimed at developing money-making products we do not need. Most people condemn animal experiments to test cosmetics as trivial and unnecessary, yet have been led to believe that all medical advances stem from animal-based work and that such experiments are therefore valid. This, although animal researchers would wish it otherwise, is a myth.

Sir George Pickering, former Professor of Medicine at Oxford University, summed it up nicely: 'The idea, as I understand it, is that fundamental truths are revealed in laboratory experiments on lower animals and are then applied to the problems of the sick patient. Having been myself trained as a physiologist, I feel in a way competent to assess such a claim. It is plain nonsense.'

The vivisection community, which never ceases to accuse animal advocates of 'wet sentimentality' and the use of emotional blackmail, itself never ceases to portray harrowing visions of babies denied treatment because animal experiments have been stopped or of anguished parents having to choose between their dog or their child. This is a hypothetical irrelevancy. In fact, you would choose your next-door neighbour or anybody else over your own family. The choice is not between dogs and children, but between good and bad science.

History proves that, time and time again, animal experiments have led us away from the path of healing and sound medical research. Unfortunately, we compound our mistakes and are still relying on conclusions drawn from animal work, despite these invariably being contradictory, confusing or totally irrelevant when it comes to human therapeutics. And in many cases of drug 'safety' evaluation, animal data applied to humans has had tragic, even fatal, results.

It is thought that side-effects, even serious and fatal ones, are grossly under-reported by doctors. One estimate puts the annual figure of drug-induced deaths in Britain at between ten and fifteen thousand, almost double the number of people killed in road accidents. This is contrary to the 'official' figure of just over two thousand deaths. Yet one medical editorial, discussing NSAIDs, associated their use *alone* with a possible four thousand fatalities. Readers will be interested to compare the pharmaceutical industry's figure of deaths caused by its products: about four hundred.

Yet we still rely on animal tests despite the fact that animals cannot tell us about headaches, dizziness, numbness, ringing in the ears, memory loss, lethargy, nausea and a host of other symptoms. Many laboratory animals are physically unable to vomit. Different species react differently and switching the results from one to another is a dangerous form of Russian roulette with the gun pointed at our heads. Aspirin causes birth defects in rats and mice but not people, whilst thalidomide works the other way around; morphine sedates us but stimulates cats;

penicillin poisons guinea pigs and hamsters. Whole books have been written full of examples like these.

Even the scientists who perform the experiments often report conclusions at variance with, or unknown to, the human situation. In one report, studies with rats and mice were aimed at predicting human cancer-causing substances. The author, Pfizer's David Salsburg, stated that on the basis of probability theory 'We would have been better off to toss a coin.' Commenting on experiments to induce ulcers in dogs, Sir Heneage Ogilvie, formerly consultant surgeon at Guy's Hospital in London, stated: 'To apply the results of experiments on dogs to the aetiology and treatment of peptic ulceration in man is as scientific as to base a course of postnatal lectures to mothers on a study of the maternal habits of the female kangaroo.'

Another area of animal research is tobacco and alcohol. Unlike many humans, animals dislike alcohol, so during experiments the substance is often forcibly administered into the stomach or else the animals may be made to breathe alcohol vapours. During 1988, 4313 animals died in alcohol experiments in UK laboratories. Animals have been dosed to study aggression, addiction, high-blood pressure, binge drinking and foetal damage in experiments conducted at over twenty laboratories. In one test, animals were forced to breathe alcohol for seven to ten days in a vapour chamber, during which many died. Survivors then allowed to breathe air experienced withdrawal symptoms within fifteen minutes – tremors, intense agitation and hair standing on end. Many suffered convulsions, with the symptoms continuing for ten to twelve hours. Yet, as with all animal experiments, the validity and scientific credibility of such work invites criticism. The Alcohol Studies Centre in Scotland has stated that 'nothing of clinical relevance has been achieved to date from the vast range of animal experiments . . . the animal models of addiction . . . are not relevant to human addiction'.

When one considers the complex social, economic and environmental factors (as well as hereditary links) which lead a person to alcohol abuse, it's hardly surprising that animal tests are irrelevant. Sadly, there seems to be no shortage of taxpayers' money for such work. Other funding bodies include the Brewers' Society, the Wellcome Trust and Action Research for the Crippled Child. Alcohol taxation earns the government some £7.5 billion annually, with a further £1 billion in exports. During 1984 the government spent £22 million on combating illegal narcotics, yet could only manage a measly £150,000 grant for Action on Smoking and Health (ASH). Action on Alcohol Abuse didn't get a penny.

After the adverse publicity surrounding the ICI 'Smoking Beagles', researchers turned to rodents, whose PR image evokes less sympathy than the dog. Although numbers have fallen, 106 animals were still used in this controversial area during 1988. Again, because animals are so unlike people, forcing them to smoke in laboratory experiments does not reproduce lung cancer, despite numerous attempts to do so.

The publication *Medical Review*, discussing animal experiments, summed up the situation thus: 'We believe that, until research switches over to the clinician and leaves the laboratory investigator to grieve over his failures, no real progress will be made.'

The cure

Thankfully, some talented and enlightened scientists are discovering that real progress can be made by discarding animals in favour of new and varied technologies. These sophisticated, humane alternatives offer greater accuracy and are often far more cost-effective and directly relevant to people.

Techniques include human tissue culture; computer-assisted safety evaluation of drugs; detecting cancer-causing chemicals in the test tube; using the normally discarded human placenta to practise micro-surgery and video and computer simulation during medical training. Scientists have often approached humane trusts – often set up by anti-vivisection groups – for financial help to develop innovative techniques after establishment sources have refused funding. Such work has led to many animals being saved and tests being developed which more reliably protect the public. Entrenched attitudes and bureaucratic inertia sadly continue to hinder the adoption of many well-proven alternatives to animal tests, and pressure groups work hard to speed up change.

A very positive initiative is being pursued by the International Association Against Painful Experiments on Animals (IAAPEA), whose Charter for Health and Humane Research, outlined on page ??, embraces the Living Without Cruelty ethic. The IAAPEA has societies operating in thirty countries and has consultative status within the United Nations. Animal Aid are UK representatives. It's hoped the Charter will help shift the emphasis towards a better system of healthcare and more reliable, humane research. You too can help by supporting the Charter and by donating to humane trusts and the IAAPEA itself, which also funds the cost of more sophisticated computer technology to replace animals in developing countries. By directing legacies and fund-raising to such organizations we help not only the animals, but ourselves too.

Teaching indifference

Education, especially within science, is the key in changing our attitudes to the way animals are perceived. At school, pressure is often placed upon children by teachers who insist on including dissection in coursework although GCSE boards no longer require it for examinations. At 'A' level, despite increasing pressure, dissection remains compulsory. The cutting up of animals methodically is upsetting for many children; it is a process which leads to the suppression of sensitivity, often in the face of ridicule. As attitudes harden, children can begin to see animals simply as disposable teaching aids who end up in a bin with the rest of the rubbish. Thousands of animals die annually to sustain this futile practice, yet animal anatomy can be learnt from diagrams, models and computer aids – as human anatomy is taught – without the need for a human corpse to be hacked about in order to impart knowledge.

Many pupils are now refusing to dissect. Pupils' feelings should be respected; they should be given alternative assignments and not penalized for taking a stance. The Animal Aid Youth Group will advise pupils and parents who face this dilemma.

Very few of the students forced into dissection will go on to a scientific career, but when they do, the pressure to conform to a system which sanctions animal abuse is even greater.

Universities, polytechnics and medical schools are licensed to carry out experiments on living animals, not just dissections on dead ones. Figures for 1988 reveal that 8247 animals died in these establishments for purposes of 'education'. Included in these figures are experiments to 'demonstrate known facts', often repeated annually, despite the fact that modern technology exists to record experiments which can then be relayed to new student intakes ad infinitum. Old habits die hard. Overall, 813,646 animal experiments were carried out within these establishments – 23 per cent of the total which, after commercial concerns, makes them the second biggest animal users.

Academics are anxious to promote the use of animals when teaching, because it validates their own animal research. Thus the whole grisly business is perpetuated, but even medical students are now beginning to question the whole approach. The National Union of Students have adopted the Charter for Violence-free Science, which upholds the rights of students wishing to opt out of vivisection and dissection. They will give full support to anyone being pressurized or threatened with academic penalties. One ex-student, now Dr Sarah Webb, stated: 'The way the technicians handled and killed the animals was so matter of fact, just another chore in the daily routine. Although it was a shock every time I witnessed it, I tolerated it, and apart from that first feeble attempt, I do not think I ever protested again. . . . I think there can be no doubt that all that slaughter was unnecessary. We were perfectly able to learn the facts without that.'

The secret war – animals and military research

In 1917, near Salisbury in Wiltshire, a farm and breeding colony of laboratory animals were added to the sprawl of buildings now known as Porton Down. There monkeys, baboons, goats, cats, dogs, sheep, rabbits, guinea pigs, rats and mice were gassed and shot to test the weapons of war. Chemicals were injected into them, bullets and bombs were aimed at them to witness the bodily devastation. Mustard gas was rubbed into their bodies and the blistering effects noted. Some animals were opened up, their internal organs smeared with mustard, then stitched back together again to suffer the consequences.

Since then, with a second world war behind us, Porton has expanded into one of the most secret and prominent centres of vivisection, where animals are experimented upon in order to find ever more effective ways of killing human beings. Such work is, of course, described as 'defensive'. Between 1952 and 1970 Porton 'used' over a thousand monkeys, nearly two hundred thousand guinea pigs and 1¼ million mice. Such experiments, conducted under the auspices of the 'Crown', do not have to be declared in annual Home Office statistics, so figures cannot be verified. MOD work includes the following experiments:

1978:	167,300
1979:	74,700
1981:	17,200
1983:	9,500
1985:	6,600
1987:	9,200

The nature of these secret tests is sometimes disclosed in scientific journals and information can be pieced together. Riot control gases have been tested, monkeys and other animals have been experimented on with nerve gases, dogs have been poisoned with cyanide, and rubber and plastic bullets have been tried out on live sheep. In one test, live monkeys were shot through the head with ball-bearings to see the effects of high-velocity missiles. In 1982, beagles were poisoned with cyanide and tested with an antidote already known to be effective in man. The animals suffered spasms, epileptic fits and collapse. The results were published in the scientific journal *Archives of Toxicology*. The Ministry of Defence refused to disclose the information (which was already in the public domain) by saying it would be 'detrimental to national security'. Perhaps a public outcry over dogs being poisoned would have been detrimental to the government's image? Cyanide tests have been going on at Porton for sixty years. Even the nerve gases first developed by Nazi chemists were being animal-tested as recently as 1979.

In recent years, Porton have added a respectable PR tool – their Public Service Health Laboratory. But when defence scientists' names appear on scientific papers connected with organisms like legionnaire's disease, one begins

to wonder just what sort of work is going on there.

One sad insight is gleaned from this statement, made by a Porton workman who lost his bearings:

> 'I thought I was ill, I thought I was seeing things. It was a little monkey enclosed in a glass cage. Its eyes seemed to be falling out and it couldn't breathe. It was in dreadful, dreadful distress. I forgot everything and went near and said something to it, and it buried its head in its arms and sobbed like a child. I never slept that night, and next day managed to go back to the same room, but it was nearly finished by then. It had sunk to a little heap at the bottom of the glass case.'

Animal suffering = human suffering = planetary suffering. And, incidentally, like so much vivisection, paid for by taxpayers' money.

Julie Christie

'Looking back, I remember two incidents in my life which helped fashion the way I feel now about animals and people. Previously, I'd had a very conventional schooling in England – we certainly never discussed any of life's real 'issues', so my education certainly didn't serve me in that way – but during the time I was a student Bardot (who now wouldn't touch a fur coat and spends all her time working for animals) was at her height of fame and I saw her dressed in a white fluffy fur hat and those huge fur snow-boots which were all the rage then. I wanted to look like that – but when I tried on the boots I began to have a tussle with myself about how great I looked, but how I really shouldn't be wearing them. In the end, my inner self overcame my vanity.

'It was part of my awakening, but it was when I was on location in Norfolk, making *The Go-between*, that I discovered factory farming. I'd lived with people who had pigs and I knew how intelligent, how full of curiosity, how naughty and how full of character they are. To think of something with all that potential being kept in this hideous concrete and steel for a lifetime was beyond comprehension. I realized they were quite mad with the torture of it – that absolute pain of a life denied. I thought, if this has to happen to them to enable me to eat meat, then I'm not going to be a part of that system which encourages a propensity towards insensitivity.

'Farmers who raise animals like that have given up a part of themselves. Of course they always have an excuse for what they're doing, as do people who carry out animal experiments or who systematically torture people in repressive regimes. I lived in Argentina for a time and came across people whose job it was to torture others. They were family men, loved their children, had pets and could offer umpteen cogent reasons to justify what they did. If you give up part of yourself – sacrifice your humaneness, your compassion – for a salary, prestige, academic acclaim . . . power, then you can excuse yourself anything, even murder.

'It's education which has to break through into people's consciousness and make the connections that animal cruelty and oppression is linked to our own oppression. Living Without Cruelty means more to me than just the animal connection, and that's what makes it such a strong

message. I buy household products like Ecover because they're not animal-tested, and for the same reasons I buy Oxfam Nicaraguan coffee because it doesn't exploit people. Everything in the struggle is inter-related.

'I know it's difficult to watch cruelty. It's easier to switch off. I was a bit like that when I narrated *The Animals Film*, but everyone should have to watch, even though we'd rather not, what goes on in those laboratories. Psychological experiments which I saw on film stick in my mind. Food deprivation, sight deprivation, maternal deprivation, aggression research, experiments into loneliness and despair. When you see those creatures who've been reduced to little bundles weeping in a corner because of the 'work' of a scientist, when I see my closest relative locked in a restraining box, his head filled with electrodes, and all he's got to reach out to you with is his eyes, then how can we respond to that if we close ours?

'In El Salvador they once filmed their tortures – they were proud of them. It's beyond imagination just how creative and inventive the torture could be. But can we then describe it as science and transform it with a credible respectability into something acceptable – providing it's not done to us? Things done to animals, in the name of science, are often no different from things done to prisoners, in the name of political expediency. The animals' suffering paves the way for our own. Sometimes the animal experiments are government-funded so we can perfect ever more subtle ways to kill or maim each other.

'Sometimes it's hard to argue with those who set themselves up as experts and who plead necessity. When I saw those visions of institutionalized hell on earth, I knew for certain that what I was watching was wrong and could never be justified – but people *did* justify it and condone it. The vivisection business has always been able to manipulate the fear that people have of illness and disease, but even here people are beginning to make connections. I wrote the Foreword for a book called *The Cruel Deception* by Dr Robert Sharpe. If people are interested in the truth about what is done in their name, with their money and for their supposed benefit, I would ask them to please read it. After all, it is we consumers who buy products tested on animals,

JULIE CHRISTIE
'. . . when I see my closest relative locked in
a restraining box, his head filled with
electrodes, and all he's got to reach out to
you with is his eyes, then how can we
respond to that if we close ours?'

whose drugs are tested on animals, even whose weapons are tested on animals. And when things inevitably go wrong, it's we consumers who pay the price. Meanwhile, of course, the animals have already paid theirs.'

Sir John Gielgud

'My parents didn't really like animals – we never had any cats or dogs – but I had an aunt who was mad about cocker spaniels (she had three or four). Auntie would bring a dog on stage with her at the end of a play, and the dog itself would often get an extra curtain call – much to the annoyance of the rest of the cast! I suppose it was she who taught me to love and value animals.'

But Sir John admits he knew nothing really about animal cruelty until he met Martin Hensla, his long-standing secretary, great friend and a vegetarian. Before the war Sir John had a cottage in Essex which he shared with five schnauzers. 'I used to take one of the dogs to the theatre with me – he loved it, but I wouldn't do it now. I think London's too difficult for animals. Exercise is so important. People who buy big dogs and live in tiny flats and never exercise them should be stopped from ever owning a dog. Confinement like that is cruelty in itself.'

Now that Sir John lives in the Buckinghamshire countryside, his present dogs have plenty of space to run about in. Home, near Aylesbury, is also home to many other animals and birds, including a peacock and a peahen. Gielgud is devoted to his animal friends. 'I have no children, but the animals are my family and I feel very strongly about them. I know I'd be terribly lonely without them and I feel I must do what I can about animal cruelty, which I abhor. Somebody actually shot the first peahen we had and the male was beside himself with grief. I was furious, but we could do nothing. Eventually we got him a new wife, and he seems happy again.

'So many things have come to my notice – the use of chimpanzees in dreadful experiments, the killing of kangaroos and wild ponies for petfood, the hunting of seals and whales . . . the fur trade. I had a fur coat as a young man, but would never wear one now. In my career I've been aware of how animals suffer in the film industry. It upsets me so much, especially the trip wires which make horses fall in battle scenes and westerns. It's terribly cruel, and they're always having to shoot animals who injure themselves on film sets.

'I suppose the thing which concerns me most is animal experimentation. I've always thought the idea of vivisection horrible. Such wonderful scientific discoveries are supposed to result – so they tell us! We don't seem to be very much better off as a result of all the suffering which animals endure. I'm not a scientist, but even I can work out that rats and mice are different from you and me. That's why I'm a supporter of humane research, which doesn't abuse animals and groups who speak up for animals in laboratories.' Sir John is patron of the non-animal research charity Quest For a Test for Cancer and Animal Aid.

'I firmly believe that young people will bring about change by their commitment and dedication to stopping animal abuse. We had some collecting outside the theatre. They were going up and down the queues in all weathers and raised several thousand pounds for humane medical work. People took leaflets and read about what they could do to stop animals suffering. That's it, isn't it? Each of us *can* do *something*.'

Whole health

Orthodox medicine, with its narrow and mechanistic approach, often fails to help because it seeks to remove the symptoms of disease without always removing, or indeed seeking, the cause. Alternative medicine seeks to do both. It's the single largest growth area in medicine today. Doctor and patient work together as a team, taking the time and trouble to find the causes of problems, both mental and physical, then taking steps to put the body back into balance through one or a variety of approaches. Because no harsh or chemically synthesized drugs are used, there are no unpleasant side-effects. No longer can alternatives be dismissed as 'quack'. The therapies may not suit the scientists but the patients tell a different story, especially orthodoxy's cast-off 'hopeless cases', who often find relief from pain and debilitating conditions after years of palliative and useless drug treatments.

A system is needed, though, which will ensure that therapies are given the respect they deserve and that any cheapskate elements are weeded out. This is being done by the Council for Complementary and Alternative Medicine, which is setting standards of practice and training for most of the major therapies, thus giving the consumer confidence and the medical establishment less to gripe about. Little would be served through evaluation via Western methodology, as the approaches differ so widely – orthodoxy traditionally discounts the value of alternative approaches in a negative and prejudiced manner. In future alternative therapies, uncorrupted by the mechanistic view, will hopefully stand side by side with the best of Western medicine and will be more readily available to all patients, regardless of their ability to pay, as the *real* health choice.

A list of therapies appears on pages oo–oo. Although it is by no means exhaustive, I have tried to confine it to professional bodies whose practitioners have undergone a recognized and often lengthy training period, who are long established and whom I personally would choose with confidence.

This is a difficult area. For instance, I personally know of two homoeopathic doctors whose knowledge has been passed on to them and who have a wealth of experience. I have consulted them through recommendation and they are excellent. Neither has any letters after his name, yet they are instinctive healers. A recommendation is often a good way to find a practitioner. Other than that it's best to obtain a list of local therapists from the professional bodies concerned. If you use Yellow Pages, look for the qualifications listed, which should give you some guidance when choosing. If in doubt, ask. Before making an appointment find out the consultation charges for both initial and subsequent visits, and ask if the charges include any medicines.

Think about what sort of practitioner might be best. Can you pin down the pain to something skeletal and muscular? One of the manipulative techniques might be best for this. Obvious internal problems might respond better to a medicinal approach. If you have a natural health centre in your town, they would enlist a variety of approaches and be able to give guidance on who best to try for your particular problem.

Diet is probably the most important factor where health is concerned, and an area you are directly in control of. The old adage 'You are what you eat' sums it up, and as diet is recognized as instrumental in promoting health, alternative therapists generally discuss individual requirements very thoroughly.

The Living Without Cruelty healthy outlook

- Give up smoking as soon as you can.
- Keep alcohol consumption low.
- Look at the healthy eating ideas in the food section and take steps to improve your diet and your health.
- Know what you're eating – become a packet-reader in the supermarket.
- Think about the stress points in your life and try to avoid or temper their effects.
- Is your trip to the doctor really necessary? Do you need yet another dose of antibiotics for yet another cold?
- Look at alternative healing systems – they might help, especially if your condition hasn't responded to persistent drug treatment; if you're offered only pain-killers; or if you suffer tension and depression or recurring disorders. Undetected allergy or deficiency may be your simple answer.
- Support ethical medical research which doesn't abuse animals.
- Avoid using dangerous chemicals in your own environment – the one you *can* control – especially garden sprays and poisons which may damage your health (see page 140).
- Use lead-free petrol.
- Support local and national initiatives for a healthy, clean environment by joining your local 'green' pressure group.

Chrissie Hynde

'I told my parents when I was seventeen that I wasn't going to eat meat any more. They said, "You're going to eat it and be 'normal'." That was over twenty years ago now, and they're finally coming around.

'It started in the sixties when I began embracing hippy values. A diet which avoided killing seemed a natural part of that. I never thought about vegetarianism from a health viewpoint, but I suppose that, even with my hectic schedule, I'm healthier than most and the diet plays its part in keeping me that way. I avoid unnecessary medicines and never take antibiotics for colds. Go out and buy six lemons and a jar of honey. Why fill yourself up with pills which can weaken your system?

'To me, the whole environmental and animal thing is all about getting people to make connections. People need to see the bigger picture and not just the narrow view. I've met people who do gigs to help save the rainforests, then go out and have a charity barbecue! Our society is all 'me, me, me' and 'ours, ours, ours'. Never 'theirs'. People say things like 'Our son will never grow up to see the seals or the great whales.' They're worrying about what they're going to miss. Even with the rainforests all they can think of is 'Hey man, there goes *my* oxygen!' – never a thought or a mention for the thousands of creatures who perish when the forest gets slashed and burnt. And not much about the burger chains who monopolize the best land for cattle grazing and perpetuate the whole disgusting business.

'I was a teenager when the burger chains started and America got its terrible taste for beef. The advertising, of course, is aimed at children. I can't understand how anyone can participate in a lifestyle that means somebody is starving to death and somebody else is dying. Why turn your child into a graveyard? Why should a kid have to wait seventeen years for the penny to drop, like I did? If you only sat down and spent half an hour thinking about it, you'd change your lifestyle.

'Don't be put off by the fact that power is in the hands of big multi-national companies. Don't feel you have no voice. We mustn't wait for the people at the 'top' to act – they'll sit on their hands as usual. The politicians should be red-faced and hold their heads in shame for what they've

CHRISSIE HYNDE
'Who are the mad ones? The animal victims who can't fight back, the so-calle[d] scientists who sit down and devise ways [to] make animals go insane, or us, for payin[g] for it and keeping our mouths shut?'

n'est pas une Vie.

allowed to happen. *We can do it – we* can put the fur and the meat industry out of business. We can force companies who test their products on animals to stop causing suffering. Each of us can actively and personally save lives by cutting out meat from our diet. And it might not just be the animals' lives we'll be saving.

'In the States, a well-known actor was seen on nationwide TV promoting meat eating for the meat industry. You'd see him in his kitchen cooking up chops and steaks and stuff. Then he had a massive heart attack. For some reason, you never saw his ads again. . . .'

The International Charter for Health and Humane Research

From the International Association Against Painful Experiments on Animals:

'In the urgent interests of both humans and animals we . . . propose the following programme for health and humane research –

(1) Emphasis to be directed towards the prevention of ill health.

(2) An essential drugs policy restricting new medicines to therapeutic areas of real need, thus avoiding the production of duplicate 'me-too' drugs for which there is no medical justification.

(3) Medical research to rely on methods of direct relevance to people.

(4) Medical training to concentrate on the study of human beings.

(5) A switch to non-animal test systems to improve the safety of medicines.

(6) Vaccines to be produced from human rather than animal cells.

(7) Governments to ensure the rapid development, validation and utilization of alternative systems.

Copies of the Charter with full explanatory text are available from Animal Aid and the IAAPEA. The Charter is an integral part of the Living Without Cruelty campaign.

Specialist anti-vivisection groups

Animal Aid
7 Castle St
Tonbridge
Kent
TN9 1BH
0732 364546
Campaigns primarily against animal experimentation and factory farming, but covers most general areas of animal abuse. Educational emphasis with thriving Youth Group. Its nationally acclaimed Living Without Cruelty campaign, together with the annual exhibition in London, has given the society deserved credibility and massive public support. Magazine, *Outrage*, for members. Local groups operate nationwide.

British Union for the Abolition of Vivisection (BUAV)
16a Crane Grove
London N7 8LB
01-700 4888
Campaigns specifically against vivisection, especially concentrating on cosmetics experiments through its national Choose Cruelty-Free campaign. Positive company vetting awards their rabbit logo which consumers can look out for. Magazine, *Liberator*. Local group network.

Animals Concern (Scotland)
121 West Regent St
Glasgow G2 2SD
041-221 2300
Formerly the Scottish Anti-Vivisection Society, Animals Concern have broadened their umbrella to take in general animal abuse issues in Scotland, although they still concentrate on animal experiments.

Scottish Society for the Prevention of Vivisection (SSPV)
10 Queensferry St
Edinburgh EH2 4PG
031-225 6039

Disabled Against Animal Research and Exploitation (DAARE)
PO Box 8
Daventry
Northants
NN11 4RQ
National group, mainly disabled membership, but also open to family supporters. Presses for health resources to help the disabled and opposes the waste, cruelty and futility of the animal experiments supposedly done for their 'benefit'.

International Association Against Painful Experiments on Animals (IAAPEA)
PO Box 215
St Albans
Herts
AL3 4RD
0727 35386
Pressure group operating at international level – representatives worldwide.

The Nurses Against Vivisection Movement
2 Hillcrest Cottage
Hillcrest
Uppertown
Bonsall
Derbyshire
DE4 2AW
National group of both student and qualified members of the nursing profession.

Student Campaign for Animal Rights (SCAR)
Mandela Building
99 Oxford Rd
Manchester
M1 7EL
061 273 1162

National Union of Students
Nelson Mandela House
461 Holloway Rd
London N7 6LJ
01-272 8900
Support and advice for students who wish to practise 'violence-free science', without animal abuse.

Humane research

The Dr Hadwen Trust for Humane Research
6c Brand St
Hitchin
Herts
SG5 1HX
0462 36819

The Humane Research Trust
Brook House
29 Bramhall Lane South
Bramhall
Cheshire
SK7 2DN
061-439 8041/3869

Quest for a Test for Cancer
Woodbury
Harlow Rd
Roydon
Essex
CM19 5HF
027 979 2233

Preventative medicine – concerned groups

Smoking
Action on Smoking and Health (ASH)
5–11 Mortimer St
London W1N 7RH
01-637 9843
Pressure group, advice and information.

Smokers' Information and Advice Centre (QUIT)
Latimer House
40–48 Hanson St
London W1P 7DE
01-636 9103
Practical advice and counselling to help you give up.

NB: The Tobacco Advisory Council is funded by the tobacco industry and exists to promote smoking. It has nothing to do with health.

Alcohol

Alcohol Concern
305 Grays Inn Rd
London WC1X 8QF
01-833 3471
Pressure group, advice and information. Charity. DHSS core-funded.

Action on Alcohol Abuse (AAA)
3rd Floor
11 Carteret House
Livingstone St
London SW1H 9DL
01-222 3454
Pressure group, advice and information.

The Alcohol Counselling Service
34 Electric Lane
London SW9 8JT
01-737 3579
Pressure group, advice, information and counselling.

Self-help

Alcoholics Anonymous
General Service Office
PO Box 1
Stonebow House
Stonebow
York
YO1 2NJ
0904 644026
Confidential service, advice and local contacts list.

The Alcohol Recovery Project
172 Kennington Park Rd
London SE11
01-582 6251
Series of London-based counselling projects.

The Greater London Alcohol Advisory Service (GLAAS)
91–93 Charterhouse St
London EC1M 6HR
01-253 6221
Counselling and information service.

Healthy eating

See pages 14–71, particularly The London Food Commission, FoodWatch International, The Vegetarian Society and The Vegan Society.

Alternative medicine

(V) next to a therapy indicates treatment also available for animals. The letters at the end of each entry indicate the qualification awarded by the various bodies.

The Natural Medicines Society
Membership Office
Edith Lewis House
Back Lane
Ilkeston
Derbyshire
DE7 8EJ
0602 440436
Pressure group formed to fight the threat against natural medicine from government policies which would deny consumers the right to choose therapies which have been available for centuries.

Council for Complementary and Alternative Medicine (CCAM)
Suite 1
19a Cavendish Square
London W1M 9AD
01-409 1440
Accrediting body which sets standards of practice and training for professional organizations.

The British Holistic Medical Association
179 Gloucester Place
London NW1 6DX
01-262 5229
Individual membership open to all; promotes holistic approach for all methods of healing. Publishes professional *Journal of Holistic Medicine*.

Institute of Complementary Medicine
21 Portland Place
London WC1
01-636 9543
Dedicated to the promotion of alternative therapies.

Oriental medicine (V)

Systems based upon acupuncture, acupressure, herbs, massage and diet and a philosophy three thousand years old. Practitioners seek to correct body disharmony by tapping into energy channels with which disease may be interfering.

British Acupuncture Association and Register
34 Alderney St
London SW1V 4EU
01-834 1012/3353
Mainly postgraduates with a medical background of some sort. BAAR.

Traditional Acupuncture Society
1 The Ridgeway
Stratford-upon-Avon
Warwickshire
CV37 9JL
0789 298798
As the title suggests, traditional Chinese methods are used. Lic. Ac. MTAS; leading to B. Ac.

Register of Traditional Chinese Medicine
19 Trinity Rd
London N2 8JJ
01-883 8431
Both acupuncturists and oriental herbal practitioners listed. Members also often practise other related disciplines such as massage. MRTCM.

International Register of Oriental Medicine
Green Hedges House
Green Hedges Avenue
East Grinstead
West Sussex
RH19 1DZ
0342 313106/7
IROM

Manipulation therapies (V)

Techniques to restore the body to balance through correcting misalignments of the skeletal frame which often go undetected by conventional medical examinations.

British Chiropractic Association
Premier House
10 Greycoat Place
London SW1P 1SB
01-222 8866
Professional body for practitioners, register of chiropractors. DC.

Anglo-European College of Chiropractic
Parkwood Rd
Bournemouth
BH5 2DF
0202 431021
Four-year full-time course leading to B.Sc. Chiropractic.

The General Council and Register of Osteopaths
21 Suffolk St
London SW1Y 4HG
01-839 2060
Largest professional body with strictest ethical training criteria. Register of practitioners. Only graduates from the approved colleges listed below are entitled to use MRO after their names.

The British School of Osteopathy
1–4 Suffolk St
London SW1Y 4HG
01-930 9254
Four-year full-time course leading to DO, MRO.

European School of Osteopathy
104 Tonbridge Rd
Maidstone
Kent
0622 671558
Four-year full-time course leading to DO, MRO.

London College of Osteopathic Medicine
8 Boston Place
London NW1
01-262 5250
Postgraduate course for interested medical practitioners only.

British College of Naturopathy and Osteopathy
6 Netherhall Gardens
London NW3 5RR
01-435 7830
Four-year full-time course leading to DO, MRO. Associated with the BNOA, below.

British Naturopathic and Osteopathic Association
Frazer House
6 Netherhall Gardens
London NW3 5RR
01-435 8728
National register of therapists £1.50 from the Secretary, or telephone for information on local practitioners. MBNOA.

Medicinal approaches

Herbalism (V)
Herbalists use whole plants, believing that nature produces her own 'balanced' treatments without the unwanted side-effects of modern drug treatments.

Institute of Medical Herbalists
41 Hatherley Rd
Winchester
Hampshire
SO22 6RR
0962 68776
Professional body and register of practitioners. MNIMH.

The School of Herbal Medicine (Phytotherapy)
148 Forest Rd
Tunbridge Wells
Kent
TN2 5EY
0892 30400
Four-year full-time course leading to MNIMH. Prospectus on application.

British Herbal Medicine Association
Lane House
Cowling
Keighley
West Yorkshire
BD22 0LX
0535 34487
Publishes *British Herbal Pharmacopoeia*. Protects interests of users, practitioners and manufacturers of herbal medicine.

Homoeopathy (V)
Healing by the 'magic of the minimum dose' formulated by Samuel Hahnemann, gives minute traces of substances to trigger the body's own healing energies.

Society of Homoeopaths
2 Artizan Rd
Northampton
NN1 4HU
0604 21400
Register. Three to four years' training; all members carry medical insurance. RS Hom.

The Faculty of Homoeopathy
Hahnemann House
2 Powis Place
Great Ormond St
London WC1N 3HR
01-837 3091
Professional body for GPs, dentists, vets, pharmacists etc. who wish to practise homoeopathy as well as conventional medicine. Register. Journal.

British Homoeopathic Association
27a Devonshire St
London W1N 1RJ
01-935 2163
Promotes homoeopathy. Advice, information, lists of doctors, chemists, vets and hospitals.★ NHS treatment available.

★Hospitals in London, Glasgow, Liverpool, Bristol and Tunbridge Wells.

Anthroposophical medicine
Based upon Rudolf Steiner's principles encompassing spiritual, artistic and scientific understanding of illness, which recognizes the inherent individual needs of each patient.

Anthroposophical Medical Association
The Old Forge
Bell End
Belbroughton
West Midlands
DY9 9UJ
List of practitioners, some partially within NHS. Information on request.

Anthroposophical Medical Trust
I Saint Hill Green
East Grinstead
West Sussex
Fund-raising trust to support the costs of clinics and practitioners. Anthroposophical practices work on the principle that medical care should be available to all who need it regardless of their ability to pay.

Healing (V)

More people attend healers than any other 'alternative' system. The power of prayer, whether linked to established religious groups or not, is utilized by mediums to convey healing energies to the recipient, either directly, through the 'laying on of hands', or distantly, through absent healing networks.

The Guild of Spiritualist Healers
36 Newmarket
Otley
West Yorkshire
LS21 3AE
0943 462708
Healing branch of the Spiritualist National Union (SNU). Trained healers operate mainly in Guild churches.

The Spiritualist Association of Great Britain
33 Belgrave Square
London SW1
01-235 3351
Free daily clinic for healing in London. Information on regional church-based healing in UK.

The National Federation of Spiritual Healers
The Old Manor Farm Studio
Sunbury-on-Thames
TW16 6RG
09327 83164
Non-denominational. National referral service. Healers operate, with permission, in NHS hospitals at patients' request.

Animal Lights
Worldwide Healing Network
66 Norbury Avenue
Thornton Heath
Surrey
Absent healing service for animals. Send an s.a.e. for details.

Hypnotherapy

Process whereby the therapist guides the relaxed subconscious mind to uncover and correct physical, mental and emotional problems such as stress, depression, phobias, insomnia and anxiety, thus enabling the patient to achieve a more fulfilling life.

Association of Qualified Curative Hypnotherapists
8 Balaclava Rd
Kings Heath
Birmingham
B14 7SG
021-444 5435

Other groups

Association for new Approaches to Cancer
1A Addison Crescent
London W14 8JP
01-603 7751
Aims to encourage the adoption of holistic cancer therapies to complement existing treatments and to support patients and their families with help and advice.

Bristol Cancer Clinic
Grove House
Cornwallis Grove
Clifton
Bristol
BS8 4PG
0272 743216
Pioneering centre for innovative approaches to cancer treatments using holistic principles.

Holistic AIDS Research Trust
17 Egremont Place
Brighton
East Sussex
BN2 2GA
0273 698698
Research and information centre on holistic approaches to AIDS treatment.

The Nature Cure Clinic
15 Oldbury Place
London W1M 3AL
01-935 2787/6213
Naturopathic clinic for patients with limited means.

The Concessions Register
55a Longridge Rd
London SW5 9SF
01-244 7578
Send an s.a.e. for list of alternative practitioners who offer reduced fees for those with limited means.

Further reading
RESEARCH AND MEDICAL
The Cruel Deception, Dr Robert Sharpe, Thorsons. A powerful indictment of current animal-based medical research and a plea for a sensible preventative approach to health based on humane and relevant systems of investigation. Excellent.
In Pity and in Anger, John Vyvan, Thorsons. Classic and historical study of man's blackest crime, vivisection.
A Higher Form of Killing, Robert Harris and Jeremy Paxman, Paladin. The secret story of gas and germ warfare.
Bitter Pills, Dianna Melrose, Oxfam. An expose of the 'ethical pharmaceutical' companies who operate in Third World countries.
Cured to Death, Arabella Melville and Colin Johnson, Secker and Warburg. How prescribed drugs can cause new diseases, sickness and even death.
Alternatives to Drugs, Arabella Melville and Colin Johnson, Fontana.
Doctoring the Media, Anne Karpf, Routledge.

The reporting of health and medical matters, and how false images are created about the medical machine.
The Diseases of Civilisation, Brian Inglis, Paladin/ Granada. Something of a classic study, full of interesting facts and perspectives.

NATURAL HEALING
The Health Crisis, Chris Thomson and Denis MacEoin, Natural Medicines Society. Explains why we should all be concerned about both the threat to natural healing from government policies, and the state of medicine today and how it affects you.
The Healing Arts, Ted Kaptchuk and Michael Croucher, BBC Publications. Fascinating read, based upon the BBC TV series on natural medicine.
The Alternative Health Guide, Brian Inglis and R. West, Mermaid Books. Very useful consumer's guide which covers seventy therapies, outlining the principles, practices and applications of each.
The National Directory of Alternative Aid, Michael Williams, Health Farm Publishing (available mail-order from Whitwell, Colyford, Colyton, Devon, EX13 6HS; 0297 52566). Details of therapies not listed here and much else besides.
The Complete Herbal Handbook for Dogs and Cats, J. de Bairacli Levy, Faber and Faber. Used by animal sanctuaries and tried and tested on hundreds of satisfied patients!
The Homoeopathy for Pets Series, Thorsons. Useful for anyone who looks after a companion animal.
The Bristol Programme, Penny Brohn, Century Hutchinson. Valuable insight into the now-famous holistic cancer treatment centre in Bristol.
Is Your Child Allergic?, Dr Jan Kuzemko, Thorsons.
Vaccination and Immunisation, Leon Chaitow, C. W. Daniel Co. Ltd (Saffron Walden). A valuable book for those parents who are worried about or question the need for their child to be inoculated. Sets the debate into a badly needed perspective.
The New E for Additives, Maurice Hanssen, Thorsons. Find out just what is in your food and learn to avoid those additives.

5 Good Housekeeping

Queen: *I will try the forces*
            Of these thy compounds on such creatures
                as
            We count not worth the hanging – but none
                human –
            To try the vigour of them . . . and by them
                gather
            Their several virtues and effects.

Doctor: *Your Highness*
            Shall from this practice but make hard your
                heart.

                            Shakespeare, *Cymbeline.*

A clean conscience?

It's new, it's bright, it's better, it's improved. Smiling housewives dash across a kitchen the size of an aircraft hanger, wielding a squirt-gun of miracle cleaner which will decimate the grease on their cookers. Women of the world are seen providing their families with whites so white you need sunglasses to look at them. A penny's worth of washing up liquid cleans the dirty dishes of the combined forces of HM Army, Navy and Air Force and leaves Nanette Newman's hands softer than ever. Meanwhile, an intruder in a light aircraft is busying himself making 'umpteen things clean' whilst Big Bad Dom lurks in the lavatory ready to eliminate unsuspecting germs who get in his way.

The hype, it seems, is easy to swallow – as were the products themselves until pressure forced manufacturers to put childproof tops on their bottles . . . and what a fight that was for the consumer groups concerned. At length, common sense prevailed and accidental poisoning decreased.

For laboratory animals, though, the poisoning regime continues. In 1988, 6916 experiments were carried out to test household products. Eleven of these animals were beagles, two monkeys, 536 rabbits and the remainder, inevitably, poor old rats and mice.

Contract laboratories are the favourites to carry out such work which, together with cosmetic, tobacco and other commercial deals, makes up the 'bread and butter' of their business. In the summer of 1984, a university student, Richard Beggs, took a job inside one of these establishments, Toxicol, in Ledbury, Herefordshire. There he documented an appalling catalogue of cruelty, ineptitude and abuse which the national press later published in an horrific exposé.

Beggs' report revealed that top companies such as Colgate-Palmolive, Johnson and Johnson, and Dunhill were amongst those involved, and that powder carpet cleaner, traffic wax, insect killer and detergents were just some of the substances being tested on animals. Toxicol, who have extensive animal houses and who list the Draize and other eye irritancy studies, and poisoning (toxicity) tests in their catalogue, maintained: 'Our rabbits are quite contented in their wooden stocks' – the devices which immobilize the animal so that it cannot use its paws to wash away the chemicals.

As with so many products of animal abuse, there are alternatives which are not only cruelty-free, but which are kinder to the environment too. Based upon long-established and safe, more natural ingredients, these products used to be available only on mail order but can now be found in many leading supermarket outlets who are beginning to respond to the demands of the caring consumer.

Although these products may seem slightly more expensive, they are usually concentrated and you need less each time. A 1 litre bottle of Clear Spring liquid detergent, for example, is the equivalent of two and a half E3-sized packs of washing powder. Many of the conventional cleaning products have also been linked to allergy problems, with skin reactions one of the major hazards – another reason for looking at the alternatives market. Companies such as Ecover helpfully list the ingredients, so you know exactly what you're getting. You don't have to be a chemist to understand it, either!

As the green consumer boom grows, some of the bigger supermarket chains have begun to sell their own environmentally friendly cleaners. Sainsburys launched Greencare during September 1989, which claims to be not only green but free of animal testing. As with own brand cosmetics and toiletries, the same dilemma applies to household products – there is no way they can be vetted if companies will not allow their products to be scrutinized. Sainsburys have indicated their willingness to do this with the Greencare range, which is a helpful step forward. Hopefully, they will also offer up their cosmetic ranges for approval. Let's hope the company policy will soon publicly come out against animal testing.

It is surely in the interests of both companies and consumers to be as open about product testing as possible. In this contentious area, secrecy can lead to suspicion which openness would avoid. For instance Sainsburys, along with many other companies, have been listed as subscribers to BIBRA (The British Industrial Biological Research Association, based at Carshalton, Surrey). This does not necessarily mean that the companies have initiated animal tests, but amongst BIBRA's research facilities are extensive animal testing laboratories.

Tesco, with an eye for the growing cruelty-free market, do not see any difficulty in collaboration with the animal movement. They have offered their toiletries range called Nature's Choice for approval by the BUAV, and confirmed their willingness to do the same for any other product which they intend to market as 'cruelty-free', including household and washing products. It is to be hoped that other companies will follow this path.

Why not try some of our approved cruelty-free cleaners when your present supply runs out? You'll feel clean all over.

Cruelty-Free cleaners

Key: see page 90.

Acdo (V)
Astley Dye and Chemical Co. Ltd
Mallison St
Bolton
BL1 8PP
0204 52577
Soap powder, net curtain whitener. Supermarkets and chemists.

ARK Green Consumer Products (V)
498–500 Harrow Rd
London W9 3QA
01-968 6780
Range of home cleaning products including detergent and washing-up liquid. Supermarkets and other outlets.

Ataka (V)
Laboratory Facilities Ltd
24 Britwell Rd
Burnham
Slough
SL1 8AG
06286 4149
Bath stain remover and kettle descaling products. Boots and hardware shops.

The Bio-D Company (V)
10 Ingleton Avenue
Anlaby High Rd
Hull
0482 571418/899505
Extensive range of home cleaning and washing products. Health stores.

The Caurnie Soaperie (V)
Canal St
Kirkintilloch
Glasgow
G66 1QZ
041-776 1218
Washing-up liquid and Des disinfectant. Health stores, chemists and mail order.

East of Eden (V)
Crossfield Industrial Estate
Appleby
Cumbria
CA16 6HD
07683 52098
Home, washing and car cleaning products. Health stores, chemists, garden centres and mail order.

Culpeper Ltd (V)
Hadstock Rd
Linton
Cambridge
CB1 6NJ
0223 891196
Furniture polish. Own stores and mail order.

ECOVER (V)
Full Moon
Mouse Lane
Steyning
West Sussex
BN4 3DG
0903 815614
Complete range of safe, bio-degradable products including: washing powder, washing-up liquid, cream cleaner, fabric conditioner, toilet cleaner, floor soap, wool wash and heavy-duty hand cleaner. Full product information on request. Health stores and some department stores. Some lines now available at Sainsburys and other big retail outlets. Mail order too.

Faith Products (V)
22 Great King St
Edinburgh
EH3 6QH
031-661 0900
Clear Spring washing-up liquid and liquid wash. Health stores, department stores and mail order.

Goodebodies (V)
Osbourne House
20 Victoria Ave
Harrogate
North Yorks
HG1 5QY
0423 500206
Home, washing and car cleaning products. Own stores and mail order.

Homecare Products (V)
London Production Centre
Broomhill Rd
London SW18 4JQ
01-871 5027/9
Shiny Sinks, Hob Brite, Microwave Plus, Bar Keeper's Friend and Copper Glo. No phosphates. Department and hardware stores, supermarkets including Sainsburys, kitchen centres. Mail order. Send for information and stockists list.

Honesty Cosmetics Ltd (V)
33 Markham Rd
Chesterfield
Derbyshire
S40 1TA
0246 211269
Washing-up liquid and all-purpose cleaning concentrate. Retail outlets and mail order. H.

Janco Sales (V)
11 Seymour Rd
Hampton Hill
TW12 1DD
01-979 7357
All-purpose washing liquid. Mail order.

Rolith International (V)
8 St George's Place
Brighton
East Sussex
BN1 4GB
0273 571221
Extensive range of household cleaners including oven, carpet, patio and toilet products as well as dishwasher liquid and rinse. Car-care products too. Sold under Little Green Shop brand name. Health stores, own outlets and mail order. H.

Simply Herbal (V)
19 West St
Wilton
Wilts
SP2 0DL
0722 743995
Laundry liquid, washing-up and worktop cleaner. Own stores and mail order.

The Soap Shop Ltd (V–) *soap flakes*
44 Sidwell St
Exeter
Devon
EX4 6NS
0392 215682
Home, washing, garden and car cleaning products. Own store and mail order.

Zohar (V)
Broom Lane Enterprises
23 Leicester Rd
Salford
Manchester
M7 0AS
061-792 7311
Household cleaners, washing-up liquid and detergent, soap pads. Chemists, department stores, supermarkets, kosher outlets and mail order.

Further information
Allergy sufferers should read about alternative medicine (chapter 4) and food (chapter 1).

DIY household cleaners
The ready-made cruelty-free cleaning products are excellent for all jobs around the home, but perhaps you might like to make a few of your own very cheap and simple preparations. The ingredients are easy to obtain, and many items are basic store cupboard essentials you will already have.

- *Good all-purpose cleaners*:
Diluted bleach or baking soda mixed to a paste with water.
- *Sinks and ovens*:
Clean with soda crystals in hot water.
- *Microwave ovens*:
Can be cleaned with the baking soda and water paste above. Remove odours by leaving an open box of baking soda inside the oven when not in use.
- *Furniture cleaners for wood and veneers*:
Store in a glass bottle out of children's reach.
  (a) Mix 1 teaspoon turpentine, 3 table-spoons linseed oil and 1¾ pints/1 litre hot water. Stir well and cool. Use on a cloth.
  (b) Three parts olive oil to one part vinegar, applied with a soft cloth.
  (c) One part lemon juice to two parts olive oil.
- *Window cleaner*:
Plain water with a dash of vinegar.
- *General stains*:
One teaspoon white vinegar to three teaspoons warm water. Leave to dry, apply a little soap powder and water solution to the stain, dry again and vacuum. Or try eucalyptus oil.
  This is good for fabrics, carpets and rugs, but check for colour fastness before using in quantity.
- *Oil stains*:
White chalk rubbed in before washing.
- *Linoleum*:
Mop with a cup of white vinegar mixed with 2 gallons/9 litres of water to clean and remove grease.
- *Toilet bowl*:
Vinegar or ammonia left overnight.
- *Mildew remover*:
Lemon juice or white vinegar, and salt.
- *Stained or burnt saucepans*:
Soak in baking soda solution before washing.
- *Air fresheners*:
Incense, pot-pourri or an open box of baking soda.
- *Fruit, grass and ballpoint stains*:
Methylated spirits.
- *Loosening dirt/restoring whiteness to clothes*:
Ammonia.
- *Water softener*:
Washing soda or ¼ cup white vinegar.
- *Brass cleaner*:
Salt.
- *Copper cleaner*:
Paste made of lemon juice, salt and flour.
- *Blocked pipes*:
Try bicarbonate of soda or 1–2 cups baking soda followed by ½ cup vinegar.
- *Car headlights, screen and mirrors*:
Use a damp cloth sprinkled with baking soda, then rinse off and dry.
- *Ant repellent*:
Wash inside surfaces with vinegar and water solution. A line of cream of tartar at the entrance stops ants.

- *Pet 'accidents'*:
Alcohol or ammonia mixed with hot water.
- *Fleas and ticks*:
Feed your animal brewer's yeast and garlic. Fennel, rue and rosemary repel fleas. Place sprigs under the furniture to clear your carpets.

Strange bedfellows

The products of animal abuse are not always apparent at first glance. Some household articles tell a story of great suffering. Not many people realize the pain which lies behind the production of a feather duvet. Yet the fillings of these and most pillows (down) comes from the slaughter-house. The cheaper duvets are often mixtures of duck, usually stated, and 'feather', which can mean a mixture containing chicken. The more duck down a duvet contains the more expensive it will be, but even these seem cheap when compared to Hungarian goose down quilts which retail at up to £300 for a double size.

Geese who are raised for down will have all their feathers plucked from their bodies four or five times during their miserable but short lives. Imagine how painful this is. Any woman who has plucked her eyebrows and found it uncomfortable will begin to appreciate what these animals go through to produce this unnecessary product.

Yet synthetic alternatives exist which are far cheaper and compare with the highest tog ratings available (the measure of warmth given to duvets). Not only that, but materials such as Fiberfill II, Polarguard and Thinsulate (chosen for Mount Everest expeditions) used for synthetic duvets are more durable and easier to dry when wet. Many can be machine-washed. Please reject feather-filled quilts and pillows. From the Living Without Cruelty point of view, 'Down is Out'!

Price comparisons of down and synthetic duvets

Costs are for a double bed-sized duvet with a 12 tog rating. The same tog ratings are available for both down and synthetics.

Synthetic	£29.00
Feather and down mix	£35.00
Duck down	£69.00
White duck	£79.00 (13.5 tog)
Hungarian goose	£295.00 (14 tog)

6 How Does Your Garden Grow?

Mary, Mary, quite unwary
How does your garden grow?
With BHC & 2,4-D
And the dead counted all in a row?

LK

As we slowly become aware of what we are eating, it may seem that nothing is safe. So much of our food is commercially adulterated, either through factory processes or by agricultural practices, that it is not surprising that the hard-pressed consumer may feel like giving up and giving in – and that, of course, is exactly what the agrochemical and food manufacturing giants would like. Unfortunately for them, however, consumers have begun to demand 'real food' which has taste and character. We have now largely rejected the mass-produced pap which masqueraded as the 'white sliced loaf' in favour of bread with a taste – real wholemeal with all the bits left in (the vitamins which nature puts into wheat) which were formally thrown away in order to make a whiter than white oblong of rubberized cotton wool.

Quality is slowly replacing quantity as the criterion by which our food should be judged. At the moment, however, the demand for healthier foods which are untainted by pesticides remains unsatisfied, and little wonder. . . .

Growers who adopt an organic policy must leave their land to lie fallow for a minimum of two years, and stringent checks are carried out to ensure that no new contamination happens. This, of course, is what the consumer wants – to be assured of organic quality – and the Soil Association are to be commended for upholding these laudable standards. The grower, however, unlike his crop-spraying counterpart who seems to be able to reap in subsidy upon subsidy for his destructive agricultural practices, gets nothing from the government to help ease him over the problems of conversion with all the worries that

this entails, such as a lack of income for at least two years. If a crop-spraying neighbour accidentally contaminates an organic grower's land, the latter loses his or her certificate of excellence. Life is certainly hard if you're a farmer with principles.

It is heartening to see, at long last, supermarket chains like Safeway, Tesco and Sainsburys introducing organic fruit and vegetables and some wines, along with other environmentally friendly lines with which they hope to tempt the aware consumer. But government and retailers should ensure that healthy eating is not undermined by unnecessarily high prices which could deter people from switching to what they know is a healthier option. Why not a penalty tax on the unhealthy, over-refined, additive-laden items which are continually foisted upon us?

Whilst we can pick and choose our way around the marketplace, there is one option which enables us to control the production ourselves – growing our own! If you have a garden, no matter how small, or even a window box or two, you can help yourself to an even healthier lifestyle by cultivating at least some produce organically. Not only will you be giving yourself valuable exercise out in the open air, you will be joining the ever-expanding ranks of those who are discovering what taste really means: home-grown tomatoes from varieties you just can't get in the shops; runner beans fresh from the garden; mange-tout for a stir-fry meal so much better than their tired and expensive shop-bought relatives; baby carrots scrubbed new from the earth with a taste you never thought could be so sweet.

There are no magic steps to establishing an organic garden, and as a convert myself the only advice I can offer is this. Treat every season as an adventure; try out something unusual and exotic to stretch your culinary expertise each year; stop worrying about 'failures' – you may lose out

BILL ODDIE
'Not only are pesticides cruelly tested on animals, they inevitably put wildlife at risk. Poisoned slugs can be eaten by hedgehogs and birds who themselves become victims of the chemical. Don't turn your garden into a deathtrap for wild creatures.'

sometimes, but so what? Re-evaluate your own standards of what you expect from your harvest – learn to accept that your vegetables will not all be absolutely uniform in size (they will invariably be bent or mis-shapen in some way, perhaps with a few chewed edges), but they will taste marvellous. Even if you live in a flat and are limited to a balcony or window sills, it's still possible to produce fresh herbs in pots, lettuces, cress, tomatoes, window-sill cucumbers, climbing beans, tub strawberries – even dwarf apple, pear and plum trees can be cultivated in tubs!

The caring gardener develops a closer affinity with the natural world around him/her, and becomes more aware of growth, life and death as the seasons pass each year. The idea of poisoning this closely interacting environment of which you are part becomes abhorrent. Every time you visit a garden centre, take a look at the vast array of chemicals for sale. Every one will have been tested on animals. Realize the chain of suffering which is entailed in producing a typical pesticide . . .

The chemical compound is tested on

laboratory animals. It will be smeared on their abraded skin, instilled into their eyes and dosed into them to discover the lethal dose. Paraquat was tested on rabbits at Hazleton Laboratories in Yorkshire in 1980. Extracts from the scientists' observation sheets revealed: 'Animal 5141 Male . . . large haemorrage from the penis, animal killed in extremis. . . . Animal 5165 Female . . . lethargy . . . animal quivering, all hind limb muscles held in contracted position (till day 2) . . . large anal haemorrhage'. Other entries at the higher dose levels recorded: '. . . severe respiratory distress . . . animal prostrate on cage floor, total loss of mobility'. Until eventually all the chart recorded, page upon page was 'Found dead . . . found dead'.

We are buying this every time we buy a pesticide.

The chemical may be utilized for both commercial and home use, where it may get into our food even though we scrub our vegetables before eating or cooking them; remain in our bodies where traces may be found in our breast milk, or stored in our livers to develop into possible problems later on in life; poison insect life, birds, small mammals, fish, farm animals . . . us; ruin the structure of the soil itself and contaminate water courses used by both animals and humans.

We are buying this every time we buy a pesticide.

There is also another unseen dimension to this situation. Small seed companies, many run for generations by family concerns, are being bought up at an alarming rate by the big agrochemical giants. Pressure and lobbying on EEC departments who govern agricultural practices has resulted in many vegetable and fruit varieties being made illegal, which means that selling seed or growing and selling produce from such seed could result in prosecution. Seed companies, who also face a heavy financial penalty for maintaining a disappearing variety, yield to pressure and delete the variety from their lists. Consumer choice is severely threatened as many old, hardy and wonderful fruits and vegetables disappear from the face of the earth, with the danger that the gene banks which maintain such a diversity of growing potential may vanish forever.

Behind this lies a sinister and worrying threat. As the seed companies become controlled by the chemical corporations, the old varieties which are made illegal are often being replaced with hybrids. Without getting too complex, essentially hybrids are very much more expensive and do not produce seed which can be saved for the following year. Generally they suit commercial interests, and often require large amounts of fertilizers and pesticides to maintain them . . . products which – what a coincidence – the new owners of the seed companies just happen to produce. And of course, with hybrids as a sole choice we would all have to buy new seed every year.

We are helping this to happen every time we buy a pesticide.

Is it worth it?

Organizations to help you go organic

The Soil Association
Freepost
Bristol
BS1 5YZ
0272 290661
Promotes organic farming and awards the Soil Association symbol to approved growers – look out for it in the shops. Anti-factory farming. Quarterly magazine, *The Living Earth*.

The Henry Doubleday Research Association (HDRA)
National Centre for Organic Gardening
Ryton on Dunsmore
Coventry
CV8 3LG
0203 303517
An excellent organization for gardeners. Lots of practical information and advice. Present *All Muck and Magic* series on Channel 4 TV. Members can help with growing experiments. Local groups. Also large retail suppliers of seed, materials and equipment. Catalogue.

The Organic Growers' Association
86–88 Colston St
Bristol 1
0272 299800

Organic Farm Foods (Wales) Ltd
Unit 25
Llambed Industrial Estate
Lampeter
Dyfed
SA48 8LT
0570 423280
Markets produce for Organic Growers, West Wales who are housed at the same address, Unit 26.

Chase (UK) Organic Seeds
Coombelands House
Addlestone
Weybridge
Surrey
KT15 1HY
0932 858511
Catalogue on request.

Suffolk Herbs
Sawyers Farm
Little Cornard
Sudbury
Suffolk
CO10 0NY
0787 227247
Catalogue on request.

E. W. King
Monks Farm
Pantlings Lane
Coggeshall Rd
Kelvedon
Essex
CO5 9PG
0376 70000
Seed catalogue on request.

Veganic Garden Suppliers
Gatehouse Cottage
Heath Farm Rd
Worsted
Norfolk
NR28 9GH

All Gain Organics
8 Netherlands Rd
New Barnet
Herts
EN5 1BN
01-449 1605
Suppliers of organic gardening products by mail order.

The Organic Wine Company
PO Box 81
High Wycombe
Bucks
0494 446557
Extensive catalogue on request. See also Chapter 1 for wine recommendations in our menus.

Vinceremos
Unit 10
Ashley Industrial Estate
Wakefield Rd
Ossett
W. Yorkshire WF5 9JD
0924 276393
Organic wines. Send for catalogue.

Also enquire for local suppliers of organic wines, beers and lagers. Some supermarkets now sell several kinds of organic wine.

Further reading
Silent Spring, Rachel Carson, Penguin.
The Seed Scandal, Socialist Countryside Group, from HDRA.
Successful Organic Gardening, Geoff Hamilton, Dorling Kindersley.
All Muck and Magic, Joy Larkcom, Channel 4 TV.
Food Growing Without Poisons, Meta Strandberg, Turnstone Books.
How to Make a Wildlife Garden, Chris Baines, Elm Tree Books.
A Month by Month Guide to Organic Gardening, Lawrence D. Hills, Thorsons.
The Holistic Gardener, M. Elphinstone and J. Langley, Thorsons.
The New Organic Food Guide, Alan Gear, J. M. Dent and Son.
Veganic Gardening, Kenneth Dalziel O'Brien, Thorsons. Successful gardening without any animal products at all.

7 Entertaining Abuse

Of all the disgraceful and abominable things
Making animals perform for the amusement of
* human beings is*
Utterly disgraceful and abominable.
Animals are animals and have their nature
And that's enough, it is enough, leave it alone.

A disgraceful and abominable thing I saw in a French
* circus*
A performing dog
Raised his back leg when he did not need to
He did not wish to relieve himself, he was made to
* raise his leg.*
The people sniggered. Oh how disgraceful and
* abominable.*
Weep for the disgrace, forbid the abomination.

Stevie Smith

The Animal Alcatraz

The zoo used to be the highlight of an otherwise tedious school summer break for me. Fascinated by all animals and birds and armed with sketchbook and camera, I would rush off to Regents Park with a packed lunch to spend whole days in rapt study, hoping I might establish 'contact' with one or two of the more lively exhibits. It was that 'wanting-to-be-close' feeling you have when you are young and 'mad' about animals. Of course, you never could get that close – the bars were always in the way, unless you opted for a camel ride or a chimpanzee's handshake after the tea party.

This is part of the appeal which keeps zoos in business. As children we're instinctively drawn towards animals, and parents look upon it as a good day out. Some advocates even argue that the experience is 'educational', but even if it is – and it can only be marginally so – at what price to the animals therein?

As I grew older and learnt more about animal behaviour and natural habitat, I began to realize that my hitherto blinkered visits had been to study and capture the activities of a moribund collection of dejected, bored and often psychotic creatures who had displayed all the symptoms of chronic neurosis before my very eyes. This was graphically illustrated one morning whilst I was sitting quite alone watching an eagle. This huge, magnificent bird swung repeatedly from his high perch into the netting overhead, eventually crashing to the ground where he sat staring out. I went over, hoping to get some close-up shots. Suddenly he flew at the mesh, ripping with his beak and talons in frustration. Then he fell back on to the concrete, wings trailing the floor, looking utterly defeated. He spent the next forty minutes staring at a bucket in the corner. In nature his territory would extend over miles of open countryside, but in the zoo his world had been reduced to the size of a taller-than-usual living room. After this I began to think about zoos in a new light and to choose the venues for days out with greater care, as more and more people are now doing.

Even the much needed refurbishment which some zoos have undertaken has done little to alter the fact that for the animals they are still contained within a prison, albeit a slightly more interesting one. Safari parks, though they have more space, are arguably little better, since the animals are exposed to all the rigours of the British weather and natural social groupings are still denied to many species. Not many people realize that the overbreeding 'successes' of such establishments mean that the cute and cuddly offspring may go off to vivisection laboratories or circuses, or are simply shot when they are no longer deemed to be a public attraction. Cubs and baby chimps often end up as the pawns of the beach photography trade.

Organizations such as Zoocheck monitor conditions within zoos, wildlife parks and dolphinaria. As a result of pressure from this and other quarters some of the more unsavoury establishments have been refused new licences, but there is still much to be done. The public can help by reporting to Zoocheck, and complaining to their local council who issue the licences and to the Department of the Environment. Better still, avoid these places altogether and teach yourselves and your children how animals

Yulia Denisenko (left) displays the results of two years' extensive 'training'.

really live by watching the marvellous nature programmes on TV. After all, you wouldn't get a balanced view on human behaviour and social interaction by visiting your local mental hospital.

Dolphinaria too are currently licensed under the Zoo Licensing Act. In a report on Morecambe's Marineland, Zoocheck examined the plight of Rocky, a twenty-four-year-old dolphin who had spent almost fifteen years in captivity, most of it in a twelve-metre-square pool and, since 1984, in virtual isolation from his own kind. He was considered underweight, sluggish and lethargic. He performed the same boring routine day after day to audiences who, it was suggested, regarded him as little more than a 'marine clown'. The pool was often dirty, with litter floating in it, the concrete sides crumbling. Since 1971 twelve dolphins had died at Morecambe.

People who visit such places learn nothing about dolphins, but are surely teaching their children, albeit unthinkingly, that such establishments are acceptable and that to laugh at these press-ganged prisoners is OK too. So please think twice before paying your entrance fee for that 'afternoon's entertainment'. You'll simply be part of the demand which requires an intelligent and sensitive creature to perform cheap tricks in a never-ending routine, and you'll be condemning it and countless others to a life of frustration, boredom and misery.

Unnatural acts

Circus Hassani, now resident at Chessington Zoo(!), was started by Coco the Clown because he was against performing animals, and is still run by the Hassani family. Jugglers, acrobats, high-wire and trapeze acts from all over the world entertain enthralled audiences with their displays of human skills, whilst Grimble the Clown steals the show with his polished slapstick routines. Circus Hassani was the forerunner of the developing, virtually animal-free 'New Circus' which is now establishing itself worldwide.

'Old Circus', with animals, on the other hand, provides an outdated and degrading spectacle, particularly when wild animals are made to perform demeaning tricks in a sawdust ring which may well be their only place of exercise. Travelling circuses keep their animals cooped up in 'beast wagons' as they go from town to town, and once encamped the animals continue to live in their mobile prisons.

Concern has long been voiced over dubious training methods, but outright cruelty here is difficult to ascertain. Suffice it to say, as with any area of life, that cruel animal trainers must exist amongst those who practise methods based upon the reward principle. Anybody who knows about horses, for example, can appreciate that kindness and patience bring far more from the animal than do beating and harsh treatment. On the other hand, even an animal as strong as that will submit eventually to fear and deprivation methods at the hands of an ignorant egotist. With these and other domesticated animals such as camels and llamas, their suffering, it could be argued, is no more than that of a horse used on the show-jumping circuits of Europe – in itself an area far from ideal in animal welfare terms. At least these circus animals can, on some sites, have access to grazing and better exercise facilities, unlike the wild animals who, for safety reasons, must remain cooped up. They undoubtedly suffer most.

I witnessed conditions inside one small travelling show on a blisteringly hot day in July 1989. Behind the razzamatazz for public view lay scenes of chronic deprivation as the animals endured the thirty-week stint around Britain: big cats living in an open-sided lorry; a solitary elephant, a chain around one ankle, whose mobile home was the size of a small furniture van; and a pathetic, solitary monkey who sat and stared at me with accusing eyes from his T-chest sized prison – a naturally social animal denied his own kind and prone, as a keeper confided, to viciousness through a life of utter tedium and frustration. The lionesses, an endangered type, looked at me with eyes which were flat and dead. They later performed their stereotyped routine with the begrudging reluctance found in those sold to slavery.

The big cats I saw, so desperately deprived, may never know release from their frustrations. Some however, are luckier. When the Cross Brothers circus folded, no one wanted the tigers and they were due to be shot, but Zoocheck had other ideas. A frantic race against time led to a sanctuary being established in India. Zoocheck

'Yes, I can see in the future circus wholly dependent on human skills, without any animals, but the demand has got to come from the public first to get the circus to change.'
Author's interview with a member of a prominent circus family who wished to remain unnamed.

trustee and founder, actress Virginia McKenna, described the release of the six ex-circus tigers into their new jungle home.

> 'The tigers took their first steps into the lush tropical bush. I found it hard to believe they had never walked through grass, bathed in a pool, had space to move at will, lain in the shade of rocks and trees in the heat of the day. The Cross Brothers tigers will never be truly free. Long years of appalling confinement . . . mean that they can only enjoy a "kind of freedom", but in the 15 acres of their new jungle home, their days in the beast wagon will hopefully become a fading nightmare.'

Although one tiger sadly died through illness, the others have adapted well to their 'kind of freedom' and are living proof against the myth that animals born in captivity cannot adjust to a freer, wilder life, given a little human help.

Facilities for animals within static outfits such as that housed within the notorious Blackpool Tower can, if anything, be even worse. There, during the season, elephants, horses, big cats and all live in the old cellars, some animals tethered by chains and only brought out for exercise periods, parades or performances. After a sustained campaign Lord Delfont, then head of First Leisure Services, who own the Tower, pledged not to renew the lease, on its expiring in 1990, to any circus with animals. For the animals' sake, let's hope this is one promise that is kept and that the circus tradition will continue at Blackpool – minus the animals.

Concerned protest has also persuaded many local councils to stop leasing their land to animal circuses. Some 120 authorities now impose a ban, though this does not affect private land in the council's area. Caring citizens can write to local councillors urging them to allow only non-animal companies permission to perform.

Business people can refuse to display posters in their shops, and the often illegal flyposting which many circuses carry out can be reported to local council cleansing departments who will remove posters, as will British Telecom when they are illegally fixed to poles and equipment boxes. Ask shopkeepers you know if they would consider removing posters accepted inadvertently, and explain your concern.

Of course, the best thing we can all do is to shun the animal circus in favour of its humane alternative and to show our children all the fun and real skills of human accomplishment.

Virginia McKenna

'Bill [Travers] and I made *Born Free* in 1964 and were in Kenya filming in 1968 when Pole Pole was caught by an animal trapper. She was to be presented to London Zoo to replace Dicksie, who had died a year earlier. We heard about her, and asked President Kenyatta if the departure might be delayed so she could appear in the film we were making, *An Elephant Called Slowly*. After filming, I wanted to ask for Pole Pole to be released, but she'd already been promised to Regent's Park, and if not her, another infant would have been caught in her place. She was two and a half years old.

'Pole Pole died in London Zoo, alone, on 17 October 1983. She was seventeen. In the wild, elephants can live 50 or 60 years if man does not interfere. When Pole Pole died in that concrete cell, a disturbed, pitiful and lonely prisoner, we knew we had to do something, and almost overnight Zoocheck came into being. I suppose it's our way of contributing something to what I believe is really a single issue – Animal Rights.

'People are fed up with what we're doing to the world, to the animals . . . to ourselves. There's no doubt that Living Without Cruelty is here to stay. There are so many young people who already know about animal exploitation and are getting involved.

'The one thing I do deeply regret is that I didn't become vegetarian years ago. My own daughter woke up to it all when she was only seven years old. It took me longer, but now I feel so well on it; the meals are delicious and much more interesting to cook. I love creative cooking, but I've found when I'm busy that the vegetarian 'convenience' foods are very good: Granose spreads, for instance, and Realeat products. Sometimes, during a hectic run in the theatre, I cook up Vegeburgers for tea – delicious. At my local Waitrose you can even get pizza made with vegetarian cheese.

'It would be great if one day there were cruelty-free or "alternative" supermarkets which sold everything, even clothes and shoes. I would so love not to wear leather shoes, but it's one area I do find difficult. Cosmetics, on the other hand, are easy and I use Beauty Without Cruelty both at home and in the theatre. I like wearing their products – the name says it all.

'Since becoming involved in the animal movement life for me has certainly taken a positive turn, even though I'm often dealing with negative elements. There comes a time in life when you have to stand up for what you believe in, and you only regret it later if you do have these feelings and don't act upon them. My son was speaking to a woman scientist about animal experiments. She told him, "There's nothing I wouldn't do, *nothing*, to gain knowledge, to understand, to find out more." I think that's one of the most terrifying things I have ever heard.

'I believe we've reduced ourselves by blocking off the "spiritual" part of us which allows us to know compassion. Society tries to put us into boxes, and we're trying to struggle out of the boxes and speak up for the truth. Of course, when you do this you're challenging the establishment. Then you attract "labels" like crank, loony, lefty etc. What does this mean? It's almost a compliment to attract derogatory remarks, because then you know you're on the right track.

'The human race is very arrogant. We do everything for ourselves. We even seem to have a prerogative on souls. I was at a conference listening to a Catholic bishop who said that he couldn't pray for animals because they had no souls. Somebody stood up and shouted "Shame!" I thought so too.

'When I was younger I used to care about being liked and accepted. I no longer worry about this or care how I'm labelled as long as I'm not like them – the abusers and maintainers of the systems of cruelty. It's *never* too late to change yourself, your diet, your lifestyle. And I should know!'

Sick pics

It seems that everywhere animals are being used so that some cheap entrepreneur can make a quick 'buck' or two. This is graphically illustrated by the beach photographers abroad, who foist on to unthinking tourists a tired, sick, often drugged baby chimpanzee or lion cub for that 'picture to remember'.

Captured in the wild by poachers who have to shoot the mother and other protective adults, these orphans are smuggled into Europe to become the focus of this tawdry trade. The animals, often with their teeth and claws pulled out, sometimes burnt with cigarette ends or beaten into submission, are plied along the seafronts of the Mediterranean until they become too heavy or too dangerous to control with drugs. At the age of four or five chimps are usually drowned. Lion or tiger cubs, often the residue from zoos and circuses, suffer the same fate or are dumped in the mountains where they starve to death. Another baby replaces them until it too. . . . This is an illegal trade, but the authorities usually turn a blind eye. If you're approached for a photograph:

- First, say *no*.
- If you can, discreetly try to take your own photographs of the operator in action, but be careful. Do not confront or argue with these people, who usually work in groups of two or three. They are criminal types, operating illegally, and are not afraid to resort to intimidation.
- Report the matter as quickly as possible to the local police. Be prepared to make a fuss. Authorities often do nothing, but on the Costa del Sol they will confiscate reported animals. However, you must act as soon as you see the photographer in operation.
- Note the time, date and place they were seen working, plus a description of the people involved. How persistent was the photographer? Note the condition of the animal. Is this person operating in a particular area throughout your holiday?
- If in Spain, and particularly if a chimpanzee is spotted, contact the local IPPL rescuer in Gerona, Simon and Peggy Templar (see address listed, and make a note of it before you travel). Let them know immediately that you've spotted a chimp in trouble. Do this whether the police have confiscated it or not, and let them have details of the incident.
- If the photographer enters your hotel with the chimp, this is breaking Spanish sanitary rules. Report him immediately to the hotel manager – not the desk clerk, who is likely to be receiving money for allowing them in. Insist that the manager calls the police. There is a risk of infection. Some rescued animals have been tested hepatitis-positive. It only takes a bite or a scratch, and you might be too.
- As soon as you return home:

(1) Write a strongly worded letter to the Spanish Embassy telling them of the incident and stating you will no longer visit their country as a tourist until they take positive and strong action against this illegal activity.

(2) Contact your MEP with details, too. He needs information, as initiatives through the EEC can have an effect and at present Spain denies that this activity takes place at all!

(3) Write to the tour company, asking why tourists aren't warned in brochures and told to avoid being photographed. Press them to include leaflets and articles about the subject.

(4) Send all your information to the groups listed who are compiling dossiers.

(5) Contact Monkey World, who are co-ordinating the rescue of beach chimps. They are operating an adoption scheme (from £50 per annum) for those rescued, and need help from humans willing to support an individual chimp.

Other delights which await the holidaymaker include real-life roundabout ponies, bought up after a lifetime of human servitude to spend nine-hour shifts toiling endlessly round and round in the fairground until they drop.

But of all the 'entertainments' on offer, the bullfight must rank as one of the most offensive. Yet it continues to attract tourists despite pleas from animal welfare groups. This financial support helps the bullfight survive. Apart from the bloody 'spectacle' seen by the public, a lot of behind-the-scenes work goes on to ensure that the bull is suitably weakened and disorientated before he goes out to meet the heroic human with his red cape.

The use of drugs and laxatives seems widespread. One vet stated that huge quantities of Epsom salts were added to the bulls' drinking water. Anti-mugging sprays or vaseline were put into the animals' eyes to blur their vision, and tranquillizing and hallucinatory drugs were administered. Their horns were shaved to impair the bulls' judgement of distances, and the animals were beaten repeatedly with sandbags.

In Portugal, holidaymakers are lulled into a false sense of security by posters proclaiming: 'No bulls are killed.' This is untrue. When the animal becomes too weak to 'fight', through injury or blood loss, it's killed – you just don't get to see it. Once again, you can easily say *no* to suffering. Why ruin a good holiday?

Your holiday may also be spoilt if you come across a distressed or cruelly treated animal. This often happens, and the feelings of helplessness are exacerbated if you cannot speak the language and know little of the laws or animal rescue services of that country. Before charging in, remember that an animal in obvious pain will bite and may be rabid.

UK visitors to Greece can arm themselves with a specially produced leaflet from the Greek Animal Welfare Fund. *Hints to Holidaymakers* offers helpful advice on what to do if you encounter such a problem.

Country pursuits

Closer to home we have our own version of the blood-for-fun rituals. The excuses for the hunting of wild animals with dogs are many and varied and when examined can all be dismissed, particularly the truly laughable proposition which promotes hunting as a conservation exercise. It simply boils down to the fact that an extremely small number of people wish to amuse themselves at the expense of the animals concerned, be they foxes, stags, pregnant deer with young, otters, mink or hares.

'Have you ever seen a chicken house after a fox has been in?' they ask, searching for justification. Well yes, as a matter of fact I have, and a pretty flimsy, hotch-potch of a building it was, giving ingress to any passing animal. The fox, being very intelligent, obviously thought the place a push-over and had a free-for-all at the expense of the hens. Such is their way.

On the other hand, my own land housed forty or so rescued battery hens and ducks in secure accommodation with free-range access. Some of my birds, after they had learnt to walk again, did eventually die from old age. Secure accommodation and proper husbandry meant there was never any fox trouble. People who lose birds in this way usually should look no further than their own shortcomings.

A great deal is also made about lamb-taking, but fox experts have found this to be a fallacy. As an opportunist, the fox will take lambs born dead, or abandoned runts, but little evidence exists which supports the contention of farmers that foxes are responsible for severe lamb losses. Between 1 and 3 million new-born lambs die annually within days of birth, due mainly to hunger, exposure and poor husbandry. Perhaps the farming fraternity should stop looking for a scapegoat and put their own house in order?

The mentality of the hunt is that which sustained bear baiting and cock fighting and continues to promote dog fights, badger baiting and hare coursing. Class has nothing to do with it; arrogance, stupidity and a general lack of brain cells, quite a lot. Contrary to popular belief, 'country people' generally do not welcome the hunt, who usually tear about with little regard for property or person, breaking farmers' fences, churning up crops and gardens, and, when hounds run out of control, tearing apart villagers' pets.

Those who enjoy an exhilarating ride around the still beautiful British countryside can go drag hunting and follow a previously laid artificial scent trail. Pre-planning the route means dangerous or out-of-bounds areas can be avoided, upsetting no one, whilst interesting and attractive rides can be selected to suit all classes of riding ability.

Every year in Great Britain alone some four hundred organized hunts bring exhaustion, suffering and, finally death to between twelve and fourteen thousand foxes, up to a hundred deer, four hundred wild mink and six thousand coursed and hunted hares, and still pose a very tangible threat to the fast-disappearing otter. Hunts provide a very close-knit and varied social life for members and supporters, so if you have the means to keep a horse and are invited to participate at least keep some perspective and investigate the facts from the animals' point of view if you are in any doubt about giving a resounding 'No, thank you'. The League Against Cruel Sports (LACS) produces excellent educational material on all aspects of the hunt and can put riders in touch with their nearest drag hunt. Ask them for advice, and if you have any complaints about your local hunt, via trespass or damage, or have incidents to report, do let them know immediately.

Badger baiting is another activity carried out by mentally deficient individuals in pursuit of a 'fun' time. The badger sett is destroyed by digging out the terrified animal, sending in terriers to flush it out. Once in the open the gaiety begins and the faces of the hunters light up as the badger is smashed about the head with a spade to weaken it, so giving the dogs an easier time. Badgers are often removed in this way, later to be baited by dogs at an organized evening's 'entertainment'. LACS has mounted an extensive campaign to save the badger, and local badger protection groups exist across the country. You can join and help too.

A survey of setts estimated that 15 per cent are blocked up on any one day. This is done by farmers, property developers and fox hunts, seeking to deprive a hunted fox a refuge. Badgers can suffocate in the setts or starve if they cannot dig themselves out again through the debris stuffed into the hole.

Hare coursing is a tiny minority bloodsport with only a thousand or so subscribers. Seventy-two per cent of the population would support a ban on this activity, where two greyhounds compete to catch a wild hare on a coursing field. Some escape, many do not. Suffering is indisputable, and many hares are torn apart as the two dogs have a 'tug-of-war' over the creature. Parliament, with many pro-bloodsports MPs, has consistently defeated bills calling for a ban. Often the vote has been close and it is here that

voters can bring pressure to bear on their elected representatives. Reports from both inside and outside the coursing fraternity record the whoops of delight from the crowd of spectators at hares squealing in terror and pain. Dame Janet Fookes MP has described coursing events as 'all that is worst in human gatherings'.

Fishing is also regarded by the animal movement as a blood sport. However, many thousands of people, often with caring attitudes in other areas, participate in this activity and regard it as an opportunity to get out into the countryside for peace, quiet and relaxation. The careless fisherman who discards line and tackle leaves a trail of mayhem in his wake, with killed or badly injured birds twisting themselves to death in his rubbish or slowly disintegrating inside due to ingesting his spilt lead shot. He is rightly condemned by his more responsible peers. There is now firm scientific evidence that fish do feel pain and distress when hooked, with increasing heart rate and breathlessness when held in nets (as in sport fishing competitions). Even when released, hook injuries and the resultant trauma often lead to death. The put-them-back angler can at least reduce suffering by using barbless weights, and all fishermen can stop using lead. Alternatives are in the shops now and have been for some time, so there is no excuse to continue to damage the environment or poison the wildlife through lack of care.

Fishermen with 'Living Without Cruelty' sympathies shouldn't think they're being presented with an all-or-nothing course of action. Animal societies are full of ex-hunters, ex-butchers, ex-factory farmers and ex-fishermen, but you must draw that line for yourselves. One word of warning though: sometimes, often a long time after the 'seed' has been planted, non-fishing partners report that the tackle has been relegated to the back of the garage or has found its way to a car boot sale!

A racing certainty

Horse and dog racing are also areas which lead to animal abuse. Despite the money involved, only a handful of animals, usually the very successful and well-publicized like Red Rum, get to live out their days in peace and tranquillity with caring owners. For the many who don't make it, the pet food industry awaits or continental

Brown Trix about to break his shoulder at Becher's Brook during the 1989 Grand National. He had to be destroyed, along with Seeandem (out of picture), also fatally injured.

slaughter. A few lucky ones may end up in sanctuaries. Ex-racing greyhounds are often sold for vivisection.

The business itself has done much to clean up its image, yet allegations of drug abuse still occur, even in 'respectable' establishments. Steeplechasing also raises criticism because the fences are often way beyond a horse's capability. Nature may have designed the equine body to be able to jump, and I know from my own experiences that many horses do enjoy it; however, the big fences in prestige events such as the Grand National have to be seen up close to be believed. It is a staggeringly cruel and testing race of endurance, which usually claims several fatalities each year. When Brown Trix died after falling at Bechers Brook during the 1989 event, and almost drowning in the stream at its foot, course officials at long last agreed to fill in the brook and flatten out the landing area at this notorious fence. One wonders how many more will have to die before the race is abandoned or the fences at least reduced to a reasonable height.

Greyhound racing has always been tainted with a rather tacky image, and has been dubbed the poor man's horse racing. Home Office statistics show that in 1988, 373 greyhounds were used in animal experiments. Investigations have revealed that ex-racing greyhounds were sold to labs through an animal supply company, Denisu. Since then this company has closed down, but others will undoubtedly step in and take the business. The National Greyhound Racing Club, appalled by the revelations, are to tighten the ruling on the re-homing of retired dogs, introducing a register and banning owners from racing for life if they supply dogs to labs. Greyhounds have been used in heart and respiratory experiments, including one in which twenty-one dogs were made to smoke four high-tar cigarettes an hour for five hours.

If you like to have a flutter at the bookmakers why not stick to cricket, tennis, boxing or other human sports? Start doing the football pools instead.

Not all tomato ketchup

The final area in the entertainment sphere is that of films, TV, video and advertising, where sadly, the opportunity for abuse arises all too often. As individuals there is little we can do here unless we are involved in the industry itself, and we can only boycott the results when and if we know that cruelty has been involved.

In Britain there is no law which demands that a vet or animal protection representative be present during the filming of animal scenes. It is left to the industry to police itself. Responsible directors do undertake consultation; the majority do not. In America the situation is far worse and almost anything seems to be condoned. Many animals are injured and killed on film sets. Despite the existence of humane societies available to inspect questionable scenes, many film makers seem content to let the animals suffer the consequences of their supposed artistry.

When *Ben Hur* was made, starring Charlton Heston, much was made of the notorious chariot race in which several horses were reported to have met their deaths. It is impossible to quantify how many animals have died since then in film-making, as there seem to be no records of incidents. Things come to light when set workers and sometimes the actors themselves complain. In the film *Heavens' Gate*, starring Warren Beatty, five horses were reportedly blown to pieces. Trip wires were used to make others fall, a cockfight was staged for real, and a dozen live chickens were decapitated so that their blood could be smeared on the actors. Well done, director Michael Comino. Another Warren Beatty film, *Reds*, which he directed, is also listed as unacceptable by the American Humane Society. In the otherwise excellent film *The Killing Fields*, a live ox was bled at the neck for the camera. In the acclaimed film *Apocalypse Now* a live water buffalo was macheted to death in a scene depicting ritual sacrifice, whilst the more recent *Babette's Feast* promoted the eating of turtle and other animals in copy-cat 'feasts' all over 'smart' America. This is one area where stringent legislation is urgently needed.

Many people may feel that animals in entertainment are outside the mainstream areas of animal abuse. Not so. Even if blatant cruelty can be set aside – and in some aspects of training it cannot – there is a greater cruelty, if anything, in confining an animal inside a world it can pace out in seconds, and in inflicting chronic deprivation so that natural instincts and behaviour are suppressed. Therein lies madness.

Many readers will recall a TV news item in

the summer of 1989 which showed a polar bear at Bristol Zoo. Although in a larger compound there, he paced within the twelve-foot square area of his previous confinement in a circus wagon . . . so many steps to the right . . . so many steps to the left . . . over, and over, and over again. He had gone quite mad. A Zoocheck survey found that of the twenty polar bears in British zoos, twelve were psychotic. Around 70 per cent born in captivity die before their first birthday. In the wild, natural losses run between 10 and 30 per cent.

Do we really want to take our children to see the mentally deranged, the pitiful, the sad, the angry and the frustrated creatures whom we imprison for the sake of a 'day out'? Is this what is meant by 'educational'? How can we expect to relate to animals completely out of sync with nature? Is it really acceptable to laugh at a dignified creature who has been made to balance on one leg, or jump through a hoop, for our amusement? Do our sniggers hide perhaps a deeper embarrassment as we grin at his difficulty in balancing on a ball? Perhaps, as with all these things, we would realize the extent of what we condone if we imagined ourselves in their place. As the poet Ralph Hodgson suggested:

> 'Twould ring the bells of Heaven
> The wildest peal for years,
> If parson lost his senses
> And people came to theirs,
> And he and they together
> Knelt down with angry prayers
> For tamed and shabby tigers
> And dancing dogs and bears,
> And wretched blind pit ponies,
> And little hunted hares.

Since 1917, when that poem was written, we have seen the last of the pit ponies. The rest has yet to come.

'New Circus' companies to look out for

UK
Circus Hassani★
Ra Ra Zoo★
Circus Senso★
Circus Burlesque★
Ship of Fools★
Zippo's Family Circus

Other European
Centre National des Arts du Cirque (France)
Archoa (France)
Volante Jean Palancy (France)
Os Paxaros (Spain)

USA/Canada
Hot and Neon★
Cirque du Soleil (French Canadian)★

Australia
Circus Oz★
The Flying Fruit Fly Circus★

Other
The Shenyange Acrobatic Troupe (China)

★ means no animals, even 'domesticated'.

Films listed as unacceptable by the American Humane Society

1979   Savage of the Cannibal Gods
Tiger's Claw
The Chisolm's Prophecy
Arabian Nights
Fist of Fury. Part 2
Mister Mike's Mondo Video
Apocalypse Now
The Black Cobra

1980   The Mountain Men
Tom Horn
The Lion Speaks
Tundra
The Long Riders
Southern Comfort

1981   Legend of the Lone Ranger
Lion of the Desert

Moments of Truth
Heaven's Gate
Crocodile
The Snakefist versus the Dragon
Heartland
Reds

1982 *Conan the Barbaric*
First Blood
Triumphs of a Man Called Horse
Suburbia
Never Say Never Again

1984 *Antarctica*
Conan the Destroyer
Heart of the Stag
Yellowhair and the Fortress of Gold
Cannibal Holocaust

1985 *Faces of Death. Parts 1 and 2*

Specialist groups

Zoocheck
Cherry Tree Cottage
Coldharbour
Dorking
Surrey
RH5 4LW
0306 712091
Primarily zoos, wildlife safari parks and dolphinaria.

Captive Animals Protection Society (CAPS)
36 Braemore Court
Kingsway
Hove
East Sussex
BN3 4FG
0273 737756
Performing animals.

World Society for the Protection of Animals
106 Jermyn St
London SW1Y 6EE
01-839 3026
Bullfights and beach photographers.

Alternativa Para La Liberacion Animal
Apdo
Postal 38.109-28080
Madrid
Spain
Bullfights.

The Conservation Dept
World Wildlife Fund UK
Panda House
Godalming
Surrey
GU7 1QU
0483 426444
Beach photographers.

International Primate Protection League (IPPL)
Claremont Hall
Pentonville Rd
London N1 9HR
01-837 7227
Beach photographers and chimpanzees.

Simon and Peggy Templar
Can Miloca
Breda
Gerona
Spain
972 870888
Local IPPL contact will travel to collect chimpanzees who have been confiscated by the authorities or rescued. Please note: facilities for primates only.

Jim Cronin
Monkey World
Nanoose Longthorne
East Stoke
Bindon Abbey
Wool
Dorset
0929 462537
Co-ordinating rescue operation and sanctuary for chimps, especially adults, to rehabilitate them after confiscation from beach photographers abroad. Adopt-a-chimp scheme now running.

Mrs G. Ware
Greek Animal Welfare Fund
11 Lower Barn Rd
Purley
Surrey
CR2 1HY
Send s.a.e. for leaflet, *Hints to Holidaymakers*.

RSPCA (Special Investigations and Operations Dept)
Causeway
Horsham
West Sussex
RH12 1HG
0403 64181
Dog fighting and badger baiting. Chief Inspector Frank Milner and his team treat all information received with the utmost discretion.

League Against Cruel Sports
Sparling House
83–87 Union St
London SE1 1SG
01-407 0979
Hunting and coursing.

The Hunt Saboteurs Association
PO Box 87
Exeter
EX4 3TX
Direct action group to disrupt hunts and save wildlife. Can be hazardous.

National Federation of Badger Groups
16 Ashdown Gardens
Sanderstead
South Croydon
Surrey
CR2 9DR
Send s.a.e. for advice on setting up a local protection group. Local list opposite.

Campaign for the Abolition of Angling
PO Box 14
Romsey
Hants
SO5 9NN

Adrian Evans
London Festival of New Circus
18b St Stephen's Avenue
London W12 8JH
Organizers of the bi-annual Festival of New Circus. This prestige event will be staged next during the last two weeks of July 1990 and bi-annually thereafter. Details from above. No wild animal acts, some dogs and horses, but rarely used, and then not to perform tricks.

Further reading
Beyond The Bars, Virginia McKenna, Bill Travers and Jonathon Ray, Thorsons.
Outfoxed, Mike Huskisson, League Against Cruel Sports.
The Hunt and the Anti-Hunt, Philip Windeatt, Pluto Press.
The Politics of Hunting, Richard Thomas, Gower Publishing Co.
Running with the Fox, David McDonald, Unwin Paperbacks. Britain's fox expert.
The Goblet of Delight, Jeanette Arnold. For children.
Badger, Anthony Masters, Methuen. Novel for children.
Hunter's Moon, Garry Kilworth, Unwin Hyman.
New Circus, Reg Bolton, The Calouste Gulbenkian Foundation, 98 Portland Place, London W1N 4ET (01-636 5513/7).
Urban Foxes, Steven Harris, Whittet Books.
Run with the Hare, Linda Newbery, Armada. For teenagers.
The Cold Moon, Aeron Clement, Penguin.
Out of the Darkness, Chris Ferris, Unwin Paperbacks.

Local badger protection groups

Avon Badger Group
15 Stanway
Bitton
Bristol
BS15 6JU

Berkshire Badger Group
c/o Dinton Pastures Country Park
Hurst
Reading
RG10 0TH

Binfield Badger Group (Berks)
The Old Oak
Coppid
Beach Hill
London Rd
Wokingham
RG11 5PJ

BROCK
61 Holmbush Rd
St Austell
Cornwall

Bucks Badger Group
'Oakleigh'
Perks Lane
Prestwood
Gt Missenden
Bucks
HP16 0JE

Clwyd Badger Group (North)
Brookdale
Ledsham Rd
Little Sutton
South Wirral
L66 4QW

Cumbria Trust for Nature Conservation Badger
Group
Church Street
Ambleside
Cumbria
LA22 0BU

Dartmoor Badger Protection League
Riverside Cottage
Poundsgate
Devon
TQ13 7NU

Derbyshire Wildlife Trust Badger Group
Elvaston Castle Country Park
Derby

Durham Badger Group
County Conservation Trust
52 Old Elvet
Durham
DH1 3HN

East and North Yorks Badger Protection
Society
Station Cottage
Warren-le-Street
Malton
N. Yorkshire
YO17 9TW

East Kent Badger Group
Park House
Stelling Minis
Canterbury
CT4 6AN

Essex Badger Protection Society
84 Clyde Way
Rise Park
Romford
Essex

Forest of Dean Badger Patrol
Lorien
Mill Hill
Bream
Gloucestershire

Glamorgan Badger Group
Carreg Pentwyn
Mynydd Alltyrgu
Ystalyfera
West Glamorgan

Gloucestershire Badger Group
15 Park Court
Park Rd
Stroud
GL5 2HQ

Gwent Badger Group
5 Deans Hill
Chepstow
Gwent
NP6 5SG

Gwynedd Badger Group
19 Ffordd y Mynydd
Llanllechid
Gwynedd

Hants Badger Link
c/o The Southampton Common Centre
Cemetery Rd
The Common
Southampton
SO1 2NM

Hastings Badger Protection Society
15 Lynwood Close
St Leonards-on-Sea
East Sussex
TN34 7HZ

Herefordshire Nature Trust Badger Group
Salsdon Cottage
Buckcastle Hill
Bridstow
Ross on Wye
HR9 6QF

Herts and Middlesex Badger Group
8 Willowside
London Colney
St Albans
AL2 1DP

High Peak Badger Group
4 Stonecliff Terrace
Cliff Rd
Fairfield
Buxton
Derbyshire
SK17 7NN

Isle of Wight Natural History Society
116 Osborne Rd
East Cowes
Isle of Wight
PO32 6RZ

Lancs Badger Group
c/o Cuerden Park Wildlife Centre
Shady Lane
Bamber Bridge
Preston
PR5 6AU

Leicestershire Badger Group
Honeysuckle Cottage
Pickwell
Melton Mowbray
LE14 2RA

Moss Brock
71 Hopefield Avenue
Frecheville
Sheffield
South Yorkshire
S12 4XD

New Forest Animal Protection Group
15 Beaulieu Close
New Milton
Hampshire
BH25 5UX

Northants Badger Group
87 The Medway
Daventry
NN11 4QX

Northumberland Badger Group
Hancock Museum
Barras Bridge
Newcastle upon Tyne
Tyne & Wear
NE2 4PT

Oxfordshire Badger Group
14a New Street
Chipping Norton
Oxon
OX8 5JJ

Plymouth RSPCA Wildlife Group
4 Waterloo Terrace
Kelly Bray
Callington
Cornwall
PL17 8ET

Shropshire Badger Group
Heatherdown
Elson
Ellesmere
SW12 9JN

South Yorkshire Badger Group
10 Main St
Ulley
Sheffield
S31 0YD

Staffs Badger Group
Westview
Longnor
Penkridge
Stafford
ST19 5QN

Suffolk Wildlife Trust Badger Group
Park Cottage
Saxmundham
Suffolk
IP17 1DQ

Surrey Badger Protection Society
15 Sanderstead Court Avenue
Sanderstead
South Croydon
CR2 9AU

Warwickshire Nature Conservation Trust
Badger Group
206 Gretna Rd
Coventry
West Midlands
CV3 6DR

West Country Badger Patrol
PO Box 94
Cheltenham
Gloucestershire
GL50 9AB

West Kent Badger Group
1a Bower Mount Rd
Maidstone
Kent

West Surrey Badger Group
14 Orchard Way
Send
Woking
Surrey
GU23 7HS

West Wales Badger Group
7 Bryn Morlais
Bryn
Llanelli
Dyfed
SA14 8QJ

West Yorkshire Badger Monitor
96 Headfield Rd
Dewsbury
W. Yorkshire
WF12 9JG

Wexford Badger Watch Group
Clonroche
Enniscorthy
Co Wexford
Eire

Wirral and Cheshire Badger Group
4 Melksham Drive
Irby
Wirral
Merseyside
L61 4YE

Worcestershire Badger Society
24 Cowleigh Rd
Malvern
Hereford and Worcester
WR14 1QD

8 A Nation of Animal Lovers?

The Bird in the Cage

'Pretty Joey, pretty Joe . . .'
The people come, the people go.
Each windstir whispers, each gleam of sun –
A bird in a cage is not worth one.

'Pretty Joey, pretty Joe . . .'
He hops from swing to perch to swing.
'Oh what a clever bird it is!
Shall we teach him how to sing?

Tweet, tweet, Joey. Tweet, tweet Joe . . .
Here's some water; here's some seed;
Here's a nice clean sanded cage;
Here is everything you need.

Pretty Joey, pretty Joe . . .
How he hops and jumps and swings!'
Pretty Joey, would you rather
Never have been born with wings?

'Pretty Joey, pretty Joe . . .'
The people come, the people go.
Each windstir whispers, each gleam of sun –
A bird in the cage is not worth one.

Fay Chivers

Carla Lane

'I can't remember a time when I didn't care about animals. They've always been a part of my life. I had parents who were in love with each other and with life, and the atmosphere at home taught me kindness and consideration both to animals and to one another. We always had cats, dogs and other creatures sharing our home, and I used to buy scruffs from the market with my pocket money and bring them home. I recall when we lived in the country the neighbours were always shooting rats and 'pests', and I'd shoo them away in an attempt to save them. I'd be upset when they were blasted, but my father never criticized my actions; he only said "Don't get bitter."'

'I've been vegetarian for twenty-three years now. I get terribly upset by what we do to animals, but I make myself know, make myself confront. I feel it's the least we can do. They are so helpless, and live or die according to our dictatorship of the earth.

'Years ago, when I was at a writers' summer school, we were having lunch and a bee flew in and couldn't get out. People were swiping at it with newspapers and trying to hit it with their spoons. Eventually a man hit it into a bowl of custard, and I rescued it. They all laughed at me, of course, and made sniggering remarks. People might say, "Well, it was only a bee", but that's not the point. It's the attitude we adopt towards other creatures which disturbs me – the attitude which assumes their life doesn't matter to them, is of no consequence.

'I get very annoyed when people say that you care more about animals than you do about people. Caring doesn't and shouldn't stop just because the species changes. You don't package up your concern into little boxes to be dished out to the most deserving cases. If you care about subjugation, oppression and exploitation, you care, no matter who's on the receiving end.

'No one can shoulder all the sorrows of the world, but Living Without Cruelty gives us the chance to remove some of the misery. If you think about it, who wants to live *with* cruelty?'

Martin Shaw

'My childhood in Birmingham was very ordinary, but I always knew I'd be an actor as I was so lousy at everything else, so I went to drama school at eighteen. In 1972, I discovered vegetarianism.

'I was already enamoured with the sixties' 'love and peace' ethic, but the animal connection had never occurred to me until I met up with an old friend and invited him to dinner. He was vegetarian and, inevitably, I asked him over dinner, "Why"? That's when I found out truth

RITA TUSHINGHAM & CARLA LANE

Rita: 'They show us trust, love and loyalty and in return we betray them utterly. Animal rights has got to be the key to creating a more loving world.'

Carla: 'If we learned to care about the other creatures, we'd learn a lot – humility for a start.'

MARTIN SHAW

'By Living Without Cruelty, I'm not the animals' enemy any more. I'm with them, not against them, and that's a good feeling.'

Martin Shaw

with a capital "T". As he spoke, I realized I was justifying killing merely because I liked the taste, and it dawned on me that the only way I could change things generally for the better was to start by changing myself. I believe that if you "try" to do a thing it becomes a struggle, and therein lies failure. If you "do" the thing, the issue is settled. I was turning my body into an animals' graveyard and it hit me like a bombshell. I became vegetarian literally overnight because of that conversation.

'In 1972 it was rather a problem, as people had little idea what to give you. I suppose Indian food was the salvation – I love spicy dishes. Now that most of my friends are vegetarian too, eating out is no problem and shopping, even for ready-meals, is simplicity itself.

'I know, to the core of my being, that I'm healthier. The diet helps make you aware of all the things your body needs – and what it could well do without. Apart from the inefficiency of meat eating and the dreadful poisons you're consuming, you are eating the very essence of fear. The animals go to their deaths in fear. Their bodies are flooded with adrenalin because of it. We then consume all that negativity.

'I do believe in following a "spiritual" path. Sometimes, when you're confronted with grotesque cruelties, it can be difficult, but I feel it's essential to keep the right "energy balance" within yourself. The only thing which defeats fear and hate is love, even to adversaries.

'Man is the only creature who has been given discrimination. We can choose not to kill, not to execute, not to hate. If we lose our sense of discrimination, and end up filled with hate for factory farmers, vivisectors, hunters and shooters, then our hate makes us just like them. I get angry and bang my fists like everyone else, but I really believe in not adding to the negativity in the world and in projecting a positive and caring energy which other people will be attracted to.

'At present, it seems we have a world governed by negative elements. Uncaring administrations, big money institutions screwing the planet for all she's worth and leaving us to swill around in the effluent. Everything seems loaded against balance and "rightness", but on the other hand, we've got a green revolution trying to counter this. Living Without Cruelty is a big part of this awareness, because the animal connections are the key factors to why the planet

is in such a mess. It's like a huge set of scales. Every person who changes towards a cruelty-free lifestyle helps tip the balance in favour of human health and happiness, compassion and love for your fellow creatures and respect for the earth itself.

'By Living Without Cruelty, I'm not the animals' enemy any more. I'm with them, not against them, and that's a good feeling.'

I wonder who first coined the term 'a nation of animal lovers'? Perhaps he or she lived in a closeted world where only well-fed dogs and cats existed, doted on by well-meaning old ladies who were rather over-generous with the tit-bits and lax with the exercise.

The reality is that we are a nation of animal keepers, animal consumers and animal exploiters. The term 'animal lover' is, in itself, disingenuous. Some would argue it is a term of offence, for those who struggle on behalf of animals do so because they see them as oppressed citizens with no course of redress. You don't have to profess 'love' for rats, mice, cats, dogs, alligators, elephants or rabbits – respect and the right to a life free from suffering and exploitation seems little enough to ask for. We may treat wild and domesticated farm animals appallingly, but surely we do better with our own 'pets'?

We profess to care, but allow the casual destruction of thousands of healthy animals every year. In 1987 the RSPCA, the largest animal welfare institution in the UK, killed a staggering 61,123 dogs – that's 176 per day – and 53,000 cats – 168 per day. Each year the problem is compounded by stray animals maturing and giving birth to yet more unwanted animals – many of whom will end up on the pile of bodies which the RSPCA seems committed to piling ever higher. If, as has been argued, the RSPCA set up low-cost spaying and neutering clinics, then the problem would at least be tackled at source and begin to diminish. At present, though, such essential work remains in the hands of small, hard-pressed groups who struggle to pay the vets' bills in a bid to prevent another batch of puppies or kittens from becoming a statistic.

Our biggest animal welfare institution believes that a dog registration scheme is the answer. This expensive bureaucratic piece of machinery, which requires animals to be either tattooed or have inserted into their bodies a microchip which can be read by a computer, is to be financed by the dog owners. How this will prevent animals being born is difficult to imagine. Perhaps the society also envisages a cat registration scheme?

Many of the animals who find themselves in animal shelters are pedigrees. Originally somebody paid a lot of money (many puppies average £100 at least), only to abandon them later, so a lack of resources cannot always be blamed. But there are other reasons. Many animals are bought as status symbols by people who have their own personality disorders. Some breeds become fashionable as if they were some sort of living accessory to go with a certain lifestyle. When the fashion changes, the animals tend to suffer accordingly. Dog and cat breeders are also responsible for adding to the numbers of unwanted animals when they should be neutering instead of profiteering from the sales of offspring.

The problems connected with unwanted animals are solely of our own making and far from easy. We domesticated the cat and the dog, and must take responsibility for the results of our human interference. The key factor is that we must limit the numbers being born. We should ask why we think we want a dog or cat, and make sure we're taking on the task for the right reasons. Buying any animal simply fuels the demand for more to be produced, so always re-home from an animal shelter rather than give a breeder business.

Apart from cats and dogs, millions of other animals are purchased annually, usually for children, and live a short, lonely life languishing in hutches at the end of the garden. In his book *Fettered Kingdoms* John Bryant wrote: 'If misery was an obnoxious gas, then tens of thousands of backyards all over the nation would be emitting an unbearable stench from old orange boxes, cabinets and tea-chests, hastily converted by 'dad' into prisons for a legion of small animals serving life-sentences.'

Will we condemn a lonely rabbit to that life sentence or can we ensure some semblance of fulfilment, with a neutered doe, proper shelter and a spacious grassy run to graze and play in? If we can't, we should think of the rabbit and scrap the idea. Are we prepared to look after an animal, feed it properly, give it exercise, fulfil *its* needs of companionship, medical care, shelter, space and attention? If we can truthfully answer 'Yes' to all of these aspects, then we won't be the sort of people who'll be bothered about fancy breeds. The next step is to approach a local animal shelter.

You'll find both RSPCA and other animal groups listed in local directories. Shelters such as the Battersea Dogs' Home and the RSPCA all make a charge in the region of £12 or so for a dog. Other groups may charge less, but vet owners more thoroughly. The Cats' Protection League is particularly good about this. It is worth asking if the shelter has a 'No destruction' policy if you feel strongly about this aspect – either way, an animal will be grateful for the chance of a happy life.

Living Without Cruelty and companion animals

- Think carefully before taking on any animal, and make sure you can look after it properly.
- Always give a home to an unwanted animal, rather than buy from a breeder and perpetuate the demand for others to be born.
- Have your animal spayed or neutered at the proper time, before it can produce a litter. If you can't afford this, or can't be bothered, don't have an animal.
- Never advertise an unwanted litter as 'free to good homes'. Be suspicious of anyone offering to take the whole litter – they could be destined for laboratories or for the fur trade. Unhomed animals should be taken to an animal shelter when weaned and the mother neutered immediately afterwards. Ask a vet for advice about this.
- Be prepared to train your dog for his own and your sake. Dog training can be fun if you have the right attitude and are not worried about the 'Crufts' syndrome. It may save your dog's life.
- Your dog will be happy and healthy on a vegetarian diet and you will find you make savings over tinned meat.

- Never give an animal as a present.
- Look at alternative medical treatments (see page 128) instead of drug therapy.

Useful addresses

RSPCA
The Causeway
Horsham
West Sussex
RH12 1HG
0403 64181
See also local telephone directory.

PDSA Headquarters
PDSA House
South St
Dorking
Surrey
0306 888291
See also local telephone directory.

The Cats' Protection League
17 Kings Rd
Horsham
West Sussex
0403 65566
Telephone for nearest local contact or consult local telephone directory.

Happidog Pet Foods
Bridge End
Brownhill Lane
Longton
Preston
PR4 4SJ
0772 614952
Vegetarian dog foods – dry meal, tinned and puppy meal. Mail order and retail outlets. Telephone for name of nearest stockist.

Green Ark
Alston
Cumbria
0434 381766
Organic vegetarian petfood/mail order, retail outlets. S.a.e. for booklet and information.

Denes veterinary herbal treatments and Denes dog foods are available from most health stores.

Vegecat – supplement for adding to vegetarian catfood. Details from the Vegan Society (see page 62.)

A list of homoeopathic vets is obtainable from the Faculty of Homoeopathy (see page 00, and look at other groups marked 'V' for those giving animal treatments).

Home-cooked vegetarian petfoods

Dogs are happy and healthy on a vegetarian diet but cats, endowed with a primitive digestion, are natural carnivores and lack a particular enzyme to extract certain nutrients from non-meat sources. Mix meat or fish into the recipes given here or include a supplement (e.g. Vegecat). Hunting cats will catch their own meat supply.

BASIC CEREAL MIX

Makes 2 meals.

6 cups water
1 cup oats
1 cup rye or wheat flakes
½ cup cracked wheat

Combine the water and grains in a large pot and cook over a medium heat until the mixture begins to bubble. Reduce the heat and cook gently for 20 minutes until the grains are soft but firm.

DRY MIX CRUNCH

Makes 4 meals.

4 cups oats
2 cups wheat or rye flakes
1 cup cracked wheat
½ cup wholemeal flour
6 tablespoons sunflower oil
6 tablespoons water
2 tablespoons honey

Pre-heat the oven to 140°C (275°F/gas mark 1). Combine the dry ingredients in a large bowl. Mix the liquids separately, then add to the dry ingredients and mix thoroughly. Bake for 1 hour in a large tray, stirring every 20 minutes to keep the mix in small bits. Serve in combination with other dinner ingredients as an effective mixer.

VEGETABLE MEDLEY FOR PUPPIES

Makes 2 meals.

2 carrots, diced
2 celery stalks, diced
1 medium courgette, diced
½ cup stock or water
2 teaspoons wheatgerm
2 tablespoons peanut butter
3 or more tablespoons basic cereal mix (as above; optional)

Liquidize the vegetables with the stock for 1 minute. Add the wheatgerm and peanut butter and blend again until smooth. Transfer the mixture to a pan and warm through slowly. Add 3 tablespoons of basic cereal mix if desired, increasing the amount as the puppy grows older.

MAIN-MEAL DOGGY DINNER

Makes 4 meals.

1 cup diced, scrubbed potato
1 cup diced carrot
1 cup each diced swede and turnip and parsnip (any root veg will do)
1 cup frozen peas
4 cups cereal mix (as above)
2 sachets Protoveg beef-flavoured chunks
1 teaspoon yeast extract e.g. Natex
1 pint/600 ml vegetable stock e.g. Vecon
Wholemeal dog biscuit mix or 4 well-toasted slices wholemeal bread, cubed

Simmer the vegetables slowly in the stock until barely tender. Soak the TVP chunks in a hot yeast extract gravy until swollen. Simmer separately for 15 minutes, then combine with the vegetables and set aside to cool. Combine with the cereal mix. Serve each portion with wholemeal biscuits or toast, adding extra gravy if desired.

SOYBEAN MASH

Makes 1 meal.

2 cups cooked soybeans
1 cup tomato juice or stock
1 slice wholemeal bread, cubed
3 tablespoons sunflower oil

Mash the beans and add the remaining ingredients, mixing well.

LENTIL AND BARLEY LOAF

Makes 2 meals.

2 cups water
½ cup dried, washed lentils
½ cup pearl barley
¼ cup chopped onion
½ cup chopped celery
½ teaspoon sea salt
A little garlic powder

Bring the water to the boil in a large saucepan, adding the lentils and barley. Reduce the heat, cover and simmer for about 25 minutes until the barley is tender. Liquidize the onion and celery and add this puree to the grains. Season with salt and a little garlic powder.

POTATO AND CEREAL DINNER

Makes 2 meals.

7 potatoes
1 dessertspoon soy sauce
1 dessertspoon tahini
1 cup cooked cereal mix (as above)

Scrub and cube the potatoes and cook them gently in a little water until they are soft enough to mash. Mash well, adding the soy sauce and tahini. Add to the cereal mix and serve when cooled.

OATMEAL QUICKIE

Makes 2 meals.

4 cups oats
9 cups water
½ teaspoon sea salt
2 thick slices wholemeal bread, cubed

Cook the oats and water over a low heat for approx 20 minutes till thick and creamy. Remove from the heat and fold in the other ingredients. Serve warm.

BUCKWHEAT AND CEREAL

Makes 2 meals.

2 cups cooked buckwheat groats
1 cup cooked cereal mix (as above)
3 tablespoons peanut butter
1 cup water

Combine the buckwheat and cereal mix in a large saucepan. Add the peanut butter and water and warm over a medium heat, stirring until combined.

ANY-KIND BEAN DISH

Makes 2 meals.

3 cups cooked beans
¼ cup sunflower oil
1 cup cracked wheat

Combine the ingredients in a large bowl and lightly mash before serving.

RICE AND MILLET VEGETABLE DISH

Makes 2 meals.

3 cups left-over vegetables
1 cup cooked rice
1 cup cooked millet
¼ cup sunflower oil
½ cup water

Liquidize the vegetables and add to the grains, oil and water. Warm through in a large pot and serve warm.

CHICK-PEA STEW

Makes 2 meals.

3 cups cooked chick peas
3 tablespoons sunflower oil
3 tablespoons peanut butter
2 cups water or stock
1 carrot, diced
1 celery stalk, diced
½ onion, chopped
1 large swede, finely diced

Mash the chick peas in a large bowl, adding the oil, peanut butter and 1 cup of the water. Liquidize the remaining ingredients and simmer the puree over a gentle heat for 5 minutes. Add to the chick pea mixture, stir well and serve warm.

BREAKFAST SPECIAL

Makes 2 meals.

5 apples, cubed
2 cups water
4 ripe bananas, mashed
2 cups cooked cereal

Liquidize the apples in the water until creamy and add to the bananas and cereal. Mix well, adding some dry mix crunch (see recipe) if desired.

POTATO SKINS

Makes 2 meals.

6–8 left-over baked potatoes
Cereal mix
Left-over cooked vegetables
1 sachet TVP mince simmered for 10 minutes in a Vecon stock

Cut the potatoes into bite-sized chunks and combine with other ingredients.

KITTY CAT SPECIAL

Makes 2 meals.

1 × 12 oz/350 g cake tofu
1 tablespoon nutritional yeast
1 teaspoon kelp
1 teaspoon chopped dulse
1 tablespoon sunflower oil

Mash the tofu and combine with the other ingredients.

BULGHUR DINNER

Makes 2 meals.

3 cups bulghur wheat
7 cups water or stock
2 carrots, diced
1 courgette, diced
1 green pepper, diced
1 small onion, diced
3 cloves garlic, diced

Soak the bulghur in 6 cups of the water. Put 1 cup of the water and the remaining ingredients in the liquidizer and blend until creamy. Combine with the bulghur, warm and serve.

9 *The Call of the Wild*

DAVID SHEPHERD

'We are beginning to wake up and we're beginning to get frightened, but we need to move fast. . . . We're destroying a species every day. It's time we realized that we're on the way to destroying ourselves . . . people-power is our only hope.'

David Shepherd

'I wanted to be a game warden, not a wildlife artist, so when I left school in 1949 I shot off to Kenya. There I discovered that I wasn't God's gift to the National Parks Service! I had no experience and they didn't want me. I thought, "This is the end, then. I'll have to be a bus driver."

'I was pushed into art as the only other option, but nearly failed that when the only art school I approached, the Slade, told me I was totally untalented. They were right, I was. I owe everything to Robin Goodwin, who for some unfathomable reason agreed to teach me privately. After three years, in 1954 he told me: "That's it, I can't teach you anything else. You're on your own."

'That's when I began painting aircraft. The RAF liked them and flew me to Kenya in 1960 to do some paintings for the officers' mess. They didn't want aircraft, however – they wanted elephants; and I'd never painted them before. Since that first picture I've never looked back, and as my success grew so did my debt to the elephants and all my other animal subjects. Kenya made me into a conservationist and led me to campaign on behalf of the animals to whom I owed so much. It was there I witnessed the sight of 250 dead zebra lying around a poisoned waterhole. You don't forget sights like that.

'I'm a highly emotional man. I still weep when I remember the elephant I saw with his foot blown off by a landmine, but over the years I've become more pragmatic in my views. The inhabitants of a country have to believe for themselves the value of protecting habitat and conserving animal life. In India there are the most beautiful reserves, lush and bountiful, but 150 yards outside the perimeter the locals are starving, the vegetation is sparse and denuded by overgrazing, and life is pretty dismal. The people there only see that they can't get to the green bit and graze their animals on it. That creates political pressure to concede the spaces reserved for animals to people. It really makes me pretty fed up – this permanent priority of human beings over animals. I believe we're all equal in this world. We all have a part to play in nature and it's supreme arrogance for man to assume, "Well, people come first", because it's a philosophy we pursue at our own dire peril. It's because of this that the world's in such a bloody mess now!

'What all this boils down to is overpopulation. Kenya has the highest birth rate (3½–4 per cent) in the world. In twenty years' time, there won't be the space to sit down. The Pope goes and tells sixty thousand young Africans they mustn't use birth control. When all those young people leave school, without the hope of a job, the social problems are going to be terrifying. The world is going to breed itself out of house and home, and to deny people birth control is in my view monstrous. It might not be popular to say it, but it's the root of all the problems we face.

'We are beginning to wake up and we're beginning to get frightened, but we need to move fast and put on the pressure to get things to change. We're destroying a species every day. It's time we realized that we're on the way to destroying ourselves. In forty to fifty years' time we'll have destroyed the rainforests and that'll be it. The planet will be devastated, there'll be nothing to eat because they'll be too many people, and the eco-structure will be beyond repair.

'I believe that people-power is our only hope. We must generate the political will to change the status quo, and to do this we need to make ourselves aware of what's happening. Knowledge changes you. For instance, some years ago I was only against 'wild or endangered species' being used for furs. Then I found out about fur farming and I'm against all of it now. It's obscene. Factory farming makes my blood pressure go through the roof. It's incredible, how we, in a supposedly civilized society, can allow it.

'I suppose the sickest thing I ever saw was the clubbing of baby seals on the ice. I was there with IFAW. I'll never forget. Soon, the ban on that will be rescinded by the Canadian government and the merchants of death and greed will be back and we'll have to go through it all again. Will they never learn?

'A so-called "quality" newspaper recently described Antarctica as a "hitherto unexploited waste". To me, a wasteland is what you get *after* man has been in – like most of the world we've wrecked. It's a wasteland after we've left, not before we arrive.'

Throughout the world, animals are exploited by man either directly, for what they yield up to his greed, or indirectly, through the pressure he puts on their natural habitat. Everywhere the pressure on the natural world is increasing, with an average loss of a species per day.

Where animal products are concerned, we know that boycotts are an effective weapon in bringing an industry to heel. Simply stop buying the goods. The continuing demise of the fur trade demonstrates this. In Africa, the rhino and elephant may be extinct by the end of the century primarily because of the ivory trade, but also through competition for land with man. Elephants are gentle, long-lived creatures who live in complex social groups. After a twenty-two-month pregnancy they make wonderful mothers who care for their children for twelve years or more, teaching them the art of elephant lore. Fifteen hundred of these extremely intelligent, caring creatures are murdered each week by poachers intent on getting the tusks. Ten years ago more than 1.3 million elephants roamed Africa. Now there are fewer than five hundred thousand. Their social structure is on the brink of collapse, the adults largely gone (bigger tusks), leaving the young and inexperienced alone and untutored in jungle survival.

The story of the elephant was well told in 1989 because of the CITES (Convention on International Trade in Endangered Species) conference in Switzerland where, after much argument, a wishy-washy two-year ivory trading ban was announced. Although most countries favoured a total trade ban, enough countries with vested interests voted against and the motion failed to achieve the two-thirds majority needed. After the two years, the mayhem will be allowed to begin again with the 'culling of managed herds' (poaching notwithstanding).

Writing in the *Guardian* on 13 October 1989, Nigel Leader-Williams from the Large Animal Research Group at Cambridge University concluded his editorial on elephants with these words: 'Given their economic potential as producers of ivory and meat, and for tourism, the loss of elephants for short-term gain is a terrible waste.' He might have added 'when, by keeping the numbers up, we could have long-term exploitation'. It is this sort of attitude which really makes me sick, because the animals are seen not as thinking, feeling individuals but as commercial assets. This is where I part company with certain aspects of 'conservation', which only seems interested in keeping a species going in sufficient numbers in order to allow greedy man a continuing profit margin.

Nobody suggests culling over-breeding humans, even though our teeth would make fine carved necklaces, our meat might be quite tasty (ask certain tribal groups in South America) and we already make good tourist attractions with the dancing, beadwork and souvenir spears. I'm not suggesting it either, but simply emphasize the point that in the race for rights, 'they' never win because 'they' carry one inescapable handicap from birth – 'they' weren't born human.

The elephant can be held up as a mirror image for all the other species thus exploited, some not big, not glamorous, not cuddly or appealing, who don't make the headlines but who nevertheless suffer man's pollution, his greed and his sentencing, and disappear from our consciousness without a whimper. Yes, we can stop buying the carvings, the jewellery and trinkets, the pathetic napkin rings, cutlery handles, umbrella stands and gorilla-hand

ashtrays. But perhaps what we need to do as much is to start to correct the 'attitude' problem we have to the creatures with whom we share our world. Nobody pretends that solutions to specific problems are simple. It does seem, though, that man is always looking for the expedient way out of the problems he has created. There is always an alternative to killing and suffering; we just have to look for it.

If there are too many animals in one place, yet overall their numbers are declining, why are ways not found to move them to areas where there are few? Why don't we put the greatest emphasis on limiting our own numbers instead of always reducing theirs? Following through ethical considerations in some areas can lead into problematical cul-de-sacs. It's all very well putting forward workable solutions to the evils of vivisection and factory farming because the alternatives are visible and within our grasp. In many Third World countries, where human life itself is a disposable commodity, giving precedence to animals can seem an irritating irrelevancy, yet here the connection is even more pertinent.

First, other countries can well do without the importation of Western animal abuse systems; many have enough of their own. The problems faced by developing nations are primarily ones requiring political and social action such as sanitation, housing and clean water. Poor economies need help with these problems, but at the same time need to resist a host of commercial parasites from the developed world, intent on profiteering from cheap labour, lax legislation and often corrupt officialdom.

Better living standards mean more surviving children so families can be kept small and healthy, instead of large and starving. To achieve this, birth control is essential.

Many Eastern countries are already primarily vegetarian: most of India, for example. They have their own spiritual philosophies to build upon, and many already embrace a 'no-killing' creed. Education then becomes the key to health and social improvement. A strengthening of animal welfare considerations and an appreciation of their own 'living world' then wouldn't seem so divorced from the reality of filling an empty belly.

Unfortunately, we may not have the time

for that. And countries may have to be jollied along and even imposed upon, if change is to be effective. The Brazilians may not like the West poking their noses into the rainforest issue, but houses obviously need to be put in order soon.

The exploitation of man, animals and the earth is inter-linked. Each is dependent on the other. If we promote the attitude that animals are expendable, that they are beneath our consideration unless a profit can be made, that they have no rights, then not only will we lose them but ourselves as well – body *and* soul. The end point of a 'them and us' philosophy means that eventually there will only be billions of 'us' and none of them. How then do we choose? How then do we 'cull'? How loud will *we* then scream out for the ethics, the compassion and the rights that we so selfishly captured all for ourselves.

Green groups concerned with life on earth/wildlife rescue

Friends of the Earth
26–28 Underwood St
London N1 7JQ
01-490 1555

Greenpeace
30–31 Islington Green
London N1
01-354 5100

The Ark Trust
498–500 Harrow Rd
London W9 3QA
01-968 6780

Population Concern
231 Tottenham Court Rd
London W1P 0HX
01-637 9587

Royal Society for Nature Conservation
The Green
Nettleham
Lincoln
LN2 2NR
0522 752326

National Society for Clean Air
136 North St
Brighton
BN1 1RG
0273 26313

Coastal Anti-Pollution League
94 Greenway Lane
Bath
Avon
BA2 4LN
0225 317094

Woodland Trust
Autumn Park
Dysart Rd
Grantham
Lincs
NG31 6LL
0476 74297

Environmental Investigation Agency
208–209 Upper St
London N1
01-704 9441
Investigates illegal trade in animals.

London Wildlife Trust
80 York Way
London N1 9AG
01-278 6612
This and other trusts are affiliated to the Royal Society for Nature Conservation. Contact them, or look in your local directory for your nearest wildlife group.

Care for the Wild
26 North St
Horsham
West Sussex
RH12 1BN
0403 50557

The Wildlife Hospitals Trust
1 Pemberton Close
Aylesbury
Bucks
HP21 7NY
0296 437373
Incorporates St Tiggywinkle's hedgehog rescue.

World Wide Fund for Nature
Panda House
Wayside Park
Godalming
Surrey
GU7 7RX
0483 426444

Elefriends
162 Boundaries Rd
London SW12 8HG
01-682 1818

The Whale and Dolphin Conservation Society
20 West Lea Rd
Bath
BA1 3RL
0225 334511

British Divers Marine Life Rescue
10 Maylan Rd
Corby
Northants
NN17 2DR
0536 201511

Local wildlife rescue and treatment centres can be found by contacting local animal contacts: RSPCA, who often refer cases on/local radio/ animal rights groups. Look in local directories for groups and societies, or ask at your local library.

Further reading
Friends of The Earth Handbook, J. Porritt, FoE.
Sacred Elephant, Heathcote Williams, Cape.
Elephant Memories, Cynthia Moss, Fontana.
Whale Nation, Heathcote Williams, Cape.
Animal First Aid, Rorke Garfield, Starprint (Northampton).
The Complete Hedgehog, Les Stocker, Chatto and Windus.
Care for the Wild, W. J. Jordan and J. Hughes, Care for the Wild.

10   *The Root of all Evil?*

All of us have, at some time, needed to call upon the services of a financial institution to help us manage our money – whether it be a large investment on the stockmarket or simply a savings account with a local building society. All companies invest and use deposits to increase their assets and offer a healthy return to shareholders and savers alike. But unfortunately, many of the companies offering shares on the stockmarket are heavily involved in both human and animal exploitation.

It is only recently, within the past few years, that ethical investment trusts have been available to the public, and it is heartening to discover that they are consolidating their position within the market and that the choice is growing as your consumer demand increases. There are now ten funds operating within the UK, some having more rigid criteria than others and excluding from their portfolios various areas of concern such as tobacco and alcohol production, the arms trade, South Africa, nuclear power, pollution of the environment, animal experimentation and the fur industry. Studies have shown that the funds perform as well as, if not better than, their 'unethical' counterparts, and 'socially responsible investors' (as they are termed in the USA) will easily find a savings or investment plan to suit them.

One fund which specifically relates to the Living Without Cruelty ethic is the Ethical Investment Fund which takes a very particular stance on cruelty to animals. The fund, which donates £20 to Animal Aid for each new investment, is the only one which imposes a total ban on any company involved in animal experimentation. Neither does it invest in companies which sell animal-tested products such as pharmaceuticals. The same company, through Scottish Equitable, also operate the Ethical Pension Fund on equally strict criteria, undertaking thorough research through EIRIS (Ethical Investment Research Service), which vets all companies quoted in the FT Share Index.

EIRIS is available to both organizations and individuals, and for a specified fee will provide analysis and information on all companies listed on the Index together with lists of firms who meet an individual's criteria. They publish a quarterly newsletter along with an investment guide, *Choosing an Ethical Fund*, which provides lots of information. Details from EIRIS.

Individually managed ethical portfolios, where you specify your own requirements, are also available. The Lancashire and Yorkshire Portfolio Management Ltd offer such a service and their minimum level is around £5000, whilst D. J. Bromidge, who manage the Ethical Investment Fund and Ethical Pension Fund already mentioned, offer private portfolio management to larger investors starting at around £50,000. If you already have a financial adviser it may be worth enquiring for information on new companies entering the ethical field. Any existing stockbroker should be able to sell your share holdings and purchase more acceptable ones over a period of time.

If you already hold shares in companies which are involved in activities which clash with your principles, you could help shape their future attitudes by attending annual general meetings and raising issues such as animal testing, declaration of product ingredients (especially on cosmetic products), factory farming and the environment. Combined shareholder action on human abuse issues such as South Africa has resulted in over one third of corporate investors withdrawing from that country since January 1986 – so pressure from within can work. A useful idea would be to retain the minimum share holding which would allow voting and attendance at AGMs, whilst switching the bulk of your money into an ethical portfolio.

For those of us with smaller sums available, we could consider the Ecology Building Society who lend on specific projects which do not harm the environment and which enhance the quality of life in both rural and urban areas, promoting such ideas as organic growing, craft workshops, energy-saving homes and a sense of community. The EBS refuses to provide finance for any factory farming activity, which it regards as both cruel and a disaster for the environment.

Lastly, for those who wish to make financial donations through deeds of covenant or leave legacies to deserving organizations or charities, it makes sense to investigate these groups, especially medical charities, to ensure they are not themselves contributing to animal abuse. Although this area is both complex and controversial it is entirely possible to ensure that your money fulfils your ideals by benefiting a humane medical research organization, thus helping your fellow man but not at the expense of animal suffering. Such organizations are examined on pages 126–7.

Societies campaigning on behalf of animals also rely on public generosity to sustain them and are well worth supporting in this way. If you are concerned about a particular aspect of animal cruelty, specialist groups are listed throughout the text. Animal Aid, who deal with all major aspects of animal abuse and finance the Living Without Cruelty educational campaign, are listed at the front of this book.

Details of companies offering ethical investment are given below.

Ethical investment UK

The Stewardship Unit Trust
Friends Provident
72–122 Castle St
Salisbury
Wilts
SP1 3SH
0722 336242 and 0306 740123
Avoids fur trade, cosmetic testing and factory farming.

The Ethical Investment Fund
10 Queen St
London W1X 7PD
01-491 0558
Total ban on companies involved in animal experiments.

The Fellowship Trust
Buckmaster and Moore Ltd
80 Cannon St
London EC4N 6HH
01-491 8759
Avoids fur trade, obvious cosmetics and pharmaceutical companies who animal test, and factory farming.

NM Conscience Fund
NM Schroder Group
Regal House
14 James St
London WC2E 8BT
01-836 8731
Avoids companies who 'unnecessarily' exploit animals, as in cosmetics testing and the fur trade.

The Ethical Trust
Abbey Unit Trust Managers
80 Holdenhurst Rd
Bournemouth
BH8 8AL
0202 297621
Avoids the fur trade and cosmetic companies who animal-test products.

Merlin Ecology Fund
Merlin Fund Management Ltd
30 St James's St
London SW1A 1HB
01-925 1277
Avoids the fur trade, obvious factory farming links and cosmetic companies who animal-test.

Lancashire and Yorkshire Portfolio Management Ltd
52/54 Artillery Lane
London E1 7LS
01-377 2727
Ethical portfolio management where clients specify own criteria. Minimum investment level approx. £5000.

Bromige and Partners
10 Queen St
London W1X 7PD
01-491 0558
Personal ethical portfolio management for larger investors, with a minimum level of £50,000.

The Ethical Investment Research Service (EIRIS)
Room 4.01
Bondway Business Centre
71 Bondway
London SW1 1SQ
01-735 1351
Provides information to individuals and organizations on a wide range of issues to help investors apply positive or negative criteria to investment.

11 Epilogue: Louder than Words

'See first that the design is wise and just; that ascertained, pursue it resolutely. . . .'

Shakespeare

This book has been aimed at influencing you, the reader, to take positive steps towards a cruelty-free lifestyle. Campaigners may plead, cajole, use emotional 'blackmail', argue and present you with irrefutable facts, but at the end of the day no one can dictate how you should live or act or feel. All I can hope is that, somewhere along the way, something has touched you, angered you or convinced you enough to spur you into action. One thing is certain: whatever action you do take will be part of a growing momentum away from the products of cruelty and exploitation – towards that 'better world' all of us wish to see.

Not only can you change your own perspective, you can influence others too. Why not lend this book to family, friends and neighbours? Better still, buy them a copy for Christmas!

Joining a group such as Animal Aid will not only encourage and inform you, but you'll be able to join with others in your local area and help, if you wish to, with local initiatives, fundraising and social events.

Living Without Cruelty can also influence the workplace. Are vegetarians catered for in the canteen? Are the materials provided for cleaning staff cruelty-free and environmentally friendly? What about adopting recycled paper products and encouraging the workforce to raise money for a worthy cause such as humane, non-animal research? Does any private health plan include alternative medicine?

Politically, it's essential that Living Without Cruelty ethics begin to permeate both local and national institutions. Is your union misguidedly trying to protect its workers by calling for the animal testing of dangerous chemicals? How 'ethical' are the companies your union invests in? What about your own investments and those of groups you belong to?

Are your children pressurized into unnecessary animal exploitation at school or college? Has your student union adopted the Charter for Violence-Free Science yet? Is there an active pro-animal/green group at your poly or university? Your intervention and support could help change things.

What does your political party *do* for animals? Does it hold forward-looking policies which will end at least the worst abuses, or is it intent on maintaining the status quo? Is profit making given preference over animal suffering? Is profit making given preference over human suffering? Are 'green' measures as green as they seem, or are they simply tinted that way for public consumption? If you're active in your local party, then you can raise questions, debate issues and put forward ideas based on Living Without Cruelty ethics. Get your MP to support Parliamentary measures which help animals, not animal abusers.

Health professionals can publicize the Charter for Health and Humane Research. Could you adopt some or all of its points? How about telling your colleagues?

Where do you worship? You could make Living Without Cruelty a part of your congregation's spiritual reality – whatever your faith. Many religions have their own internal lobby group to speak up for those who cannot.

Whatever you do, and whatever walk of life you occupy, Living Without Cruelty can influence it, improve it and spread its message of compassionate living.

Political groups

The Green Party
10 Station Parade
Balham High Rd
London SW12 9AZ
01-673 0045

Socialist Environment and Resources Association (SERA)
11 Goodwin St
London N4 3HQ
01-263 7424

Socialist Countryside & Agriculture Group
Tidy's Cottage
School Lane
West Kingsdown
Sevenoaks
Kent TN15 6JN
0474 852326

SLD Animal Protection Group
Hay House
Haytor Vale
Devon
TQ13
03646 383

Green Democrats
'Bramblewood'
Staythorpe
Newark
Notts
NG23 5RH
0636 73430

SLD Against Bloodsports
51 Russell St
Gosport
Hants
PO12 1DU
0705 528017

Tory Green Initiative
1 St Michael's St
London
W2 1QT
01-402 5065

Conservative Anti-Hunt Council
c/o Danesbury Lodge
Danesbury Park Rd
Welling
Herts
AL6 9SD

Religious groups working for animals

Quaker Concern for Animal Welfare
Webb's Cottage
Saling
Braintree
Essex
CM7 5DZ

Catholic Study Circle for Animal Welfare
39 Onslow Gardens
London E18
01-989 0478

The Christian Consultative Council for the Welfare of Animals
11 Dagmar Rd
London N4 4NY

The Anglican Society for the Welfare of Animals
10 Chester Avenue
Hawkesbury
Tunbridge Wells
Kent

Jewish Vegetarian Society
855 Finchley Rd
London NW11 8LX
01-455 0692

Further reading

The Living Without Cruelty Diary, Mark Gold, Greenprint, £3.50. Available annually – the essential pocket-sized diary for the green movement.
The Unkindest Beast. An Animal Aid Anthology, compiled by Maureen Duffy, £1.95 from Animal Aid. Many of the poems quoted herein are taken from this anthology.

Photographic Credits

COVER
Photography: Neil Barstow
Model: Janet Kay
Handcare and colour lacquers: BWC
Digby is appearing at Heavens Gate Animal Sanctuary, Langport, Somerset. Donations warmly appreciated.

SEAL
Photo courtesy International Fund for Animal Welfare.

PETER GABRIEL
Photo courtesy Virgin records.

HOWARD JONES
Friar's Management

DAVID ESSEX
London Features International Ltd.

LINDA McCARTNEY
Photographer: John Swannell
Make-up: BWC

URI GELLER
Photographer: Alan Shawcross
Vegetarian ready-meal by Mange Tout Foods – Vegetable Hot-pot at under £1, suitable for vegans. Other quality dishes use only free-range eggs and vegetarian cheeses. Exceptional quality and generous helpings.

TWIGGY
Photo courtesy London Management.

RICHARD ADAMS
Photographer: Alan Shawcross

JULIE CHRISTIE
Photography: Greg Gorman

CHRISSIE HYNDE
Photographer: Jill Furmanovsky
Body painting: Lorraine Kay
Technical assistance: Branco

BILL ODDIE
Press Association

POLAR BEAR ON ICE SKATES
Associated Press Ltd

CIRCUS HASSANI
Photographer: Jill Furmanovsky

FALLING RACEHORSES AT BECHERS BROOK
Photographer: Ed Byrne

CARLA LANE & RITA TUSHINGHAM
Photographer: Tim Bret-Day
Own make-up: Body Shop and BWC.

DAVID SHEPHERD
Photographer: Stuart McLeod

MARTIN SHAW
Photographer: Mathew Anker
At: Heavens Gate Animal Sanctuary, Langport, Somerset

JOANNA LUMLEY
Photographer: Tommy Candler
Make-up: BWC
Hair: Simply Herbal Chamomile shampoo and conditioner.
Food: Afternoon Tea Treats
Veeze and Tomato Sandwiches, Plamil Carob Spread, Whole Earth Blackcurrant Preserve, Meridian Raspberry Spread and Mexican Honey, Holly Mill Carob Chip Cookies, Plamil apricot

and apple bars. Pot of Luaka de-caffeinated tea with soya milk. Living Without Cruelty big T-shirt from Animal Aid.

ENGLISH SUNDAY BREAKFAST
See pages 51–2 for recipes.
Photographer: Ian Kalinowski
Cook: Oded Schwartz
Silverware, Sheffield Scene/white utility china, Cookshop Sheffield/Menu ingredients, Holland and Barrett and Whole Earth foods.

SOPHIE WARD
Photographer: Karena Perronet-Miller
Make-up: Lisa Butler
Hair: Arno at Pin-Up
Make-up: Colourings 001 and 01 mixed foundation, 01 powder shaker, 02 pressed powder blusher/Eyes: CTG Mocktail, Barry M. Natural Dazzle, BWC black mascara, BWC grey eye definer + Barry M. Natural Dazzle on brows/Lips: BWC Rosewood, Colourings 01 gloss.
Hair: gel by Crimpers.

BARBECUE
See pages 56–7 for recipes.
Photographer: Ian Kalinowski
Cook: Oded Schwartz
Wine: Organic Wine Company Ltd/Menu ingredients, Holland and Barrett and Whole Earth foods.

BARBARA DICKSON
Photographer: Robyn Beeche
Make-up: Barbara Daly
Hair: Frank Warner, Michaeljohn
Make-up: All Colourings from Body Shop. 01 and 02 foundation mixed, 01 and 02 Concealer, 01 loose powder, 02 powder blush/Eyes: 03 shadow, 04 pencil shadow, pale gold shadowlight, dark brown mascara, 02 eye definer/Lips: 01 liner, 02 stick, eyebrow make-up.
Barbara and son Colm tuck into a Vegeburger lunch.

ORIENTAL DINNER
See pages 57–8 for recipes.
Photographer: Ian Kalinowski
Cook: Oded Schwartz
Menu ingredients, Holland and Barrett/antique dishes, Filibuster and Booth Antiquarians, Sheffield.

WEDDING FEAST
See pages 52–6 for recipes.
Photographer: John Welburn
Recipes and photograph, kind permission *Health Express*.

CHRISTMAS DINNER
See pages 60–61 for recipes.
Photographer: Ian Kalinowski
Cook: Oded Schwartz
Silverware by Sheffield Scene/Wines: The Organic Wine Company Ltd/Menu ingredients supplied by Holland and Barrett.

MARIE HELVIN
Photography: David Bailey.

CAROL ROYLE
Photographer: Tommy Candler
Make-up: Body Shop Jojoba moisturizer/Colourings translucent bronzer/BWC cover-up stick/BWC loose powder/Barry M

blusher No. 13 with Cosmetics To Go Terracotta/Eyes: Colourings 03 Shadowlight + Barry M. No. 13/ BWC pencil liner, brown and BWC brown mascara/ Lips: BWC pink lipliner/Colourings 04 + Barry M. 31.
Carol uses Body Shop Orchid Oil Cleanser.
Carol washed her hair in BWC's Lotus Flower shampoo.

VICKI MICHELLE
Photographer: Trevor Leighton
Make-up: William Casey
Hair: Lawrence Falk
Stylist for set: Jaleh
Make-up: CTG Pagoda fruit moisturizer/BWC Cool Beige foundation, translucent loose powder/Blusher CTG Za Za/Eyes BWC smudged black pencil, black mascara and black pencil on brows/Lips: BWC red lipliner, Colourings No. 11 lipstick.
Cleanser, toner and moisturizer, Naturally Yours Lettuce and Linden range.
Hair: Crimpers gel and spray
Bathtime products: Foam – Honesty Coconut and Pineapple Bath Products on show include soaps by BWC, Pacific Isle, Neals Yard and Barry M. Bath salts, seeds foams and oils by Bodyline, Montagne Jeunnesse, Fleur and Honesty.

ANNIE LENNOX
Photographer: Sanders Nicholson
Make-up: Barbara Daly
Foundation 01 and 02 mixed + concealer, 01 loose powder, 01 powder blusher/Eyes: 01 shadow crayon + 04 crayon for lids, 01 shadowlight crayon. 04 Eye definer, 04 mascara/Lips: 02 liner, 04 stick.

BEAUTIFUL HANDS
Photographer: Bob Marchant
Model: Janet Kay
Products: Hand and body lotion by Animal Aid, BWC Nailcolour Peach Dream.

VIRGINIA McKENNA
Photographer: Tommy Candler
Virginia in her dressing room making up for a performance of the musical *Winnie*, using make-up from the Beauty Without Cruelty range. Honey Beige foundation/translucent face powder/Blush Rose blusher/Eyes: Sapphire pencil and eyeliner/brown eyebrow pencil/Lips: brown lipliner, Amber Pearl lipstick.
BWC Calistra cologne keeps her cool and fragrant during the performance.
Everyday Make-up: BWC coffee beige tint, translucent powder, powder blusher/Sapphire eye crayon, Brandysnap lipstick, Natural Nailcolor.

KATE O'MARA
Photographer: Trevor Leighton
Make-up: Barbara Daly
Hair: Lawrence Falk
Make-up: All Colourings from Body Shop – Jojoba moisturizer, 01 and 02 foundation mixed, 01 loose face powder, also on brow-bones, 02 blusher to highlight/Eye: 04 shadow + brown 02 eye-definer pencil, Black 05 mascara/Lips: 01 liner, 02 + 02 liner for lip colour.
Hair: Crimpers gel and spray.
Kate sprays Fichu perfume by Yvonne Gray.

TOYAH WILCOX
Photographer: Tony McGee
Make-up: Linda Burns at Lynne Franks
Hair: Joseph Carney for Sparks, Kings Road
Make-up: Cosmetics To Go moisturizer/Colourings 01 foundation/BWC translucent powder/Barry M. No. 14 blusher/Eyes: lids CTG Mocktail and Shanghai, Barry M. No. 1 lashes/Brows Body Shop 02 pencil/Lips: BWC Rosewood.
Cleanser – Yvonne Gray Royal Jelly.
Hair: Michaeljohn spray and sculpture lotion. City Range.

SUSANNAH YORK
Photography: John Swannell/Courtesy *Woman and Home* magazine
Make-up by Barbara Daly
Hair by Annie Russell
Cosmetics used: Colourings by Barbara Daly from Body Shop. Foundation 02 followed by loose translucent powder 01 and warm apricot blusher 01. Taupe coloured shadow 05, contoured with grey/brown 05 crayon. Dark brown 02 mascara applied in several coats highlights lashes, and brows emphasized with eyebrow powder make-up. Lips outlined with 01 brown/pink pencil liner followed by combination of lipsticks 02 and 07 to give a dusky pink.

HAYLEY MILLS
Photographer: Trevor Leighton
Make-up: William Casey
Hair: Drew Jarrett at Pin-Up
Make-up: BWC moisturizer, Foundation CTG No. 1, Colourings loose powder mixed with BWC translucent/Eyes: BWC Shy Seal on lids, BWC navy and black mascara on lashes/Lips: BWC pink liner, Cosmetics To Go Rusty Nail, Colourings 03 gloss.
Cleanser, toner and moisturizer all BWC.
Hayley's own fake fur by Astraka from Harrods.

FOX
Photographer: Gary Treadwell

LYSETTE ANTHONY
Photographer: Trevor Leighton
Make-up: Theresa Fairminer at Image
Hair: Francesca Crowder at Image
Make-up: All BWC – Cool Beige foundation, translucent pressed powder, Beige brown blusher/Eyes: Ginger Cat on lids, black pencil eyeliner, black mascara/Lips: red liner, stick and gloss. BWC Avocado cleanser.
Hair: sculpture lotion, spray and slicker dressing from Michaeljohn, City Range.
Fox fur and leghold trap kindly loaned from LYNX.

JOHN GIELGUD
Photographer: Patrick Lichfield

PETER CUSHING
Personal photograph.